STUDYING DRAMA

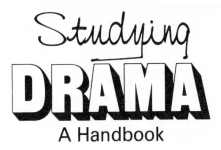

Studying DRAMA

A Handbook

David Bradby, Philip Thomas and Kenneth Pickering

Illustrations by John Parkinson

CROOM HELM
London & Canberra

© 1983 David Bradby, Philip Thomas and Kenneth Pickering
Croom Helm Ltd, Provident House, Burrell Row,
Beckenham, Kent BR3 1AT

British Library Cataloguing in Publication Data

Bradby, David
    Studying drama.
    1. Drama — Study and teaching — Great Britain
    I. Title   II. Thomas, Philip.
    III. Pickering, Kenneth
    792'.07'041   PN2078.G7

    ISBN 0-7099-0650-1
    ISBN 0-7099-3219-7 Pbk

Typeset by Leaper & Gard Ltd, Bristol
Printed and bound in Great Britain
by Billing & Sons Limited, Worcester.

CONTENTS

PREFACE

This book is intended primarily for undergraduates and 'A' level students following courses in drama and theatre arts, but we hope it will also be of value in a wide variety of courses in drama at higher and further education levels. It is written as a result of our experience of teaching in schools, colleges and universities in an attempt to provide both a methodology and a structured programme of work for the study of drama. The underlying principle of our approach is that *active* involvement in the processes of drama is an essential prerequisite of its study and accordingly our sections dealing with Staging, Acting and Contextual Issues include both theoretical and practical considerations. In attempting to enter into a dialogue with the reader we have aimed for a variety of practical responses to the material and have provided both exercises for personal development and starting points for further study. Teachers are encouraged to use such material from the book as may be appropriate to their needs and situation: the three sections of the book may be used in isolation whereas the entire text will provide a complete course of study.

D.B., P.P.T., K.W.P.

1 INTRODUCTION

The concept of an academic subject is a curious one. Conditioned as we are by years of schooling, in which timetables are broken up into little blocks, like chocolate bars, with each block labelled English, French, Maths or Physics, the concept seems quite natural. It is only when we confront a new area of study, like drama, that we realise what an artificial division of knowledge is involved in the concept of a subject. In fact this concept has come into being mainly for the convenience of teachers and academic institutions. It is linked to the notion of a course of study, that is the amount of information or conceptual ideas that a person may be expected to master in a given period of time.

Most of the subjects that we now take for granted were at one time considered illegitimate or confused or a rag-bag of disparate elements having no internal coherence or reason to hang together. Psychology, for example, was long considered to be an ill-fitting mixture of experimental physical science and philosophical speculation. Those who accused it of incoherence were strengthened by the fact that individual psychologists tended to entrench themselves in one or other of these positions, insisting that they were essentially scientists or that they were chiefly philosophers. Controversies of this kind generally centre on methodology. The argument becomes a matter of which methods and techniques of scholarly work are most fruitful or appropriate. It becomes impossible to define the subject area to be studied without also defining the manner in which it is to be studied.

Drama, in the 1980s, must be seen as an emergent subject. Although courses are now offered in drama at CSE 'O' and 'A' level as well as in further and higher education, its position is precarious. The University Grants Committee demonstrated considerable hostility towards drama in its 1981 review of courses. The 'A' level course went through several versions before it was finally approved in 1979 and is still offered by only one Examining Board. Drama is, in this way, partially accepted as a subject but there is still considerable disagreement, among its supporters as well as its critics, about both the nature of the subject and about an appropriate methodology.

A clear definition of drama as a subject is made particularly difficult by the fact that the word is not new to academic programmes. Traditionally it has been seen, not as a separate subject, but as a genre within literary studies on the same footing as the novel, the epic, the short story, etc. This represents a decline from the state of affairs in the early medieval universities, when dramatic works had pride of place in the study of literature. A major part of medieval literary studies was devoted to the tragedies of Aeschylus, Sophocles and Euripides and to the works of Aristotle, especially the *Poetics*, in which he sets out a complex definition of tragedy. With the rise of the novel in Europe during the eighteenth, nineteenth and twentieth centuries, literary studies have gradually changed their emphasis, devoting more time to prose and less to drama or poetry.

At the same time the words 'drama' and 'dramatic', along with other associated terms such as 'scenario' and 'role', have been extended to use in new areas quite distinct from the theatre, their place of origin. This tendency is already two centuries old: 'Dramatic, in the sense of an action or situation having qualities of spectacle and surprise comparable to those of written or acted drama, dates mainly from the eighteenth century' (R. Williams, *Keywords*). But it has accelerated rapidly in recent times, and this can be attributed largely to the development of television. The people who make television programmes have discovered that almost any piece of information can be put across more effectively on the small screen if it is cast in dramatic form. Because of this, the study of dramatic forms, and of how they achieve their effects, has become extremely important for anyone wanting to know how television can be most effectively used.

The new currency that television has given to the forms and concepts associated with drama would be quite sufficient to make it difficult to define as a discrete subject even if there were no further complications. But one further complication presents itself immediately: it is difficult to study drama without reference to the theatre. This is reflected in the titles of many further and higher education courses: 'Drama and Theatre Arts' or 'Drama and Theatre Studies'. To study the theatre means to study the history of the theatre and for this it may be necessary to use the methods of the archaeologist, especially if we want to know anything about the Ancient Greek and Roman theatres. Archaeology will tell us about the shape and size of early theatre buildings, but if we want to know about the place of theatre performance in human society, especially its religious and political functions, then we must turn to social anthropology. In addition, theatre practice incorporates a number of different skills and disciplines, some of which are classed as separate artistic disciplines in their own right (mime, dance, music) whereas others, like lighting, sound, property and scene construction, are seen as specific technologies of the theatre.

Drama, defined as an academic subject, must therefore cut across a number of different disciplines. Clearly, courses in drama will combine the different skills and methods we have sketched out in different combinations according to the presuppositions of the course plans. To study drama may simply be to study a branch of literature if the course concentrates exclusively on the words of the playwrights. Or it may be to study a branch of mass communications if the course centres on forms and modes of transmission. Again, it may be to study a branch of social anthropology if the course concentrates on the social process out of which these things are constructed. It should come as no surprise to find that existing drama courses are, in fact, every bit as varied as this list would suggest.

The pressures of tradition and vested academic interest have usually forced drama courses to develop as offshoots of English departments, whether in colleges or universities. So far no drama course exists as an offshoot of a sociology or technology department. This handbook is therefore addressed to people studying or teaching in departments that have their place within a Faculty of Arts or Humanities. The exclusively arts background introduces a further difficulty in the attempt to define drama as a coherent subject: where it is not seen as a messy monster, it is viewed as nothing more than an eccentric branch of English Lit. — an overgrown genre course. In order to counter such misunderstandings, it is important to be clear from the outset about the specific and peculiar nature of drama study. We take this to be the study of plays performed in theatres.

Such a definition calls for qualification of the words *play* and *theatre*. By 'play', should be understood any represented action between fictitious people; by 'theatre', any space separated from all the other spaces around it, marked out for a special purpose. Implied also in both notions is the presence of an onlooker: 'A man walks across this empty space whilst someone else is watching him, and this is all that is needed for an act of theatre to be engaged.' This is how Peter Brook lays the foundation for a theoretical lecture course on dramatic art (*The Empty Space*, p. 9). Brook's formulation is typical of many such attempts to state a lowest common factor for all theatre of all ages. Such reductions can be useful for their emphasis, which falls upon things done rather than things said, actions rather than

words, and upon the presence of the onlooker. When we *read* a story
(or a play), we understand it first, and only as we begin to understand
it do we begin to visualise it. In the theatre this process is reversed — a
play viewed in performance is *seen* first and understood only second.
The importance of this is enormous: it means that theatre communicates in a way that is radically different from either everyday speech
or the written media. It therefore follows that the language of this
communication is not the same as that of the written media. It has its
own grammatical and syntactical forms which require analysis and
practice like any other language.

The analysis of theatre language is no easy task and there are a
number of reasons for this. The most important is the fact that plays
done in theatres are ephemeral: they cannot be fully recorded
without changing their nature in important ways. But it is obviously
necessary for drama students to be able to study certain plays irrespective of whether they can see a performance and it is equally
obvious that for every performance that is given, a host of other,
different performances could be imagined. For these reasons
students have to deal with the printed texts of plays more often than
with live performances. It is therefore necessary, in the first place, to
distinguish between what is conveyed by the printed text and what is
conveyed by the performance. A printed text consists of only two
codes of communication: dialogue (sometimes monologue) and
stage directions. The stage directions may be explicit or merely
implicit but they are present in the text of every play at least in the
minimal form of *who* is speaking and *where.* The experience of seeing
a play performed in a theatre, on the other hand, is a very different
experience: a variety of codes of communication present themselves
to the spectator simultaneously and all compete for his attention. The
settings, the costumes, the music, the lights, the movements as well as
the words, all offer to the spectator their peculiar sequence of sign
systems. What is more, each has its own rhythm of change and
development. The settings, for example, will change rarely or may
even be the same throughout the performance. The actions will
present moments of rapid change and moments of stability. Now one,
now another element of the production will move into the foreground
of the spectator's attention, while the rest becomes background. In
other words, each separate sign system will be decoded by the
spectators with reference to all the others: an actor going through
movements representing a sword fight will be understood quite
differently according to whether he does so in the setting of a

medieval castle or of a modern padded cell.

The example just given presents us with no difficulty in deciding what shall be seen as foreground, what as background. But if more than one action is taking place on stage the spectator may be invited to choose between two equally plausible possibilities of ways of reading (i.e. constructing a meaning) for the scene: either to see action A as a background for action B, or vice versa. Other difficulties may present themselves in a production that deliberately sets out to challenge accepted stage conventions. Theatre-goers are used to treating the set as a background for the actors' movement, dialogue, etc. A recent production of *La Dispute* (Marivaux) included a moment when the walls of the set began to move. Becoming active, their movements occupied the foreground of the spectators' attention instead of retaining their customary place as passive background. Some productions offer more scope for this than others, but even in quite traditional productions different interpretations of the same play can be accounted for by the varying weight that the spectators give to the different sign systems.

In using terms like 'codes of communication' or 'sign system', we are borrowing from the school of criticism usually termed 'Structuralism'. Applied to literature, this method has demolished the traditional assumption that the text could function like a transparent screen between writer and reader. The identity of both reader and writer and the meaning of the story had previously been assumed to be fixed, in some sense *there*, waiting to be discovered. The Structuralist critics have shown that the identities of both reader and writer are constructed by and through the process of exchange of communication. If meaning in literature is constructed rather than found, then the theatre is doubly complex, since meaning is constructed both by performers and by spectators. The traditional view, which was that the text alone could be reliably preserved, has been called into question. It has been asserted that the process of reading a text is no more reliable than the process of reading (i.e. constructing a meaning for) a performance.

These new approaches to literary criticism serve to remind us that any approach to theatre must somehow take account of the variety of different sign systems through which the theatre communicates. The idea of the sign system has been developed by Structuralist critics, especially Roland Barthes, to show that we are perpetually 'reading' messages in the objects that surround us, but they are messages not communicated in words. Almost everything around us, from traffic lights to the latest dress fashion, conveys a meaning to us, or, rather, offers us a specific set of coded signs which we interpret, often sub-consciously. In the theatre, it is clear that costume does not convey the same sort of message nor does it communicate in the same way as speech. But the spectator certainly interprets it, or attaches a meaning to it, whether he does so consciously or subconsciously. The world of costume constitutes a sign system by means of which meanings can be constructed, meanings which may denote (i.e. state explicitly) or connote (i.e. suggest by means of association). The same is true of all other aspects of theatre production. Lighting, sound, sets, properties, actions, dances, music, sound effects are all separate sign systems available to the actors and producer/director in the construction of a performance.

When we witness a performance, the meaning of the play presents itself to us as a totality. We do not ask whether this lighting effect or that movement serves to reinforce or to contradict a particular line of thought: we think alongside the performance, that is to say we construct a meaning as it goes along, responding to a whole variety of signs which we do not necessarily separate out and disentangle from one another as the performance unfolds. But each movement, light, colour, sound that is presented on stage is the result of a choice by the director (or somebody on the production team) and it is necessary to find some way of categorising these different codes of signification. No two structuralist critics of the theatre agree about how this is to be done, but in order to provide an example of how such a method operates we can suggest four basic and clearly differentiated codes.

(1)   The linguistic. This includes the dialogue (or monologue) that is spoken and also words as they appear in any shape or form: projected on to a screen, written on the set, sung to music, etc.
(2)   The perceptual. This, a rather loose category, groups together anything that makes a direct impact upon the senses of the audience: sound, colours, images, movements, and all those elements that have a significance not filtered through language.
(3)   The socio-cultural. The significance that will be attached to elements of both (1) or (2) above will depend on conventions peculiar to specific societies and cultures. Hanging white sheets from the windows will be construed as signifying that a death has taken place (in Sweden) or that it is washing day (in Italy). For people working within their native culture and tradition, those kinds of associations will be taken for granted. Such conventions

will operate both at the level of connotation and of denotation.

(4)   The theatrical. More specific than the socio-cultural, and not necessarily recognised by every member of a socio-cultural group, are the theatrical conventions or codes of signification. These vary considerably, even with the same social and cultural tradition.

Of these four categories, only the first is included with any thoroughness in the printed texts of plays. As a result of this, the study of drama is bound to call upon creative and imaginative skill, as well as skills of a critical and analytical nature. This is evident as soon as we begin to analyse the speeches in a play. In order to be able to hear the voice with which they should be spoken, we require all sorts of information not contained in the text. For what survives of a play, once its original production has disappeared (or what exists of a play that has never been produced) is not characters or a story (although these can be reconstructed by the use of inference and imagination) but a sequence of speeches attributed to a set of names. These speeches are better described as *speech acts*. By speech act is meant the performative function of speech which is normally implied rather than stated. Most statements contain a function of this kind: they promise or threaten or enquire or command but often fail to include the explicit statement 'I promise', 'I threaten', etc. In order to bring these speech acts back to life in a performance, the performer has to attend not only to the statements themselves but also to the conditions in which they are uttered. Statements made by a character in a novel will also be affected by the conditions in which that character utters his words but the novelist is able to provide a precise delineation of the circumstances of his choosing. But the situation of the stage character is one of those elements of freedom and flexibility that necessitate a genuinely creative act on the part of the performer. For while certain circumstantial details are given by the playwright, others need to be found in the course of rehearsal and production work.

The conditions or circumstances that have to be considered by the performer are of two distinct kinds: the material conditions and the imaginary conditions. Material circumstances condition statements in a very obvious way: the words 'I am hungry' are spoken in a different voice when the character uttering them is rich and well fed from the voice that will be used by someone starving to death. In the theatre material conditions of this kind have to be *materialised,* shown in concrete form and the shape that they take will depend on the scenic vocabulary and stage technology employed. Sometimes the form in which these conditions should be materialised is specified by the playwright. In *Endgame*, Beckett specifies that Nagg and Nell should be placed in dustbins, a situation which only too clearly conditions their statements about life, whether they are understood to rise above this degrading position, or thought of as merely 'talking rubbish'. In other cases the playwright could not possibly have suspected the material conditions in which the performer of his words is placed. In Peter Brook's production of *A Midsummer Night's Dream*, many of Oberon's lines were delivered while swinging on a trapeze.

The dustbins in *Endgame* or the trapeze in *A Midsummer Night's Dream* are both unusually concrete, non-metaphorical examples of conditioning. More common is the case where the performers themselves convey the imaginary situations that condition and define the meaning of the speeches. In a scene from Brecht's *Galileo*, we see the Pope at first expressing ideas quite sympathetic to Galileo. In the course of the scene he is dressed up in the papal regalia for a public audience: the more robes are put on him, the less able he is to resist the demands of the Cardinal Inquisitor, who wants to interrogate Galileo. In this case the change in an imaginary relationship is being presented to the audience by concrete, visual means: those of the papal regalia. Often, an essential condition which gives meaning to a statement is created simply by means of the attitudes and statements of other characters. In a celebrated scene from *The Man of Mode* (Act 3 Scene 1) Harriet and young Bellair decide to put on a show of love for their respective parents who are observing them. Their lines, taken out of context, do not read like a love scene at all. In the context provided by the presence of the onlookers they take on a different meaning. It is the peculiarity of theatre dialogue that what is important is not so much the statements themselves as the conditions in which they are uttered.

Drama has often been studied with a view to extracting and discussing the philosophy of its author. But it is not so easy to extract a line of thought from the speeches of a play. For, as we have just seen, the speeches are seldom intended to be taken at face value, but rather within the context of a total situation. An author who has suffered particularly in this respect is Molière. Volumes of criticism have been devoted to a study of this author's thought and to elucidating the philosophies of the different characters of his plays. But Tartuffe's famous statement that 'il y des accommodements avec le ciel' is not interesting as a philosophical proposition. It is interesting as the kind of thing a man will say when he is trying to play the saintly celibate but is in fact aflame with a lust he can neither deny nor control. Similarly, the statements made by Alceste and Oronte in the discussion of the sonnet (*Le Misanthrope,* Act 1) are in themselves too extreme to be foundations of a philosophy. Their interest lies in the context. This shows that the protestations made by the two men are quite out of proportion with the rather trivial occasion. If taken separately and out of context, both the statements of Alceste and those of Oronte seem absurdly extreme. But taken in their place in the scene as Molière wrote it, each character's statements are explained by the extremism of the other and the point of the scene can be appreciated, i.e. to extract comedy from the contrast between the man who believes that one should always say exactly what one thinks and the opposite attitude, that maintains that one should always flatter and deceive.

So a play can be seen to function more by presenting a number of conflicting ideas than by developing a single philosophy. In studying plays, we shall find that we have to pay attention to a number of different 'voices'. It is not simply a matter, as in a novel, of assessing the author's meaning. The task is to be attentive to all the different voices in a play. Among these different voices we can sometimes even distinguish the voice of the public. When Winnie, in Beckett's play *Happy Days,* recalls a bystander looking at her and asking, 'What does she mean, planted there up to her titties in the sand,' the natural response of the average observer is being built into the fabric of the dialogue.

If we look only at the printed words of the playtext, we encounter another interesting problem for the study of drama. This has to do with the action of *character* in literature. Much dramatic criticism treats characters in the theatre as if they were similar to characters in a novel. But the novelist does not rely solely on dialogue. He is able to provide a wealth of information concerning the character's thoughts, dreams, upbringing, ancestry. He can even tell us things that the character himself does not know. But a 'character' in a playtext is literally only a set of disconnected speeches set down against a name. The one factor giving unity to the character is the actor who portrays him. This actor must find a mask, costume, voice, way of moving, etc. that integrate all the things set down for his character to say. If any privileged information of the kind supplied by the novelist is to be conveyed to the audience, then it must be by other characters speaking about him behind his back and such information is always suspect — an audience will wait for the character to confirm by his *behaviour* the truth or otherwise of the assertions made about him. When Polonius tells Ophelia that Hamlet is going mad, we do not immediately believe him, but wait to see how Hamlet will behave. In this situation, a novelist would be able to tell us *both* what Polonius thought *and* what was really going on in Hamlet's mind. But the dramatist has voluntarily limited himself to the perspective of his characters, chosen to speak through their voice alone.

The unity of character that the actor must supply is as complex as the unity of people in real life. The best playwrights are those whose lines allow the actor to build into the unity of his role some of the contradictory movements of characters in real life. In doing this, he is assisted by the nature of dramatic development which is not linear but tabular. That is to say that the audience perceives the character as a series of images, situations, relationships. In each separate scene, the character's behaviour is governed by a particular logic of aims and achievements or frustrations, but this logic may change from scene to scene. At the extreme, each new scene may be designed specifically to establish discontinuities of character. This is the case in Brecht's *Good Woman of Setzuan*, in which the central character is exposed to pressures of so contradictory a nature that she splits in half, 'becoming' two different characters, the kindly Shen Te and the ruthless Shui Ta.

Tabular development is simply one aspect of a particular set of dramatic conventions. All the speeches contained in a playtext have been set down with the assumption of certain precisely defined conventions for mimetic and representational actions by the actor. Broad differences of convention are easy enough to spot. Shakespeare would clearly have constructed his speeches differently if he had written for the late nineteenth-century proscenium arch stage. Part of the task of the student will be to rediscover these performance conventions and to fill in the subtler details that are not immediately apparent. This does not mean he has to be slavish in following original conventions. A recent Shakespeare season by the Théâtre du Soleil has shown that by employing some of the conventions of Kabuki theatre Shakespeare's characters can be made to come to life in surprising ways. But the purpose of understanding the original conventions will be partly to decide how far they can or should be followed in production.

To work on the text of a play in this perspective quickly raises questions about the theatre space in which it is to be performed. No two theatres are exactly alike and over the centuries the size and shape of acting spaces has varied enormously, as also have the social connotations of the theatre as an institution. The depth and complexity of a good theatre performance is the result of a two-way influence: the theatre space influences our perception of the text and the text influences our perception of the space. To a person accustomed to seeing Shakespeare performed in a proscenium arch theatre, where the spaces for audience and for action are strictly separate, a performance in an assembly hall, warehouse or similar open space will seem very different. This has been the experience of visitors to the Edinburgh Festival. The influence also flows the other way: in an age when theatres were a convenient place for men to encounter prostitutes the plays performed on stage were treated with some disdain, even plays now considered 'great'. Contrariwise, a play performed in the National Theatre acquires a certain status irrespective of subject matter or dramatic merit.

Since the play performance is the object of our study, the space in which that performance takes place requires analysis as much as the text and the conventions of acting, costuming, setting. Certain characteristics of the performance space can be seen to hold good for almost any play, while others are more specific to particular periods or places. Among the generally valid, four can be distinguished by way of introduction. We shall return to consider refinements upon these basic positions in later parts of the book. In the first place, a performance space is always defined by means of its limitations: it is separated off from the world of everyday reality that surrounds it. It is raised up or hollowed out or marked off in some other fashion and it is empty. It presents itself as a space not yet filled with either objects or people. In the second place, this emptiness can be defined by reference to the purpose for which it is reserved. The purpose cannot be defined in one word because it is a double purpose, both concrete and imaginary, neither quality having a separable existence of its own, each existing by virtue of the other. It is *both* the physically defined, measurable area in which actors of flesh and blood can deploy their muscles, vocal chords, etc., and into which objects of various kinds may be introduced *and* it is an imaginary space in which the laws of time, space and mass can be overruled. In the third place, this space possesses characteristics having a conventional or codified relation to the real world, both in its material aspects and in its social relations. An object, when it enters this space, will be understood to 're-present' something, as Quince explains to his actors in *A Midsummer Night's Dream*; it may, or may not, be a real object, but as soon as it enters the theatre space its function alters: it becomes representational. The same is true of social relations. The actor playing Macbeth may in fact hate the actor playing Macduff but when they confront one another on the stage they re-present a fight, they do not fight as they would in any other place outside the theatre. A fourth characteristic needs to be mentioned as part of this introduction not because it is invariable, but because it is a characteristic always potentially present, whatever the type of theatre. This is the ceremonial or ludic quality. In Ancient Greece, in medieval Europe (and in many societies or subcultures scattered around the world today) the theatre space was also a space reserved for devotional purposes or for public games, occasionally both at once. The place was thought of as a precinct or space especially inhabited by divine power. This is why it was empty. There was danger attached to entering the space and one only did so after complicated preparations and with an official seal of approval.

Of course theatre spaces change and develop. Among the many shaping influences upon them, one or other may predominate for a while but then another will reassert itself and bring about a return to earlier patterns. The recent history of the European theatre shows a theatre shaped chiefly by the demands of a public who wanted to be able to scrutinise one another (the horse-shoe-shaped italianate theatre), giving way to a theatre more suited to a convincing, even illusionistic depiction of reality (the late nineteenth-century proscenium arch theatre). This in turn has given way to a theatre in which the demands of the actor are the predominant shaping influence — either by establishing an open arena with a minimum of illusionistic equipment as in the case of Brook or Grotowski's theatres, or in the less extreme form of the thrust stages that are so common in theatres built during the last two decades.

Any act of theatre, however modest in means, involves a complex interplay of the various elements that have been identified: stage directions and dialogue, theatre technologies and social conventions, sign systems and the spaces in which they are deployed. In this book we have attempted to elaborate a method for studying each separate element in an appropriate manner while at the same time maintaining an overview of how each finds its place in the complete performance of a given play in a given theatre.

PART I

STAGING PROBLEMS

2 THEATRE: SPACES AND AUDIENCES

Studies in the origins of drama in almost every culture have revealed its relationship with religious practice, sometimes sacrificial, sometimes in the form of enacted myths in which the stage became a metaphor for the human condition. In such conditions an act of theatre was the celebration of a shared belief and was possible because of a broad consensus, within a given society, concerning the relationship between natural and supernatural forces. Forms of drama emanating from such religious or ceremonial gatherings possess a power that is recognised, even by people who know very little of the cultural conventions from which they sprang. For this reason, the Noh plays of Japan, the miracle plays of medieval Europe or the tragedies of Ancient Greece are often thought to possess qualities of pure theatre that we have lost in the modern Western dramatic tradition. Accordingly, critics and theatre practitioners seeking to revitalise our drama have often turned to ancient forms for their inspiration, in the belief that ritual drama can somehow crystallise central human concerns.

An example is the work, in the early years of this century, of W.B. Yeats. Yeats and his followers were excited by the revelation of the Japanese Noh tradition in the translations of Ezra Pound and Ernest Fenellosa. They began to write plays based on Japanese models, including detailed instructions for their staging, employing methods that ran contrary to the commercial theatre of their day. They wanted special small theatres to be constructed and plays performed in private homes so as to create a sense of shared space between performers and audience. They aimed to recreate a communal ritual experience by means of theatre performance which made use of deliberately non-representational forms of staging. The performance began with the ritual designation of the acting space, and employed anti-naturalistic devices like the use of masks, stylised gesture, dance and music. During the same period in England the new translations of Ancient Greek plays by Gilbert Murray gave rise to similar ideas. Murray was responsible for some striking productions of plays by Euripides at the Court theatre between 1904 and 1908 through which it was felt by contemporaries that ritual theatre was being rediscovered. Murray made use of chorus movement, dance, music

15

and heightened verse forms in similar ways to those suggested by Yeats.

The renaissance that such developments were intended to herald never, in fact, occurred in Britain. Yeats's and Murray's concept of ritual theatre only throve in private or heavily subsidised perform-ances and, as Arnold Bennett noted in his Journal, created only a depressing elite. This was the result of a double error: the error of assuming that an act of theatre involves solely the action presented on stage and the error of supposing that the ceremony of theatre can be meaningful without relating to the society in which it is presented. Each society creates the ceremonies that are appropriate for itself. Theatre is not shaped only by playwrights, directors, actors, but also by audiences and by the cultural norms of the society to which all belong. It follows that performance styles, the signs by which communication is effected, even the content of the plays themselves, must be analysed in relation to the expectations of the audiences for whom they are intended. An analysis of a piece of anti-nuclear street theatre designed for performance at a CND rally could not confine itself to style and content of the play alone, for the very meaning of the performance is to some extent dictated by the manner in which its audience receives it. At the anti-nuclear rally, the play would be celebratory, inspirational, confirming the shared beliefs of the onlookers, whereas if the same piece were performed on the lawn of the White House it would be deemed agitational, divisive and propagandist.

As soon as we begin to consider problems of staging, therefore, we have to consider first the nature of the audience, for what is done in the performance space is guided by a calculation of its effect on the observing audience. If that calculation is wrong, and the audience does not react as expected, the performers will begin to alter what they are doing. So the key to understanding questions of staging lies in the nature of the relationship between the performance and its audience. When they buy a ticket and step into a theatre, or when they decide to stop in the street to watch an open-air performance, the people who make up the audience are entering into a kind of contract. They are, literally, putting themselves in a position to be amused or shocked, moved or affected. Audiences allow themselves to be manipulated in remarkable ways. They suffer insults, physical dis-comforts, excessive noise, or even physical violence, and they watch acts that they would not tolerate in their own homes. This is because they believe that the experience, as a whole, will offer them something of interest. As we shall see in the course of this discussion, the audience's willingness to be manipulated can be used in very different ways by those responsible for creating the performance. In the modern theatre all those whose work contributes to the creation of a performance are, at least nominally, under the control of the director, and so our consideration of staging methods will deal largely with the approach of the director, although we shall assume that the director works in collaboration with set designer, costume designer and lighting designer.

The director's attention will be focused mainly on the stage space, that is the space separated off from the audience and staked out for the actors, invested with the power to transform itself into other, imaginary spaces. The various methods and techniques employed in pursuit of this transformation constitute the art of the director. It is an art practised by everyone who picks up a play and reads a few pages for it is impossible to read a play without some mental reconstruction of a three-dimensional space in which the action could take place. The reader of a play will often allow several contradictory images or spaces to coexist in his mind. While reading *Macbeth*, he might think, at different moments, of a Scottish moor he has walked over, of images from the Japanese film version, and of a drawing of Shakespeare's stage. The director will be able, if he chooses, to build allusions to all of things into his production, but first of all he must settle on the size, shape and character of the three-dimensional space in which his flesh and blood actors will move and speak. This will entail a series of fundamental decisions such as whether the setting should remain the same throughout the play or change for different scenes; whether there should be a curtain to hide the preparation of the imaginary space; whether the settings should be constructed from three-dimensional or from flat elements, natural or man-made substances; whether the treatment of space should appeal to the audience's sense of verisimilitude or to its powers of imagination.

In any performance there is a dynamic relationship between action and setting, each contributing to the meaning of the other. We might take the example of Sartre's play *In Camera*. The stage directions give a careful description of the exact type of room in which the action of the play is to take place: it is a bourgeois drawing room furnished in the Second Empire style (i.e. massive Victorian) with both window and fireplace bricked up. The total effect Sartre intended to have on his audience was of stifling claustrophobia. The walls, bricked-up apertures and heavy furnishings serve to increase the audience's awareness of the finality of the characters' situation: they are in Hell for all eternity and can never escape. Sartre's choice of the Victorian drawing room as an image for Hell was a kind of practical joke played on his audience, for the expectations of that audience would have led them to assume, once the set was revealed, that they were about to witness a typical French comedy of adultery. The dawning realisation that the action takes place in Hell was made all the more frightening for the audience because they had at first been led to expect something light and frivolous. When the audience comes with different expectations, a different method of staging may be necessary. When Harold Pinter produced the play for BBC television, he clearly felt that the associations of Second Empire furniture would be lost on British audiences and that he could achieve the effect of anguish and claustrophobia equally well by setting the action in a dark limitless space. Any director, when he comes to stage a play, must assess the setting specified by the playwright and reinterpret it, using the scenic means at his disposal, in the light of the effect he wishes to have upon his audience.

No director starts from a position of total innocence, however much he might wish to. He is influenced by received ideas and by images that he has seen. These are not confined to the theatre productions he has seen, but include every example of representational art to which he has been exposed. In the modern period, representational methods such as photography or cinema can be as important an influence on a director's imagination as anything he has seen of a purely theatrical nature. In the medieval period painting, sculpture and stained glass had a similar function. At any given period, certain ideas of represented space will be commonly accepted, others will seem old-fashioned, and the most innovative will appear unfamiliar. In the theatre we see a dialectical process at work whereby stage practice is shaped by such ideas, but also, in its turn, helps to shape and change them. This process can best be understood by reference to a particular, historical example: Chekhov's play *The Seagull.* The circumstances of this play's earliest productions demonstrate the importance of the director's work in shaping the responses of his audience. At its first performance in 1896, *The Seagull* was a failure. To audiences and critics alike it seemed neither comedy nor tragedy nor melodrama and it was taken off after only five performances. But two years later it was given a second production by the new Moscow Arts Theatre, directed by Konstantin Stanislavsky, and this time it had a considerable success. The difference between the two productions was that only Stanislavsky had understood that the words of Chekhov's text pointed to another reality, unstated but evident, and that it was the work of the director to make this reality visible to the audience. This 'other reality' can be expressed in a number of ways. It can, for example, be expressed in terms of psychology by pointing out that what the characters say almost always conceals something else, that their superficial statements cover profound emotions.

It can also be expressed in terms of space, as is shown by Stanislavsky's production work on the play. In his production notes, he pointed out that the reason why these people felt that they had no purchase on life was partly explained by their position as town dwellers visiting their country estate. The first two acts of the play are set in the estate park and Stanislavsky employed every means he could think of to stress the associations with fading happiness and irrecoverable dreams of youth that the space holds for most of the characters.

The novelty of Chekhov's writing, in contrast to the accepted theatre of the late nineteenth century, was that the lines spoken by the characters were constantly hinting at their own inadequacy to express the speakers' profound, often painful, feelings. The famous opening exchange of the play illustrates this point:

Medvyedenko. Why do you always go about in black?
Masha. Because I'm in mourning for my life. I'm unhappy.

Both characters mean to convey much more than the words, on their own, can express. Medvyedenko longs to persuade Masha that she has no cause for unhappiness and could in fact find fulfilment in marriage if she would accept him as a husband. Masha longs to get rid of Medvyedenko so as to be able to indulge her melancholy infatuation with Konstantin, who she knows to be in love with someone else. For his production, Stanislavsky opened up additional spaces in the text by introducing lengthy pauses in which location and subtext were conveyed by a variety of means. His production note for the opening reads as follows:

The play starts in darkness, an (August) evening. The dim light of a lantern on top of a lamp post, distant sounds of a drunkard's song, distant howling of a dog, the croaking of frogs, the crake of a landrail, the slow tolling of a distant church bell — help the audience to get the feel of the sad, monotonous life of the characters. Flashes of lightning, faint rumble of thunder in the distance. After the raising of the curtain, a pause of ten seconds. After the pause Yakov knocks, hammering in a nail (on the stage); having knocked the nail in, he busies himself on the stage, humming a tune. During the first half of this scene Medvyedenko and Masha enter. They come out on the right of the audience. Stroll about after dinner. (Medvyedenko is smoking — he smokes a lot during the whole of the play.) Masha is cracking nuts. Medvyedenko carries a small club in his hands — not a walking stick. (*The Seagull Produced by Stanislavsky*, p. 139)

This use of pauses filled with sound and action was not unique to the opening but continued throughout the performance. The Russian scholar S.D. Balukhaty explains that they varied

from a tiny pause, a little pause, a pause of five seconds, ten seconds, fifteen seconds, ten plus five seconds, ten plus ten seconds, fifteen plus, a long pause and a very long pause. Their number (over one hundred) and their role in the scenic movement and in the conduct of the dialogue is exceptionally great. (ibid, p.114)

The purpose of these pauses was to impress the audience as strongly as possible with the impression of a real action set in a real time and place. For the poignancy of the characters' understated emotions to be fully appreciated, the staging of the play had to convey a quantity of other information about their relationship to the house, park and estate.

The achievement and force of Stanislavsky's work on *The Seagull* was to have found a way to represent on stage the interaction between people and the spaces they inhabit. In doing so, he was influenced by contemporary developments in science, in literature and in the visual arts which stressed the close connections between human beings and their environments. The Naturalist school of writers had taken up with enthusiasm the implications of Darwin's theories, particularly the idea that people's behaviour could be explained by the forces in the environment with which they had to contend. Painters of the Realist school such as Courbet and Millet had also depicted people as fashioned by their environments. But if Stanislavsky was influenced by the intellectual and artistic trends of his time, he also influenced them in his turn. His introduction of long periods of silent action and his use of stage space to suggest that what was visible to the audience was only a small part of a larger reality stretching far beyond the wings of the stage became a paradigm for Naturalist productions. It was so widely copied that it came to be thought of as 'natural' to present people in their environment in this way.

The above example has involved the use of scholarly reconstruction by historians of the theatre, and we shall be examining their mode of working in some detail in our section on Contextual Issues. The first productions of most plays are too remote to be recaptured by modern reproductive means or by using the memories of original audiences. In the case of *The Seagull* reconstruction is made much easier by the survival of Stanislavsky's production notes, contemporary descriptions and a few photographs. But even these are of little help without an informed idea of the expectations of his audience. Every element of his production was conceived with a particular effect on his particular audience in mind. The production succeeded because the audience recognised and responded to that image of people in their social and spatial environment. This explains why productions recorded on film or television often seem so stale to audiences who see them even a few years after their first performance. What had appeared electrifying to the first theatre audiences seems predictable or overplayed on the screen. The explanation lies not in the imperfections of the medium but in the fact that the expectations of the audience are no longer the same. In order to understand the force of Stanislavsky's work on *The Seagull*, we need to be made aware of the artificiality of much theatre production work in the 1890s.

So to reconstruct a historical production is also to reconstruct its audience. As well as knowing the size of the performance space, the movements of the actors, the arrangements of the settings, we have to know the composition of the audiences, where they came from, what class they belonged to and what pleasure they anticipated from a visit to the theatre. The audience at a medieval Mystery play may have been drawn from more than one social class, but all came together with the common purpose of reaffirming a shared faith. They did not differentiate the pleasure to be derived from attending a performance from the pleasures of feasting, celebration and worship. On page 238 in the section on Contextual Issues we have set out a comparative table of the different attitudes of modern and medieval audiences.

If we turn our attention to the audience for a Restoration play, we shall find that they came together for a very different kind of pleasure.

This audience was drawn from a more homogeneous class group, the aristocracy and upper bourgeoisie, and they could remember the years of Cromwell's rule, when all public performances were banned and the theatre denounced as a breeding ground for sin. Now that the Restoration had brought about the reopening of the theatres, these people were determined to enjoy that pleasure which had been denied to them for so long. Many of them had spent time in exile at the court of Louis XIV, where they had discovered the pleasure of going to the theatre simply to see and to be seen by other members of their caste, to hear the social gossip and to curry favour with the leaders of fashion. For them, the play was something of a pretext and so those who staged plays had to compete with other distractions for their audience's attention. It is not surprising if the subject matter of their plays was sometimes bawdy or that the dramatic rhythm was that of short, brilliant bursts, rather than sustained development, or that they depended on the cultivation of a glamorous star system.

Different again from both of these was the audience brought together for the production of *The Seagull* in 1898. Drawn from the Moscow intelligentsia, this group shared an interest in a new theatre that had only been open for a few months and that claimed by its name to be offering a new repertoire of high artistic standards for a broad audience — it was first known as the People's Art Theatre. They did not share the common religious beliefs of the medieval audience: some would have been atheists, some agnostics and some believers. But they did share a belief of a different kind: a belief that the latest developments in artistic style were important enough to merit serious, even reverential, consideration. Stanislavsky describes the play's first night as follows:

> I do not remember how we played. The first act was over. There was a gravelike silence. Knipper fainted on the stage. All of us could hardly keep our feet. In the throes of despair we began moving to our dressing rooms. Suddenly there was a roar in the auditorium and a shriek of joy or fright on the stage. Then there were the ovations to Lilina, who played Masha, and who had broken the ice with her last words which tore themselves from her heart, moans washed with tears. This it was that had held the audience mute for a time before it began to roar and thunder in mad ovation. (*My Life in Art*, p. 356)

This reaction suggests very clearly a collective state of mind of a group of people lost in rapt attention to what is being portrayed, awaking, as it were, from a dream at the end of the performance and taking some time to recapture the critical faculties which then find expression in applause. This is an audience that does not expect to participate in the manner of the medieval audience, nor does it engage in other activities as a Restoration audience might have done. Instead, it comes for the pleasure of losing itself in a fictitious story presented with maximum realism. In order to increase this sensation, the lights in the auditorium are not left on as they were in the Restoration theatre, but everything is darkened, except the stage area so that the audience appears to be observing a slice of real life that takes place as if unobserved, and whose agents never show that they realise that they are being watched.

This audience, which became the model for many 'art' theatres all over the world in the twentieth century, is defined chiefly by its level of education and interest in a particular idea of art. The pleasure that its members expect to derive from a visit to the theatre will not always be accounted for simply by the extent to which the play absorbs them. It will also relate to a sense of being part of an elite group — those who know about and can follow the latest developments. But this social function is firmly subordinated to belief in the value of the work of art. Such an audience is prepared for a play that demands a lengthy attention span presenting a single dramatic movement involving the same half dozen or so people and restricting itself to a single location, usually a drawing room similar to the one they have left behind in their own houses. The visit to the play flatters their belief that the most important events do indeed occur within their restricted caste and are located within their own special space: the four walls of the middle-class drawing room.

In his book *A Good Night Out*, John McGrath evokes a working-class audience that contrasts sharply with the middle-class audience we have just considered. Very amusingly, the author stresses the vitality, participation but unwillingness to pay attention that characterises a working-class audience unless it is sure that what is being presented really concerns it. Working in the theatre in Germany during the 1920s, the director playwright Bertolt Brecht was even more critical of the self-importance of the established middle-class theatre and sought to draw on the model of working-class entertainment:

All those establishments with their excellent heating systems, their pretty lighting, their appetite for large sums of money, their imposing exteriors together with the entire business that goes on inside them [he wrote of the middle-class theatres] all this doesn't contain five pennyworth of fun. ('Emphasis on Sport' in Willett, *Brecht on Theatre*, p. 7)

His ideal audience was like the public at a boxing match — both passionately involved in the action and yet prepared to stand back and take a dispassionate view of the technique of the participants. In the preface to *In the Jungle of Cities* (1923) Brecht addressed his audience in these terms: 'Don't worry your heads about the motives for the fight, concentrate on the stakes. Judge impartially the technique of the contenders and keep your eyes fixed on the finish.' Just as a boxer or a musician tries to show off his technique, so Brecht wanted the theatrical means and techniques to be plainly visible to the audience. From this followed all the familiar aspects of his production style: the half curtain that did not attempt to hide the preparations going on behind, the use of very bright, even light from visible lighting rows and an acting style that aimed to 'demonstrate' rather than 'incarnate'.

Brecht's view of the right relationship between action and audience was developed during the 1920s and early 1930s, a period when he was becoming convinced of the need to take sides in the political struggle then dividing Germany. In these circumstances, it seemed vital to prevent the audience from identifying itself in rapt, dreamlike attention with the action being portrayed. Instead, his model became the café or pub audience that McGrath later evoked. Such an audience not only remained detached and retained its independence of mind; it was also prepared to intervene if it disliked or diagreed with what was being presented for it on stage. Thus Brecht wrote a number of plays specifically for production in halls, schools or workers' clubs which were designed to generate political discussion in their audiences. In Brecht's view, far from making theatre performance boring, this type of approach could re-introduce some of the fun that he had found missing in the middle-class theatre. He anticipated that his audience would experience a particular pleasure: that of discussing, learning, confronting new ideas:

The theatre of the scientific age is able to make dialectics pleasurable. The surprises of development as it proceeds logically or by leaps and bounds, the instability of all states, the humour of contradictions, etc., these are enjoyments of the vitality of men, things and processes, and they heighten the art of living and the joy of living. ('Appendix to Short Organum' in Cole, *Playwrights on Playwriting*, p. 84)

A different kind of relationship between action and audience was envisaged by Jean Genet, when he wrote *The Blacks* (1959). It is one of the rare plays to go so far as to specify in so many words that it has been designed for performance before a particular audience:

> This play, written, I repeat, by a white man, is intended for a white audience, but if — which is unlikely — it is ever performed before a black audience, then a white person, male or female, should be invited every evening. The organizer of the show should welcome him formally, dress him in ceremonial costume and lead him to his seat, preferably in the front row of the stalls. The actors will play for him. A spotlight should be focussed upon this symbolic white throughout the performance. (Preface to the published edition, trans. Frechtman, 1960)

This shows an exceptionally sensitive attention on the part of a playwright to the function the audience performs in constructing a meaning for his play. The reason for his insistence on the presence of a white audience is that his play is not a story but a ritual; it does not describe events, it attacks attitudes. It is a ceremony for exorcising the European or white view of Africans or blacks. The ceremony is directed at the traditional white-skinned view of black skins as representing everything that is primitive, obscure, threatening, disgusting. The ceremony aims to realise as fully as possible this figment of the white imagination, in order, ultimately, to destroy it. Since it does not represent the reality of the blacks, but only the image imposed upon them by white people, it is essential to have a white audience. In other words, Genet requires a quality in his audience that is very like the quality of belief in a medieval audience. The images presented on stage only acquire their force as a result of the beliefs of the white audience. If we ask what kind of pleasure the white audience might be expected to derive from attending a performance of *The Blacks*, the answer must also be couched in something like religious terms. It is certainly not the pleasure of flattery or self-indulgence. It can only be described as the pleasure of seeing an indefensible myth undermined and exploded from within and the sense of release that may come from recognising the evils embedded in one's own culture.

3 PRODUCTION MODES: NATURALIST THEATRE, EPIC THEATRE AND THEATRE OF COMMUNION

The key question for the staging of any play is therefore 'for what audience and to what effect?' All the choices that a director makes concerning the type of staging, styles of acting, costumes, settings, etc. follow from his response to this initial question. The variations in production style available to a modern director are almost infinite, but it is possible to identify three broad modes of theatre production and these will enable us to focus a discussion of staging problems by reference to concrete examples of the work of twentieth-century directors.

Naturalist Theatre

The first category is the theatre of imitation, or Naturalist theatre, and we have already discussed an example of this in Stanislavsky's production of *The Seagull*. Stanislavsky's deployment of atmospheric detail bathed his actors in an environment that came as near as possible to evoking the real world in which the characters they were portraying lived and moved. The settings designed by Stanislavsky's designer Simov were variations on the basic pattern of the 'box set' that had been in use since the early years of the century. By joining together a series of canvas flats and inserting panels containing windows, doors, fireplaces and other solid pieces, designers had discovered that it was possible to create a very accurate reconstruction of an interior. In this way, not only could the play convey visually to its audience a great deal about the tastes and economic condition of the characters, but the actors portraying the characters were greatly helped by inhabiting an environment which gave realistic support to their performances. In a box set, the actor is enclosed within the walls of a setting and by assuming that there is an imaginary fourth wall on the side where the audience is placed, he can recreate imaginatively the feeling of living in a real room. Among modern directors, André Antoine (1858-1943) was the most extreme exponent of the idea of the fourth wall:

For a stage set to be original, striking, and authentic, it should first be built in accordance with something seen — whether a landscape or an interior. If it is an interior, it should be built with its four sides, its four walls, without worrying about the fourth wall, which will later disappear so as to enable the audience to see what is going on. (*Directors on Directing*, p. 95)

The development of these new staging techniques by Stanislavsky, Antoine and others was at first heralded as a move towards greater truth and vitality in the theatre. But the danger of theatre resembling life too closely is that it becomes merely an inert copy of it. The Russian director, Nikolai Evreinov (1879-1950) argued that if Stanislavsky had followed his logic through when directing *The Three Sisters*, he would have rented a house in the suburbs of Moscow, 'the audience would have come under the pretext of looking for apartments and then looked through the keyhole or half-open door' (Styan, *Modern Drama in Theory and Practice*, vol. 3, p. 90). He was implying that Stanislavsky's theatre was barely theatre at all and involved its audience in the dangerous hypocrisy of pretending that the stage world was real and that the characters had independent existences. The end-product of such theatre could only be passive observation, sentimentality or, at worst, voyeurism. Though the audience might feel sympathy for the characters portrayed, they would, he maintained, acquire no larger understanding of the way the world worked, nor discover any desire to change it.

Epic Theatre

In reaction to Naturalism, there emerged an approach to production and to playwriting that has come to be known as Epic theatre. It embraces many different styles, including the productions of Brecht, Meyerhold, Piscator and Joan Littlewood and the stylistic modes of Expressionism, Epic and Constructivism. In recent times, the work of such companies as Red Ladder or 7:84 and of playwrights such as Edward Bond, Peter Weiss and Peter Handke come within its scope. Despite their many differences, these all share the common concern with an appeal to the minds and social consciences of the members of the audience. They are of interest to us because they offer alternative staging rationales to those of Stanislavsky and Antoine. The various theatre workers mentioned shared at least four basic attitudes: they were opposed to indulgence in theatricality for its own sake, they were opposed to the economic and political system of capitalism, they sought to emphasise the social and economic determinants of human behaviour and they wished to counter the tendency of the audience to identify with the world and characters of the play.

The term 'Epic theatre' was coined, in modern times, by Erwin Piscator (1893-1966) to describe a direct form of theatre which acknowledged its own artificiality, denying the audience an eavesdropping role, using the actor to show not only the result, but the thought which created the result. Motive had to be transparent and clearly perceptible. Piscator had derived the term 'Epic' from the Aristotelian idea of a narrative unconstrained by the unities of time and place. By rejecting Naturalist imitations of real life and appealing to audience-identification, he hoped to make it possible to analyse a social or political issue directly.

In lieu of private themes, Piscator wrote, we had generalisations, in lieu of what was special, the typical, in lieu of accident, causality. Decorations gave way to constructiveness, Reason was on a par with Emotion, while sensuality was replaced by didacticism and fantasy by documentary reality. (Quoted by Willett, *The Theatre of Erwin Piscator*, p. 107)

The formative period of Piscator's work was between 1918 and 1933 in Germany when, in company with many young intellectuals, he had been appalled by the experience of the First World War. Socialism seemed to him to be the only appropriate response to the economic disarray and social malaise of the country. He formed a Communist theatre group, whose work was of an 'agit-prop' nature. The word derives from 'agitation' and 'propaganda', and the climactic lines from one of his early productions *Russia's Day* serve to illustrate the form of his communication.

Voice of the Russian Proletariat: Proletarians, into the struggle.
World Capitalism: Hell, devil, plague.
The German Worker: Struggle, struggle, struggle.
Voices (from all directions): Struggle, struggle, struggle.
World Capitalism (going off right): Down with Soviet Russia!
The German Worker. All for Russia. All for Russia. Long live Soviet Russia!

Whilst the play was more ideological than dramatic, the staging method, which used a map for scenery, heralded a scenic technique whose objective was to illustrate the plot and issues in the play rather than localise a setting. The set became a counter-point to the action, a function which later was taken over in part by use of projected slides and film. By announcing the content of a scene before it was played, much of the dramatic tension was removed, allowing the audience to focus on the meaning rather than the facts of each episode. In his *Despite All* (1925) there were 24 scenes which were interspersed with documentary film. The play was a historical revue from the years 1914-19, the setting was merely a large revolve with a simple construction of steps and platforms which were backed by a large projection screen. The final scene was a clear celebration of the Communist movement and fifty members of the Roter Frontkampferbund (a Communist paramilitary force) marched on to the scene and formed up waving eight enormous flags. This became a prototype for much of Piscator's work: a historical period dramatised in short scenes supported by documentary evidence on a sparse set which relied on technology with the intention of bringing art to the people and thereby explaining the meaning of history and the forces which shaped their lives.

The use of film was not new, but Piscator explored and exploited the medium for his own purpose of relating reality to fiction. He called his screen 'the theatre's fourth dimension' and argued 'In this way the photographic image conducts the story, becomes its motive force, a piece of living scenery (Willett, pp. 94-5). In *The Drunken Ship* (1926), Piscator used backing slides drawn by the cartoonist George Grosz on three screens which both identified place and made comment. Thus a prison scene was played with the central character sitting on a chair on a bare stage. He was backed by a large slide showing a prison exercise yard which was flanked by two other screens with slides of a grotesque warder on one side and a grotesque priest on the other. All of the figures were very large and dwarfed the prisoner himself. Piscator referred to his use of slides as the 'literarisation of the theatre' and stated that he used film for three purposes, to instruct, for dramatic reasons and as commentary. According to Willet (p. 113) instructional film was documentary and historical, extending the subject matter in terms of time and space. He writes that dramatic film 'furthered the story and served the dialogue' and commentary film 'pointed things out to the audience and emphasised the mood'.

This emphasis on film had a counterpart in the use of other technology and one of Piscator's principal devices was to have a stage of which some part could move. The revolve was commonplace, but a more ambitious device was the treadmill on which an actor could walk against a background of moving and changing projected scenery, thus giving a sense of journeying which was particularly suitable for his production of *Schweyk* with its adventuring and picaresque central character. For that production Piscator used two parallel treadmills each 55 feet long crossing the full length of the stage.

The production of *Schweyk* (1928) is discussed in detail by John Willet in *The Theatre of Erwin Piscator* and we include below an extract which gives a graphic description of the techniques and their effect.

A horrifying cartoon by Grosz ... showed soldiers arresting spies or hostages, their faces changing into those of snarling dogs; their prisoners are hanged and a dapper officer gets out his box camera to photograph the result. Schweyk finds his unit and goes on by train with his friend the gluttonous Baloun and other notabilities from the book. Again a filmed landscape rolls by on the screen, then for the scene where Schweyk and Baloun are made to do physical jerks beside the tracks a careful full-scale mock-up of a waggon comes in on the treadmill, with cut-out figures representing the 48 Men (or 6 Horses) it might contain. At this point Pallenburg tells the story of the waggon he has sent astray: a virtuoso monologue, delivered with all Schweyk's obstinately subversive gentleness. Then as they get nearer the front Grosz's images become grimmer and less caricatured: a bombed village is carried past, a Red Cross waggon with wounded soldiers changes on the screen into a coffin, a solitary sentry stands in the snow-covered landscape as the moon goes down; after which come almost Goya-like cut-outs of fighting, a skeleton releasing poison gas, with on the screen a pit full of bones and skulls, and one last paragraph sign dwindling into a question mark. (pp. 94-5)

Perhaps the best indicator of the sort of theatrical event which Piscator was trying to achieve is the total theatre which Gropius designed for him in 1927. Although the theatre was never built the principles were clear. There was a rejection of a tiered seating arrangement such as obtained in conventional theatres which

Piscator saw as reflecting and reinforcing the class divisions in society. Through a system of three huge revolves the space could be converted to provide thrust, arena and proscenium staging. Around the auditorium and behind the auditorium there were seventeen projection points so that the audience could be completely surrounded. The overall aim was, according to Gropius (quoted in

Figure 1: Grosz's Drawings for the Film, *Schweyk in the Second World War*

These relate to Part II, probably to Schweyk's Anabasis through the rear areas of the Austrian army.

Willett, pp. 117-18) of 'building in mechanical and light-generated fields of force which can be shifted in all three spatial dimensions and by their components and their cubes of light permit the director to conjure up the dreamspaces of his imagination with infinite variability within the invisible network of coordinates imposed by the neutral, blacked-out auditorium (p. 118). The theatre was to be a place in which social relations were changed by both the piece presented and by the organisation of the theatre itself.

Whilst Piscator was certainly innovative it is dangerous to emphasise this aspect of his work for such emphasis detracts from his central ideological ambitions. His staging ideas were evolving experiments with the communication of a Marxist interpretation of events. Perhaps this is best illustrated with reference to his experimental work with lighting. One of the techniques he developed was the use of lighting sources behind and to the side of the stage which were in full view of the audience. His objective was to 'make things clear' or 'clarify facts'. One of his most radical works was *Salome* (1964). Hans Ulrich Schmuckle who worked with Piscator wrote of the work:

> One of Erwin Piscator's great problems was the stage floor. He eventually decided to transform it into yet another source of light ... he ... was watching the sunlight which shone into the aeroplane from the depths of the horizon. Waves of light flooded up through the cabin-windows from below. Yet there were no shadows to be seen on the passengers' faces. Their faces were exceptionally clearly defined ... Later we tried to get the same effect with a transparent stage-floor made of glass. We laid lighting strips across the stage and inserted the sources of light underneath ... By this means we were able to literally 'bathe' the characters in light. (Schmuckle, 'Erwin Piscator and the Stage' p. 21)

The point which Schmuckle iterates is that the technique served to undermine any illusionistic or decorative effect and focus on the action of the opera's meaning, not to appeal to the audience's pleasure in spectacle.

Piscator's working method was also radical. He developed his scenic ideas during the rehearsal process as he and the actors felt a need for a development of the scene's meaning or a structure which would support and amplify the action.

Both Brecht and Meyerhold (Brecht worked with Piscator inter-

Figure 2: Walter Gropius's Design for 'Total Theatre'

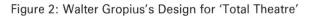

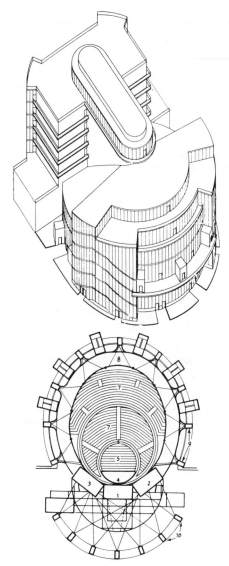

Note: 1, 2, 3 & 4 are the acting areas; 5 can be used as a revolve, with or without seating; the inner circle of seating at 7, together with 5 can be swung right around to create a theatre in the round; 8 shows the beam of light from one of the projectors housed in the pillars all round the theatre, e.g. at 9 and 10, making it possible for a director to surround his audience with an uninterrupted wall of images (using back-projection).

mittently during the twenties) felt that in the end Piscator's emphasis on staging actually detracted from the ideological impact of the performance and Meyerhold wrote in 1928 that he was 'on the wrong track' and that he 'had not grasped the problem'. In trying to create a revolutionary theatre he had focused on 'developing the *material* aspects of theatre technique'. Whereas he should have recognised the 'stage and theatre as a framework', 'to which the actor's voice and gestures have to be accommodated' (Willett, p. 125).

Meyerhold (1874-1940) had his early experience of theatre in Stanislavsky's Moscow Arts Theatre. Like Piscator he was a Communist, but unlike Piscator most of his important work was carried out within a Communist state.

It is worth noting here that the ideology of virtually all of the key theatre figures in the twentieth century has had a democratising purpose and has been partly didactic. Even Stanislavsky said in a speech to his company in 1898, 'What we are undertaking is not a simple private affair but a social task ... Our aim is to create the first intelligent, moral popular theatre and to this end we are dedicating our lives' (Quoted in Braun, E. *The Theatre of Meyerhold,* p. 23).

However it would seem that this stated purpose was not so clear in practice and in 1899, while a member of Stanislavsky's company, Meyerhold wrote, 'We need to know *why* we are acting, *what* we are acting, and whom we are instructing or attacking through our performance ... to understand which society or section of society the author is for or against' (ibid.).

One of Meyerhold's arguments with Stanislavsky was that the Naturalistic theatre was necessarily conservative. He left the MAT in 1902, but returned to run a studio theatre there in 1905. One of his objectives was to develop his ideas on 'stylisation'. He argued that the term was

indivisibly tied up with the idea of convention, generalisation and symbol. To stylise a given period means to employ every possible means of expression in order to reveal the inner synthesis of that period or phenomenon, to bring about those hidden features which are deeply rooted in the style of any work of art. (p. 42)

Fundamentally, he was arguing that theatre should find the essence of the matter with which it was dealing and find symbols which expressed that essence. In staging terms this had, for Meyerhold, to be a paring-down process which readily associated with the socialist puritanism in a post-revolutionary social context.

The artistic policy which was formulated to describe this 'essential' staging was 'Constructivism'. Put simply, Constructivism was based on a socialist utilitarian principle that art should serve the people rather than elaborate on itself. Sheldon Cheney wrote in 1927:

> The out-and-out Constructivists have announced that the stage setting must not only be stripped of every shred of adventitious decoration but must be conceived *anti-decoratively*... The typical Constructivist setting may be described as a skeleton structure made up of the physically necessary means for acting ... an agglomeration of stairs, platforms, runways etc., ... stripped to their basic and structural forms, held together by plain scaffolding ... Every plank and part of it is tested by the rigid question of its functional use. It is the 'practicable' of the old pictorial scene plucked out of the picture, skeletonised and nailed together for safe usage. (*Theatre Arts Monthly* (November 1927), p. 557)

Meyerhold's personal interpretation of Constructivism led to some interesting experiments. He staged Ibsen's *A Doll's House* by propping up stock flattage back to front against the stage walls (1922). In *Earth Rampant* (1923) Meyerhold used utilitarian objects, cars, motor cycles, field telephones, lorries, a threshing machine and a field kitchen and the one exception to the real objects was a gantry crane which had to be made of wood because the stage floor was not strong enough to carry the weight of the real thing. This functional staging was complemented by lighting from actual search-lights placed in the auditorium, 'real' costumes and actors without make-up. *Earth Rampant* was dedicated to the Army and from collections made at early performances an aeroplane was bought for the Army which was given the name 'Meyerhold'. The play's cele-bratory nature was fully achieved at the Fifth Congress of the Comintern in Moscow in 1926 when a cast of 1,500, including infantry and horse cavalry, took part performing before an audience of 25,000.

Meyerhold's Constructivism was clearly shaped by the enthus-iasms of the post-revolutionary period; after a while, people tired of its constraints and of the jingoism associated with the sort of celebration which we have described. Whilst maintaining the principle of art serving ideology Meyerhold moved on to use many of the staging techniques which we have discussed in relation to

Piscator, employing multiple-staging, slides and film. Many other elements of his staging strategy are also of interest. One is his use of both individual actors and group for their sculptural value and another is his use of props in order to relate the minutiae of behaviour to general human issues. Both of these strategies were also to be used by Brecht.

Meyerhold referred to his actors as 'actor-tribunes' who acted 'not the situation itself, but what is concealed behind it and what it has to reveal for a specifically propagandist purpose' (*The Theatre of Meyerhold*, p. 192). He continued, 'When the actor-tribune lifts the mask of the character he does not merely speak the lines ... he reveals the roots from which the lines have sprung.' The task demanded considerable technical clarity and pointing up of the actors' behaviour. This was helped by a process which Meyerhold called 'pre-acting' whereby according to Braun (ibid. p. 192) the actor employed 'mime before he spoke his lines in order to convey his true state of mind'. It can be seen that the slowing down of the acting and removal of the 'real' temporal and psychological context turn the actor into a kinetic sculptural form rather than a 'person'. The sort of impact deriving from the individual actor could also be achieved by the group.   Meyerhold's most celebrated production was of Gogol's *The Government Inspector* (1926) in which tableaux vivants served to provide a visual comment and metaphoric amplification of the action of the central characters. The scenes were choreographed and orchestrated rather than directed. The performance has been described by Emmanual Kaplan, who wrote the following with regard to the opening scene.

Introduction. Dark. Somewhere, slow quiet music begins to play. In the centre of the stage massive doors swing silently open of their own accord and a platform moves slowly forward towards the spectator, out of the gloom, out of the distance, out of the past — one senses this immediately, because it is contained in the music. The music swells and comes nearer, then suddenly on an abrupt chord — *sforzando* — the platform is flooded with light in unison with the music.

On the platform stand a table and a few chairs; candles burn; officials sit. The audience seems to crane forward towards the dark and gloomy age of Nicholas in order to see better what it was like in those days.

Suddenly, the music grows quiet — *subito piano* — gloomy like the period, like the colours of the setting: red furniture, red doors and red walls, green uniforms and green hanging lampshades: the colour scheme of government offices. The music is abruptly retarded and drawn out expectantly; everybody waits — on the stage and in the audience. Smoke rises from pipes and chibouks. The long stems 'cross out' the faces of the officials lit by the flickering candle flames; they are like fossilised monsters: crossed out and obliterated, once and for all. There they sit, wreathed in a haze with only the shadows of their pipes flickering on their faces; and the music plays on, slower and quieter as though flickering too, bearing them away from us, further and further into that irretrievable 'then'. A pause — *fermata* — and then a voice: 'Gentlemen, I have invited you here to give you some unpleasant news ...' like Rossini in the Act One *stretto* with Doctor Bartholo and Don Basilio, only there the tempo is *presto*, whilst here it is very slow. Then suddenly, as though on a word of command, at a stroke of the conductor's baton, everyone stirs in agitation, pipes jump from lips, fists clench, heads swivel. The last syllable of 'revizor' (inspector) seems to tweak everybody. Now the word is hissed in a whisper: the whole word by some, just the consonants by others, and somewhere even a softly rolled 'r'. The word 'revizor' is divided musically into every conceivable intonation. The ensemble of suddenly startled officials blows up and dies away like a squall. Everyone freezes and falls silent; the guilty conscience rears up in alarm then hides its poisonous head again, like a serpent lying motionless, harbouring its deadly venom.

The dynamics of this perfectly fashioned musical introduction fluctuate constantly. The sudden *forte-fortissimo* of the Mayor's cry 'send for Lyapkin-Tyakpin!' The terrified officials spring up in all directions, hiding their guilty consciences as far away as possible — under the table, behind each other's backs, even behind the armchair where the Mayor was just sitting. It is like a dance-pantomime of fright. The District Physician begins to squeal on the letter 'i', first a long drawn-out whistle then jerkily on 'e' *staccato*, then the two 'notes' alternately rising and falling, whilst the next lines are 'embroidered' onto this background. In orchestral terms, it is like a piccolo with double bass *pizzicato*, just like the comic scenes in Rimsky-Korsakov's *May Night*. A sudden screech *glissando* from the Doctor and a new 'dance of terror' begins. The plastic pattern of the characters' movements corresponds to the rhythmical pattern of their voices. Their brief pauses seem to foretoken the dumb scene of the finale. (quoted in Braun, *The Theatre of Meyerhold*, pp. 221-2)

The use of props to point up the character's inner emotions and as a cross-reference to general issues can also be seen from Meyerhold's production of Chekhov's 'vaudeville pieces' *The Bear, The Proposal* and *The Anniversary,* which he entitled *33 Swoons.* In *The Proposal* Lomov and Natasha fought over a tray and a napkin whilst disputing the ownership of the meadows. In *The Anniversary* the deputation of shareholders ironically presented Chairman Shipuchin with a stuffed bear rather than an address and silver tankard (see *The Theatre of Meyerhold,* p. 260).

In the work of Meyerhold we have a clear example of an artist trying to share in and shape the evolution of a society, using as rationale for his staging the rationale of his political ideology. The fact that in the end Meyerhold was deemed to have deviated from the correct association, and was shot in prison, tends to indicate that to employ the criteria which he himself lived by underwrites tyranny rather than artistic expression. It might be argued however that the fault lies not in the principle of art serving ideology, but in the narrow perspective of political leaders.

No discussion of Epic theatre can ignore the work of Bertolt Brecht (1896-1956). We have purposely left him until last in order to show that he was part of a larger artistic movement. Our discussion will be brief because he has been written of so comprehensively in other sources and we particularly recommend the reader to John Willett's books, *The Theatre of Bertolt Brecht* and *Brecht on Theatre.*

Probably the clearest statement that Brecht made about his objectives was in an essay called 'The Modern Theatre is the Epic Theatre' (in *Brecht on Theatre,* pp. 37-42). He compares his Epic theatre with what he calls Dramatic theatre and creates a parallel analysis which identifies the 'shifts of accent' between the two.

The working method most often associated with this comparison is that of the 'distance' method of acting, through which the actor attempts to demonstrate rather than to impersonate his role, commenting upon the character he is portraying and thereby revealing the relationship between motives and constraints. Discussion of this will be found in our section on acting. But Brecht was also responsible for developing new staging techniques, also devoted to highlighting the real material causes and effects of human action. He often achieved this by means of a striking, but contradictory central image. A good

Dramatic Theatre	Epic Theatre
plot	narrative
implicates the spectator in a stage situation	turns the spectator into an observer, but
wears down his capacity for action	arouses his capacity for action
provides him with sensations	forces him to take decisions
experience	picture of the world
the spectator is involved in something	he is made to face something
suggestion	argument
instinctive feelings are preserved	brought to the point of recognition
the spectator is in the thick of it, shares the experience	the spectator stands outside, studies
the human being is taken for granted	the human being is the obect of inquiry
he is unalterable	he is alterable and able to alter
eyes on the finish	eyes on the course
one scene makes another	each scene for itself
growth	montage
linear development	in curves
evolutionary determinism	jumps
man as a fixed point	man as a process
thought determines being	social being determines thought
feeling	reason

example of such an image is Mother Courage at the end of the play of that name, alone between the shafts of her cart on an otherwise empty stage. The whole action of the play has been building up to and explaining the significance of this stark image with which the audience leaves the theatre.

In his staging methods, Brecht was constantly searching for new ways of presenting vividly the contradictions of life under the capitalist system, or, as he put it, of making dialectics pleasurable. *The Good Woman of Setzuan* illustrates the interplay of character and setting contributing to the dialectical presentation of a contradictory situation. The setting is a tobacconist's shop and the central character's predicament is how to survive in business whilst remaining a compassionate human being. She can only resolve her contradictions by literally splitting in two: she adopts an alter ego, Shui Ta, the ruthless businessman. Once Shui Ta has set the business in order, by adopting the ruthless morality of the market forces, she can reappear as Shen Te, the good-hearted girl who has compassion on the sufferings of her fellows. The contradictory qualities of the commerce which provides the means of both survival and exploitation are reflected in the contradictory qualities of the two-in-one character. The audience is led towards an understanding of the play's issues through this paradox-in-action. The setting of the shop itself represents the essential contradiction.

In the work of both Meyerhold and Piscator, the text of the playwright was often distorted almost out of recognition to allow them to develop the staging forms and to make the ideological points that they wanted. Brecht, as both playwright and producer, was able to match his material and his methods more evenly. As a result of this, it is very difficult to study his plays satisfactorily without considering the appropriate performance methods. Over the four decades of his work in the theatre, his ideas were constantly developing and so it is only too easy to misapply the ideas of one period to a play written at a different time. One of the most celebrated of Brecht's suggestions was that the audiences in his theatre should be able to smoke and chat during the performance. This suggestion was made in the middle twenties, when he wished to develop an informal atmosphere in which people could feel relaxed enough to ponder on the performance's issues. Round about the same time he was also thinking of the theatre in similar terms to sporting events. In 1926 he wrote an article called 'How to Apply the Principles of Good Sports Promotion to the Theatre'. The objective was to bring to the theatre the same perceptual approach as we bring to, say, a boxing match. The boxing promoter's aim is to reveal rather than disguise the contest, the system of 'rounds' gives time for reflection and discussion. These approaches have to be compared with Brecht's quite conventional methods of staging with the Berliner Ensemble.

Perhaps the most characteristic attitude of Brecht towards staging was expressed in his statement to Mordecai Gorelik regarding the latter's production of *The Mother* in New York in 1935, in which he said:

Forget about settings ... Let's have a platform, and on this platform we'll put chairs, tables, partitions — whatever the actors need. For hanging a curtain give me a wooden pole or a metal bar; for hanging a picture a piece of wall. And I'll want a large projection screen ... Let it all be elegant, thin and fine, like Japanese banners, flimsy like Japanese kites and lanterns; let's be aware of the natural textures of wood and metal ... We'll place two grand pianos visibly at one side of the stage; the play must have the quality of a concert as well as that of a drama ... And we'll show the lighting units as they dim on and off, playing over the scene. (quoted in *The Theatre of Bertolt Brecht*, p. 149)

The intention is clear. The staging must be functional and there must be no attempt at disguising the theatre. The qualities of texture and appearance must be observed. The occasion must be pleasurable. There must be the projection screen for the inevitable commentary and illustration. Brecht's actual work was not so stark as this implies, but it was always simple and direct.

The most striking characteristic of Brecht's staging method was his use of properties. A character's relationship with any object which he used had to be revealed by the way in which he used it. Willett tells us (p. 159):

> the jobs done by his characters, whether plucking a chicken or mending a motor tyre or scrubbing a man's back in the bath, always have to be done properly, as if they had a life-time's practice behind them. They could never be allowed to degenerate into 'business'; a botched up imitation of activities which to Brecht were at once beautiful and socially important.

The material world of objects was almost as intense as that of a Balzac novel. Though not so cluttered, the material world partly defined and illustrated the psychological world of the character. Use of properties indicated the character's economic basis, a point which is well illustrated by the way in which Brecht had Helene Weigel as Mother Courage bite a coin to see if it was genuine and then put it into a purse which shut with a loud click. The incident was both amusing and illustrative of the character's situation and attitude.

Brecht has influenced the modern theatre more than any other single director or playwright. Epic theatre has been developed and refined by a great many of the serious or innovatory playwrights since the war. His work has shown that political theatre does not need to rely on the over-simplifications of agit-prop to be effective and his mastery of a style showing the interaction of people and objects on the stage has helped to inspire the work of directors as different as Mike Leigh, Max Stafford-Clark and Peter Brook.

Theatre of Communion

As we saw at the beginning of this section, it has frequently been assumed that theatre has its origins in ritual rather than in demonstration or communication of the kind found in Epic theatre. A director believing that the function of theatre is to unite his audience in the experience of a ritual of common affirmation will make very different choices in how to stage and present his plays, than a director whose aims are those of Epic theatre. The possibilities open to directors wishing to create a theatre of communion can best be outlined by reference to the work and theories of Antonin Artaud and Jerzy Grotowski.

Artaud was born in 1896 and died in 1948. He was a French actor, writer and director who worked with Lugné-Poë, Dullin and Jean Louis Barrault. For much of his life he suffered from mental illness and the effects of drugs. He is best known for his theoretical collection, *The Theatre and its Double*. Whilst his ideas have had a profound influence on the theatre of the last fifty years he was never able to achieve any great theatrical success himself.

Artaud wrote in 1926:

The illusion we are seeking to create has no bearing on the greater or lesser degree of verisimilitude of the action. By this very act, each show becomes a sort of event. The audience must feel a scene in their lives is being acted out in front of them, a truly vital scene. In a word, we ask our audiences to join with us, inwardly, deeply ... Audiences must be thoroughly convinced we can make them cry out. (*Collected Works*, vol. 2, p. 18)

Artaud later elaborated on this ambition in terms of both practice and rationale, evolving the concept of 'theatre of cruelty'. The imagery he uses is both religious and revolutionary. Religion and revolution both relate to absolute principles and to fundamental and frequently 'holistic' attitudes, and together they imply, at least in Artaud's terms, the discovery of new and purer socio-political and personal relationships. Artaud wished to reveal an 'occult equivalent' (p. 22) of the moribund religion of the time. He wanted to extirpate 'our world's lies, aimlessness, meanness and ... two-facedness' (ibid.). Believing that a 'real stage play upsets our sensual tranquility, releases our repressed sub-conscious, driving us to a kind of potential rebellion' (p. 19), he sought a new communion, a new sign system, and a new priesthood in the theatre to give form to his ideas and achieve his objectives.

The 'communion' element of Artaud's schemes was at the core of his beliefs. The audience was to be 'encircled' so that direct contact could be made. Seated in the centre of the action the audience, in swivel chairs, would change their focus according to the movement of the drama around the hall, which was to be similar architecturally to a 'holy place'. There was to be no vacuum in the audience's 'mind or sensitivity' (p. 84): their attention was to be persistent and persistently committed. 'Intensities of colour, light or sound ... vibrations and tremors, tonality of light ... tremoring gestures' were to fuse, to create discords and to envelop the whole space and people so that the experience was immediate and primal, 'as exactly localised as the circulation of blood through our veins' (p. 70).

Artaud sought 'true magic' and the 'hypnotically suggestive mood where the mind is affected by direct sensual pressure' (p. 84). However the performance was not aimed to entice just the minds or the senses of the audience but their 'entire existence', plumbing and revealing 'the most secret recesses of the heart'. Artaud likens the experience he sought to inspire to that of the snake which is charmed: 'I intend to do to the audience what snake-charmers do and to make them reach even the subtlest notions through their organism.' He had argued that it was not just the music which affects the snake, but the vibrations which its long body contacts through the ground.

It is this profound and complete experience which identified what Artaud meant by 'Theatre of Cruelty', a theatre in which the 'unconscious' was to be liberated and the individual's driving force revealed and recognised. It was to be 'cruel' in that it denied the audience a 'Peeping Tom' perspective, and forced them into a 'tangible laceration', a full and 'whole' commitment to the occasion.

> The theatre
>   is the state
>   the place
>   the point
> Where we can get hold of man's anatomy and
> through it heal and dominate life
>
> ('Aliener l'acteur', 12 May 1947,
> quoted in Esslin, *Artaud*, p. 76)

These ideas of new theatre language and forms were confirmed for Artaud by the experience of watching a company of Balinese dancers, not in Bali, but in Paris, in 1931. What particularly impressed him was the supremacy of movement and sound rather than verbal language. He saw in the dancer's behaviour the creation of a novel and essentially theatrical language. He wrote:

by language I do not mean an idiom we fail to catch at first hearing, but precisely that kind of theatrical language foreign to every *spoken language*, where it seems a tremendous stage experience is recaptured, besides which our exclusively dialogue productions seem like so much stammering. (p. 39)

He wrote very precisely of his experience, speaking of

those angular, sudden, jerky postures, those syncopated inflexions found at the back of the throat, those musical phrases cut short, the sharded flights, rustling branches, hollow drum sounds, robot creaking ... a new bodily language no longer based on words but on signs. (p. 37)

The actors were like 'moving hieroglyphs', the whole appearance one of 'theatre conventions' with profound symbolic meaning too deep for 'logical discursive language'.

Whilst it has been argued that Artaud was probably mistaken and the signs he perceived had more literal meaning than he realised, what is important is his stress on the concept of potential symbolic and metaphoric value of all elements of theatre.

This was not new: it may even be a necessary law of perception. When we see things we can only understand them if they relate to our previous experience. We therefore continually place those things we see into a framework of meaning and everything which we can see simultaneously which appears to belong to the same event is placed within the same framework of perception. Therefore all things on and around the stage are likely to be 'read' unless conventions of dis-attention are established which tell us not to consider certain elements which are not designed for our perception at that moment. The most obvious attention/disattention convention in theatre is the use of stage-lighting to focus on the desired action and place.

What was comparatively novel was the extra-intellectual, sensuous, but none the less precise nature of the sign system. Artaud was creating a 'total' environment, bringing about 'real' experiences. His aim, and it must be remembered that he never fully achieved this, was to discover and present an absolutely controlled system of symbolic experiences which would have exact sensory effects on his audiences. In order to achieve this he needed a high priest, a director who could orchestrate and choreograph a complex web of experiences for actor and audience.

What Artaud was seeking to remedy was man's partition of himself into body, mind and spirit and his separation from his fellow men. We have seen that one of Artaud's immediate influences was the theatre of Bali, but he was also part of the general revolution away from the superficial and the vulgar, a revolution which he shared with Stanislavsky, with Brecht and almost every person working in the serious theatre, all of whom sought to inspire a new consciousness.

Whilst the Balinese dances had a striking effect on Artaud, a more profound and persistent influence was his study of eastern mysticism and medicine which seek to confront and treat the 'whole' man. In fact he began to formulate acting techniques based on Chinese acupuncture points and on breathing methods derived from the Jewish Cabala.

He outlined the principles and techniques of acting in an article which he called 'An Affective Athleticism'. Deriving his rationale from 'holistic' thought, Artaud developed two fundamental principles. One was that just as the athlete can command very isolated muscular action, the actor can identify very particular areas of his body to discover and convey emotion. In the article Artaud only discusses the solar plexus, the small of the back and the breasts, but suggests that as Chinese acupuncture recognises 380 pressure points, many of these must be available to provide the source of the actor's emotional behaviour. He argued, 'The secret is to irritate those pressure points as if the muscles were flayed' (*Theatre and its Double*, pp. 94-5). Acupuncture points were not to be seen as just points on the body's surface, but as key points in the 'meridians' through which 'vital energy' passes, providing a network of channels throughout the body similar to the nervous system.

In developing his argument Artaud notes the Chinese belief in pairs of opposites, most notably the '*yin*' and '*yang*', which explain all human behaviour. An increase in one automatically leads to a decrease in its opposite. A balanced person is one in whom all of the opposites are in equilibrium. The art of acupuncture is to stimulate or decrease the body's 'vital energy' according to a person's needs. Artaud was arguing that in order to expose deep emotion the actor should learn to exploit acupuncture's 'points' through his own will.

Of Artaud's second principle concerning the relationship between emotion and breathing, he wrote 'All breathing has three measures, just as there are three basic principles in all creation and the figures that correspond to them can be found in breathing itself' (pp. 90-1). The three basic principles add a neutral state to the Chinese opposites so that in addition to 'male' and 'female' we have 'androgynous' or to 'expanding' and 'attracting' we have 'balanced' and so on. In acting terms the aim was to rediscover the breathing associated with 'every mental movement, every feeling' so that we can have access to the origin of emotion and thus convey it, thereby expressing the 'soul's flowing substantiality' creating what Artaud referred to as 'breathing tempi' the source of the emotional flow of drama or 'passionate time'. The end-product of this process is that the audience will lock into the breathing rhythms and subsequently the physical, emotional and spiritual tempi, merging with the actors and moving to a 'magical trance', the essence of 'divine theatre'.

It is important to note here that in spite of the mysticism and emotion Artaud was still looking for a 'code' whereby his theatre could communicate. He speaks of 'breathing hieroglyphs' as his medium and scorned the primacy of verbal coding, but he identified the central need of all theatre to encode its meaning in such a way that the audience can share this meaning. Artaud's unique quality was that he sought a primal, innate and universal code as opposed to an abstract code of conventions which have to be artificially created.

The imagery of religion and belief in the need for 'holism' in life and the theatre are at the core of all of the 'total theatre' pioneers. In more recent times the practices and process have tended to be inspired by the work of the Polish director Jerzy Grotowski.

In his 'Statement of Principles' (*Towards a Poor Theatre*, p. 256) Grotowski wrote:

> Theatre — through the actor's technique, his art in which the living organism strives for higher motives — provides an opportunity for what could be called integration, the discarding of masks, the revealing of the real substance: a totality of physical and mental reaction.

Whilst his work over the years has evolved from fairly conventional staging methods to the point where he has abandoned the whole notion of theatre, preferring to think in terms of a 'meeting', he has consistently pursued the twin objectives which are embedded in the statement we have quoted. The first objective has been to strip down the barriers which inhibit communication, including the theatrical paraphernalia of staging and the masks, 'the daily mask of lies', behind which both actor and audience hide their sensitivity and vulnerability. The second objective has been to take these exposed and receptive parties to a confrontation with their cultural myths in a communal 'trying out' of traditional values.

So far as staging is concerned, Grotowski has reflected his 'inductive technique' or 'technique of elimination' in acting by the concept of the 'poor' theatre which dispenses with the notion of theatre as a 'synthesis of disparate creative disciplines — literature, sculpture, painting, architecture, lighting, acting'. Grotowski accuses this 'synthetic' theatre of suffering from 'artistic kleptomania'. Whenever possible he has reduced reliance on any element other than the actor himself, attempting to distil the theatrical experience to the core. For Grotowski that core must allow us to 'transcend our stereotyped vision, our conventional feelings, our standards of judgement' so that 'in a state of complete defencelessness we can 'discover ourselves' and 'entrust ourselves to something we cannot name, but in which live Eros and Charitas' (p. 257). In other words, discover the essence of our humanity.

Grotowski has sought to put an end to the actor/audience, stage/ auditorium separation. His audiences have been witnesses to his actors' nakedness; the confrontation was to be an 'osmosis' and the stage eliminated in favour of a 'chamber theatre'. The characteristics of such a theatre are that it permits the 'proper spectator/actor relationship for each type of performance' in which it is possible to 'embody the decision in physical arrangements'. Experiments with these principles have led Grotowski to set *Kordian* (1962) in a psychiatric ward with the spectators sitting on and around the two-tiered beds as though they were patients. Marlowe's play *Dr Faustus* (1963) was set as though at a Last Supper. The spectator/guests were welcomed by Faustus and seated at two long refectory tables whilst Faustus finally sat at a smaller table at one end rather like the prior in a refectory. The action took place on the tables. For *The Constant Prince* (1965) the 'spectators-peepers' looked down over the wooden walls of a rectangular bear pit. The only staging element in the pit itself was a low oblong dais just long enough to take a man's body. Of *Akropolis*, Flaszen, Grotowski's literary adviser, wrote, 'it was decided that there would be no direct action between actors and spectators'. The actors were 'to be dead; the spectators represent those who are outside of the circle of initiates, ... they are the living' (*Towards a Poor Theatre*, p. 63). The idea was that the separation, combined with the closeness of the spectators, gave the impression 'that the dead are born from a dream of the living'. The only material element present at the beginning of the piece was a large box with metallic junk piled on top of it, 'stovepipes of various lengths and widths, a wheelbarrow, a bathtub, nails, hammers. Everything ... old, rusty ... picked up from a junkyard.' During the action of the performance all of these objects became elements in an evolving civilisation whose ultimate metaphor was the gas chamber. Costumes for *Akropolis* served not to identify characters or social group, but became metaphors for the torn human body. They were bags full of holes, the holes lined with material to suggest torn flesh. The spectators looked through the holes as though through the person's skin. This experimentation with space reached its final point when for *Apocalypsis Cum Figuris* the space was completely undifferentiated and actors and audience shared a large empty hall.

In spite of the remarkable effects of this sort of drama and staging, for Grotowski a division still remained, identified by the idea of 'performance' which essentially denied the possibility of the fusion of appearance which he sought. Noting that true communication between human beings depends on an 'understanding that goes beyond the understanding of words' and that when that point is reached concepts of performance and the theatre were no longer relevant, he decided that 'it was necessary to eliminate the notion of theatre' (an actor in front of a spectator) and what remained was a 'notion of meeting'. The search for theatre became a search for what Grotowski calls 'active culture' (quoted in Menne, 'Grotowski's Paratheatrical Projects').

Like Artaud, Grotowski's imagery and point of reference are religious. Although he is an atheist he speaks of the 'holy' actor who 'sacrifices' his body. He writes:

> If the actor by setting himself a challenge publicly challenges others and through excess, profanation and outrageous sacrilege reveals himself by casting off his everyday mask, he makes it possible for the spectator to undertake a similar process of self-penetration. If he does not exhibit his body, but annihilates it, burns it, frees it from every resistance to any psychic impulse, then he does not sell his body, but sacrifices it. He repeats the atonement, he is close to holiness. (*Towards a Poor Theatre*, p. 34)

It is not difficult to understand the sort of event and communication which Grotowski sought. He seems to resent the spiritual monopoly which the church has claimed of man and sought to replace its moribund 'services' with his own penetrating and dynamic 'confrontations' or 'meetings'. It is worth noting in parentheses that the church itself has made similar sorts of changes. The 'evangelical' movement searches for greater emotional commitment, the Quakers in fact hold 'meetings' and the whole non-conformist movement was in part a rejection of the church itself in favour of the simple Christian witness.

Grotowski accepts the fundamental matter of the primitive theatre, the cultural myths of the parent society, but he turns the ritual purpose on its head. His aim is not to perpetuate the myth but to 'confront it', to discover through a total commitment to the myth's human sources what it can mean to the individual living at a later and different historical period. Somewhat paradoxically he asks the spectator to become absorbed in the drama whilst consciously showing and perceiving his mutual commitment with other spectators. However the effect of this dramatic experience is not to be conformity, but change. Like Artaud, Grotowski's purpose is to create a fundamental revolution in man's sensitivity and relations.

Grotowski's staging techniques are really the inevitable outcome of this purpose. He wants communion so he must get rid of theatre's physical divisions. He believes in the essential 'human' quality of his communion so props and furniture are likely only to get in the way. His theatrical experience is to be 'real' so he cannot afford to use any of the devices of illusion which are the conventional theatre's stock-in-trade. Costumes and props must serve as metaphors which give resonance and relevance to the myth being enacted. The lighting must serve to enhance, but not elaborate, the communication. Grotowski wrote, 'we forsook lighting effects and this revealed a wide range of possibilities for the actors' use of stationary lighting sources by deliberate work with shadows, light spots etc.' He continues, 'It is particularly significant that once a spectator is placed in an illuminated zone ... he too begins to play a part in the performance' (*Towards a Poor Theatre*, p. 20). Grotowski develops from this a belief in the actor's personal ability to become a source of 'spatial light', meaning that by the intensity of his performance and the efficient concentration of his energies he can become a powerful visual focus.

The division of society had led to a need to package and sell theatre in order to widen its potential audience. As soon as this sort of compromise is made it is a short step to 'commercial' theatre and the bartering of performance for money. It was this commercialism which Grotowski particularly opposed. He refers to the conventional actor as the 'courtesan' actor who has accumulated skills to sell on behalf of a director/pimp. The spectators are more and more individuated in their relation to the myth, 'group identification with myth — the equation of personal, individual truth with universal truth is virtually impossible' (p. 23). The selling process itself is a barrier to the process of a 'sharing' communication which Grotowski sought. He also recognises the difficulty in making a profound communication across cultural barriers: 'The performance is *national* because it is a sincere and absolute search into *our* historical ego'.

The relation between Artaud and Grotowski is deceptively close. Grotowski did not read Artaud until long after he had begun his work and he denies most of the parallels which have been drawn between their work. Artaud was really only a man of inspirations which, according to Grotowski, were impossible to work in practice. His emphasis on puppetry would detract from the communion and his staging form with the action around the audience would only change rather than destroy the audience actor frontiers. His breathing techniques derived from the Cabala were based on a misunderstanding and were quite impractical.

The similarity which we wish to emphasise is their equal belief in the need to create a 'communion'. The idea of 'communion', or at least the greater intimacy between audience and actor, has been one of the greatest dynamics in the evolution of twentieth-century theatre. It has been complemented by a desire to destroy the artificial theatricality of the stage. Whilst Grotowski and Artaud are most clearly identified with the movement, so too are a host of others, including such disparate names as Stanislavsky, Alan Ayckbourn and Brecht.

4 THEATRE FORMS

The form of the theatre building is the first thing a director must consider when he begins to confront staging problems. At some periods in the history of western theatre forms a particular arrangement of stage and auditorium has predominated, at others a great variety of forms have co-existed. In the history of English theatre forms, two periods stand out as having been marked by the predominance of a particular theatre form: the Elizabethan age, when a *thrust stage* was common, jutting out into an audience that surrounded it on three sides, and the Victorian age, when the theatre was virtually divided into two separate rooms, stage and auditorium, separated by a *proscenium arch*.

The main difference between a thrust stage and a proscenium arch stage lies in the relationship established between the actors and their audience. On a thrust stage the actors inhabit the same space as their audience. They may therefore find it easy to address the audience directly. It is often maintained that the use of soliloquy in Elizabethan drama was particularly suited to thrust stages like that in the conjectured reconstruction of the Swan theatre (Figure 1). On this kind of

Figure 1: Inside 'The Swan'?

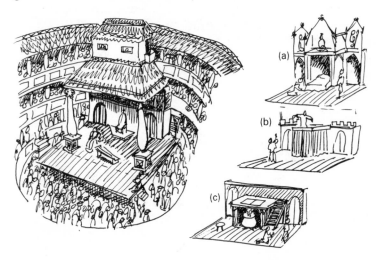

(a), (b) and (c) are possible temporary structures.

51

stage any scenic elements used need to be three-dimensional and practicable. There has been much discussion of the use made, on the Elizabethan stage, of the area between the two entrances in the back wall. Inserts a, b and c suggest scenic elements that might have been constructed for particular productions.

In the masques that became popular at the English court in the first part of the seventeenth century, new Italian methods of providing spectacular backgrounds came into use, involving elaborate machinery for 'flying' scenery in and out (Figure 2). In the Restoration period (i.e. the years following 1660), new theatres were built to enable the use of perspective scenery, painted on backcloths and on flats placed at intervals on each side of the stage (Figure 3). But the scale of such theatres was much more intimate than the Elizabethan theatre had been, part of the stage remained thrust out into the auditorium and a door at the front of the stage on each side allowed for entrances and exits in close proximity with the audience. This was a theatre form in transition between the Elizabethan thrust stage and the proscenium arch stage that was to predominate in the eighteenth and nineteenth centuries.

Figure 2: Court Masque

Figure 3: A Restoration Playhouse: Richmond Theatre

A proscenium arch stage is ideal for the creation of illusion and picture effects. Because the audience cannot see behind the surface of the proscenium it is possible to hide from view a great deal of machinery, lighting equipment, constructional reinforcement and scenery in preparation for several transformations of the stage picture. By the careful use of perspective, a designer can create the illusion of a larger space. Single flat surfaces can be painted to resemble buildings or landscapes or to make whatever visual statement the director desires. By cunning use of gauze and lighting, characters and scenes can appear and disappear at will.

Such was the dominance achieved by the proscenium form by the end of the nineteenth century that it is still often referred to as the 'traditional' method of staging. This is misleading and inaccurate, for the period during which the proscenium arch was used to make a complete separation between stage and auditorium was a comparatively brief one. The proscenium arch itself is ancient; it was only during the late eighteenth and nineteenth centuries that theatres were built in such a way as to ensure that the audience's view of the entire stage was framed by this arch. The invention of first gas and then electric stage lighting, together with the innovation of darkening the auditorium for the performance, both enhanced the new sense of the proscenium arch as a barrier dividing actors from audience. The most extreme expression of this idea of a barrier was to be found in the staging methods of Antoine (see p. 27), who encouraged his actors and designers to think of the stage as just a room from which the fourth wall had been removed to allow the audience to see inside.

In the twentieth century, especially since Gropius' work (see p. 33) theatre architects have tried to design flexible buildings which will allow for many different theatre forms under the same roof. The National Theatre, for example, includes three auditoria (see Figure 4). The Olivier has an *arena* stage, whose design borrows elements from both the Elizabethan thrust stage and the Ancient Greek open-air theatres; the Lyttleton has a proscenium arch stage and the Cottesloe is a flexible space in which a number of different arrangements are possible: a stage may be constructed at one end of the auditorium and part of the space used for tiered seating (inset drawing) or the whole space may be used for the dramatic action with spectators looking down from the first and second galleries which run right round the auditorium.

A number of flexible spaces like the Cottesloe have been built in recent years. They allow a director to vary the shape of his stage space for each new production, erecting a proscenium arch to frame the action if he so wishes, seating an audience on three sides of a thrust stage or on both sides of a traverse stage. An example of such a building is the Manchester University Theatre (Figure 5).

Another theatre form that has attracted revived interest in recent years is *theatre in the round*, in which the audience entirely surrounds the action. During the 1950s and 1960s, Stephen Joseph became Britain's leading exponent of this form of theatre and his book, *New Theatre Forms* took on the force of a manifesto for all those who felt stifled by the dominance of permanent proscenium arch theatres. Joseph gathered round him actors, directors and playwrights who shared his enthusiasm and in the small Library Theatre at Scarborough they carried out their experiments. A permanent theatre in the round at Stoke on Trent and the new theatre named in Stephen Joseph's memory at Scarborough, together with many other new buildings, such as the Manchester Royal Exchange (Figure 6) are a measure of his influence.

The central arena, of a theatre in the round, which might be circular, square or many-sided, ensures that an audience, viewing from all sides, is always relatively near the action. Entrances and exits must

Figure 4: National Theatre

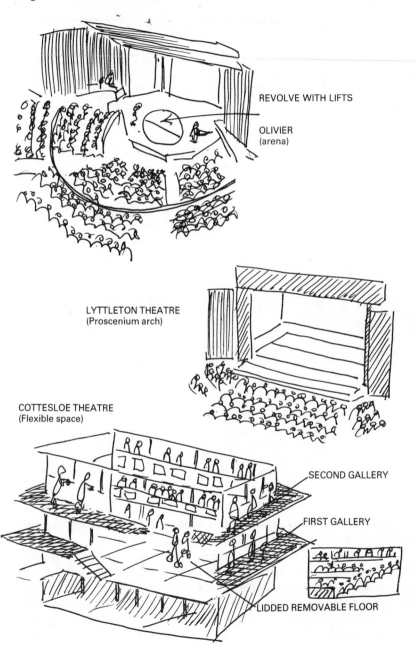

REVOLVE WITH LIFTS

OLIVIER
(arena)

LYTTLETON THEATRE
(Proscenium arch)

COTTESLOE THEATRE
(Flexible space)

SECOND GALLERY

FIRST GALLERY

LIDDED REMOVABLE FLOOR

Figure 5: Manchester University Theatre

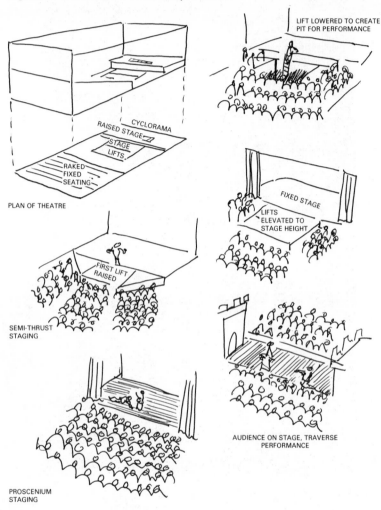

LIFT LOWERED TO CREATE PIT FOR PERFORMANCE

CYCLORAMA
RAISED STAGE
STAGE
LIFTS
RAKED FIXED SEATING

PLAN OF THEATRE

FIXED STAGE
LIFTS ELEVATED TO STAGE HEIGHT

FIRST LIFT RAISED

SEMI-THRUST STAGING

AUDIENCE ON STAGE, TRAVERSE PERFORMANCE

PROSCENIUM STAGING

be constructed through the auditorium and these, usually placed on opposite corners or sides, allow great fluidity of movement across the stage. The only background against which the actors perform is that of the spectators and the actor and director have to discover ways in which they may all be meaningfully involved in the performance. Old rules about projection, the dominance of various parts of the stage, and the grouping of figures are no longer applicable and, because of the sight lines, the stage must be virtually free of decor.

Figure 6: A Permanent Theatre in the Round: The Royal Exchange, Manchester

Photo: Kevin Cummins.

The situation today, then, is one in which no single theatre form is predominant. Because of this, parallels can be drawn with the medieval period, when a variety of different theatre forms were also in use. As modern staging methods have become more flexible in recent years, so interest in medieval stages has grown, and it is for this reason that we shall conclude our discussion of theatre forms with a brief mention of four types of medieval stage. The great English cycle plays appear to have been performed on a number of different mobile stages or *pageants* (see Figure 7), each one representing a particular location in the course of the cycle. Other plays were performed in *rounds*, which appear to have been common in western Europe during this period (see Figure 8). Here the performance space consisted of a central *platea*, or acting area, with a number of raised structures around the edge. The audience crowded into the round with the actors and were kept in order by attendants, who would clear spaces for the actors and help direct the audience's attention.

A simpler, and very common form of staging was the *booth stage* (Figure 9), consisting of boards on a trestle with a curtain behind which actors could change costumes and from which they could make a surprise entrance. Finally, many plays, like the Valenciennes passion play of 1547 (Figure 10) were performed on a long stage or a town square, forming a central *platea* while behind it were ranged a sequence of *mansions* or small, separate stage sets, representing different locations, from heaven (on the left of the drawing) through to a hell's mouth (on the right). Most theatre histories deal with these and other forms of staging; a particularly interesting discussion of the subject is Richard Southern's book *The Seven Ages of Theatre*, in which he emphasises the relevance of early theatre forms for understanding modern staging methods.

Transforming the Stage

Design

Once the form, the actual physical space for performance, has been defined, the director and designer can set about transforming it into 'artistic space' as part of a unified concept. We owe much of the inspiration for modern design ideas to the writings of Gordon Craig (1872-1966) who insisted on the importance of seeing a production as a whole and although some of his own designs were visionary rather than practical they set new standards in ways of thinking about

Figure 7: A Pageant Waggon

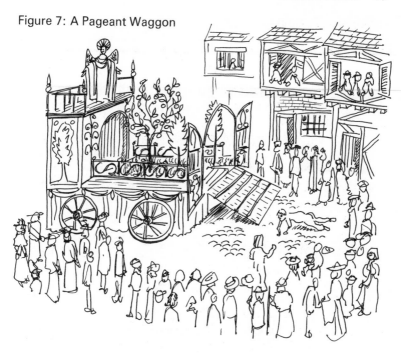

Figure 8: Medieval Theatre in the Round (conjectural)

Figure 9: A Booth Stage

Figure 10: Valenciennes Passion Play, 1547

the visual presentation of drama. In his most famous and influential book, *The Art of the Theatre* (1905) Craig writes in the form of a dialogue between a playgoer and a stage director. The playgoer has been attempting to define the nature of the art of theatre and the director replies:

> No; the art of the Theatre is neither the acting nor the play, it is not scene nor dance, but it consists of all the elements of which these things are composed: action, which is the very spirit of acting; words, which are the body of the play; line and colour, which are the very heart of the scene; rhythm, which is the very essence of the dance. (*The Art of the Theatre*, p. 102)

Craig is extending the idea of design to include far more than scenery and drew on his friendship with Isadora Duncan, who did much to liberate dance from the rules of classical ballet, to formulate his belief that the arrangement of bodies in space can shape a performance as powerfully as a piece of scenery.

The options available to us in the modern theatre in determining what the audience will see are considerable and they constitute the set of decisions which follow the establishing of the chosen theatre form. We can change the shape of the stage space in a variety of ways as Craig demonstrated and his designs always show the stage area transformed by lighting, scenic structure and live figures. By constructing and decorating certain types of scenery and by lighting the environment created appropriately, the stage can be made to precisely resemble somewhere else; alternatively we can provide sufficient visual clues for the setting to *suggest* another location. In other circumstances the designer may decide to provide a deliberately *distorted* representation of somewhere else in order that the audience views it with new interest or so that a particular quality of the environment is highlighted. Fashions in scenic representation have changed and compared with the early years of this century recent designs have tended less towards architectural or landscape accuracy and more towards economy and symbolic suggestion, but most designers are mainly concerned to create an image which makes its own statement. Such images may evoke a mood, a theme or an idea or, like the single tree in Beckett's *Waiting for Godot*, may remain essentially enigmatic yet organically linked to the nature of the play.

Various areas of the stage may be clearly defined by lighting or setting and one effect of this may be to divide the stage into a number of different parts, each with its own function. By dividing the stage horizontally the action can be made to move between two or more levels; such levels may be created with rostra, steps, ramps, scaffolding or even ladders or swings and in some theatres the facility exists for raising or lowering parts of the stage mechanically. The division of the stage in this way is an ancient device and a good deal of speculation exists as to how, for example, the upper level of the Elizabethan playhouse was employed. The stage may also be divided vertically so that characters move from one location to another, each representing different places, as they must have done in the simple journey in the medieval play of *Abraham and Isaac*; or various pre-set areas of the stage may be lit in rotation to show the action going on in several rooms or situations. In Brecht's *The Seven Deadly Sins*, the stage is divided vertically to allow the play to be acted and danced simultaneously and a similar technique enables the director to show both the inside and outside of a house at the same time.

The introduction of various levels and special areas of the stage is not always a temporary arrangement imposed on a bare and level stage. Some theatre designers have insisted that certain permanent features be constructed in new theatres to provide, for example, a number of possible levels and locations for the action. Directors may find it extremely stimulating to work with the possibilities of such staging arrangements and may equally find inspiration in working in outdoor auditoria or in buildings such as warehouses or churches which provide unusual stages.

So far we have examined the methods by which the shape of a stage may be modified according to the needs of the director; but the stage environment is also transformed by colour and texture. The colour of light used can create moods of tension, gloom or optimism; pools of shadow, shafts of bright light, large expanses of rich colour can all create a powerful image; or the director may elect to have his cast lit with constant bright and even light. Light from the lanterns falls on the surfaces of the décor and the effect will vary greatly depending on the materials and colours used in the scenic construction and decoration. In recent years there has been an enormous extension in the range of materials available to the designer: in addition to wood and canvas he may now use lightweight synthetic materials which are both strong and versatile and there has been a particular advance in the recognition of the importance and impact of surface textures. This, coupled with several new techniques for the application of paints and dyes, has encouraged designers to create settings composed of bold and strikingly textured surfaces. Such experiments have produced environments in which the substance itself is the central feature and justification for the design; and some modern settings appear to be an exploration into the structural and aesthetic possibilities of mirrors, marbled blocks, rope, stainless steel, chrome, wire, moulded plastic and other substances. In other words, the material composing the actors' surroundings has become the subject of carefully considered, artistic choice.

One of the major problems facing the designer is the combination of the 'real' with the artificial. An actor entering a bare stage and telling a joke to the audience is simply that; but the same actor entering a stage which is shaped and painted to look like a room in which he, as some fictitious character, lives is a far more complex idea, especially if he then turns out from his interactions with other characters in the play and tells a joke to the audience. In a similar way there is a distinction between the walls of that room which we know not to be made of plaster and the furniture which is as real as any in our own home. In some ways the effect of placing a natural object in an artificial environment is to sharpen the audience's awareness of the importance and function of that object and this is particularly the case where a play shows characters whose personal property is particularly meaningful to them. The junk with which Aston surrounds himself in Harold Pinter's *The Caretaker* is not only a feature of the setting but an extension of his predicament and Brecht, who included several artificial theatrical devices in his productions, always insisted on absolute accuracy and reality in the stage properties used by the actors.

One of the objections that Appia had towards the scenic conventions of his day was that the surface on which the actor moved was always false:

> This painting which is supposed to represent everything, is forced at the outset to renounce representing the ground ... there is no possibility of relationship between the vertical flats of the set and the stage floor ... so the ground cannot be reproduced by painting. But that is precisely where the actor moves. (*Directors on Directing*, p. 139)

In an attempt to overcome this problem some designers have experimented with natural substances such as sand, earth or water as part of the stage setting: in the National Theatre's production of *The Creation* for example, Adam and Eve emerged from a mound of clay and in a production of Wallace Salter's *Crusade to Surly Bottoms* in Cardiff the entire stage was covered with green turf and scrap metal.

Whatever ideas the designer and director may have concerning the staging of a play before rehearsals begin, it is quite possible that modifications may become necessary. In another production at Cardiff the designer had proposed a setting for *Macbeth* which consisted of a huge spiral ramp of textured wood supported on polished chrome columns. In the completed model the setting appeared to provide a whole range of performance possibilities and satisfied the need for those scenes in which the director wanted characters to appear 'above'. Once the set was constructed, however, the cast who had been undertaking their early rehearsals on a level floor found it quite impossible to move with any certainty on the ramp. The struggle to remain still or upright proved so physically exhausting that the cast insisted that the gradient of the ramp be lowered. On the other hand, the director found that the physical struggle was in itself productive and produced performances of great intensity and inventiveness. The modifications continued until after the dress rehearsal and formed an integral part of the evolution of the performance.

Adaptability on the part of designer and director is now seen as an essential quality if the creative process is to persist throughout the preparation for a production and many theatre companies recognise the importance of the interplay between the actor and his environment. This has led some theorists to suggest that there must always be some physical risk involved as the performer struggles against his human weakness to release latent energy. Performances in which actors run round precarious catwalks, swing from ropes, leap from towers, demonstrate astonishing feats of agility and acrobatics or retain uncomfortable poses for long periods have become part of the legacy of post-Artaudian theatre.

The tendency towards more economic and adaptable forms of staging has received additional impetus from the emergence of hundreds of small-scale, experimental 'fringe' theatre groups in recent years. The demands of touring, of setting up in variable performance spaces, the economic necessity of quick 'get ins' and 'get outs' together with the fact that actors themselves often form their own stage-management crew, have all militated against elaborate settings and forced designers to construct portable 'minimal' scenery. Commercial theatres have also found that their budget, their approach to performance and the growth of their own 'lunch time' or studio theatres have restricted the scale on which scenery is built.

The one exception to the situation appears to be opera, which continues to demand lavish settings on a scale comparable with those of the late nineteenth century. Recent productions of *La Bohème* and *Aida* by English National Opera were both staged on massive 'realistic' sets in which the performers resembled insects inhabiting a giant world: the spectacle was breathtaking but the visual and musical landscape relegated the human bodies, the so called 'characters' of the drama, to almost marginal significance, and it is noticeable that many modern designers see their most exciting opportunities lying in the fields of opera and dance, in which the need for a forward projected picture remains constant.

When we first open a playtext the suggested setting for the play is one of the earliest impressions we have of it. The playwright's instructions may range from a brief indication of the location: 'a wood, a castle, etc.' to a most elaborate description of the visual impact intended. Before the construction of 'scenery' became a normal part of theatrical presentation, the indications of the scene were often embedded in the text of the play so that the audience was asked to use its imagination to picture the setting. For example, the character called Rumour who speaks the prologue to Shakespeare's *Henry IV Part 2* asks us to imagine ourselves in 'this worm eaten hold of ragged stone' — Northumberland's castle. Theatre technology has advanced a great deal since Shakespeare's day and like all other forms of technology was accelerated enormously by the Industrial Revolution, so that since the nineteenth century playwrights have had an ever increasing range of stage machinery, lighting equipment, sound effects and constructional techniques at their disposal. The effect has been for playwrights to conceive their plays in visual as well as aural terms, to include powerful visual images and, if they so wish, to simulate real life with greater accuracy.

Costume

The move from Naturalism to Symbolism which was discernible in the European and American theatres during the closing years of the last century had a considerable impact on the design and function of costume. We have seen how the design of any production includes the human body moving in space and nothing transforms the body so completely and variously as the wearing of clothes. Indeed, it may well be that in 'dressing up' we have one of our first experiences of drama and throughout our lives the clothes we wear are part of the role which we play and the impression of ourselves that we wish to project. Many clothes are so personal to us that they virtually become an extension of our body, affecting the way we move, enhancing our character, changing our shape, enlarging the space we occupy, denoting our loyalty or reflecting our mood. Additionally, clothes are the most immediate symbol of changing fashion, and in some cases have become synonymous with the idea of fashion; they are recognisable as belonging to specific periods of history, geographical regions or nationalities, and are presumed to make a statement about the wearer.

In the theatre, costume not only embraces all the functions we have outlined, but is also part of a larger design scheme. It appears to be the one constant element in all forms and periods of theatre, for evidence suggests that in every type of drama, even when the stage was a bare platform or space on the ground, the choice of costume was a conscious artistic decision. This is because in dramatic action the performer is the focus of attention and careful thought must therefore be given to the visual impact of the body. The question of visibility is, however, one of the issues which affects theatre costume and sometimes changes the principles by which it must be designed in comparison with the clothes of everyday life.

In the first instance, detail which is visible in the intimacy of a room may be lost in a theatre; accordingly designs may need to be bolder and on a larger scale. At the same time it is possible to simulate fine detail with alternative techniques and materials, so rich embroidery may be achieved by piping paint or drawing with felt-tipped pen, costly jewellery constructed from nuts and bolts sprayed gold and decoration of fabrics may be applied by stencil, paint spray or paint roller.

Under powerful stage lighting and at a distance a different range of fabrics compared with those used for normal wear will produce better results. Loose woven materials such as hessian or calico, or those with a broken surface, like velour velvet or rough wool, all take on richness and depth when made into stage costume. Such fabrics may be dyed, textured, cut, stuck or layered to produce an infinite number of shapes and effects and stage designers are constantly experimenting with unusual and unexpected materials with which to enhance the human body.

Costume-making has become a highly specialised aspect of theatre design, although it is usual for the design to be executed by the set designer. Fortunately, the costume sketches from many past productions have survived and it is relatively easy to find illustrations which enable a student to trace the development of the art, at least during the past hundred years. A particularly rich source of costume design is found in the work of the group of artists who worked in Russia from the 1880s under the patronage first of Savva Mamontov and later of Diaghilev. Their contribution to the success of directors like Stanislavsky and Meyerhold or to the leading choreographers and dancers of the day is very well documented in Edward Braun's *The Theatre of Meyerhold* and demonstrates an area in which both opera and dance have contributed to the development of the wider aspect of theatre.

Historical accuracy of costume has not always been considered of paramount importance, although at other times it has been the subject of much careful research. Whereas the productions of the mid-nineteenth century frequently employed absolute accuracy of dress and architecture down to the finest detail, illustrations from earlier periods show characters either dressed in contemporary costume or in a strange mixture of historic and modern attire. 'Modern dress' versions of older plays continue to excite rather special interest and are frequently accompanied by statements from the director anxious to point out the topicality or continuing relevance of the play. There are, of course, certain plays which appear to be firmly rooted in the social conditions or historic events of one particular period but in recent years, quite apart from the frequent transmigration of Shakespeare to different times and places, Molière has had 1960s settings, Ibsen has been set in Scotland in the 1940s and Marlowe in futuristic dress.

One of the arguments for retaining some accuracy in the costume is that fashion extends to movement, posture, physical shape, language and manners, and that a production must leave the language unchanged. What happens then if we are to tamper with one of the details while others remain constant? Some designers and directors have attempted to solve this problem by making their costumes *suggest* rather than reproduce the style of a particular period whilst others, such as Jarry, have aimed for a style of costume that was somehow placed out of time. In a letter which Jarry wrote concerning the possible production of hs play *Ubu Roi*, he asked that the costume be divorced as far as possible from local time or chronology (which will thus help to give the impression of something eternal): modern costumes, preferably, since the satire is modern, and shoddy ones, too, to make the play even more wretched and horrible. (*Selected Works*, p. 68)

Another solution which transcends the time element is to dress characters in certain traditional performance clothes such as clowns, pierrots, other characters originating in the *commedia dell'arte* or in top hat, white gloves and cane of the music hall; this technique was used most successfully in *O What a Lovely War*, the popular rock musical *Godspell* and Caryl Churchill's *Vinegar Tom*, to cite but three examples.

As we have seen, another of the considerations is the way in which costume establishes and extends character: the elaborate and outrageous dress of the 'fop' in Restoration comedy, the austerity of the puritan inquisitors in *The Crucible*, the short cloak of Henry II in *Curtmantle* or Osric's hat in *Hamlet* demand an understanding of the whole play before the designer can produce a suitable set of designs for a production. Many performers also find that they are greatly helped, even in early rehearsal, by being able to wear a key piece of costume.

5 LIGHTING

Of all the inventions which changed the face of the theatre none was so influential as the introduction of, first, gas and, later, electric stage lighting. Gas was in use in British and European theatres from about 1817 onwards and this was gradually replaced by electricity during the 1880s. In subsequent years, lighting equipment has reached a very high level of sophistication but from the early years of the last century the control of intensity, direction, colour and quality of light has been seen as an integral part of the art of theatre.

When Shakespeare's mechanicals in *A Midsummer Night's Dream* are discussing how they will achieve the effect of moonlight for the meeting of Pyramus and Thisbe, the best they can suggest is that they leave open the casement window to allow the moon to shine in to the chamber and to have a character carrying a lantern and thorn bush and bringing in a dog to represent moonshine; yet we read that in Samuel Phelps's production of the play in 1853, moonlight and sunrise were 'exquisitely presented'. The imagery of the lantern, thorn and dog, no doubt understood by the original audiences, had been replaced with the moon shining to order as the mechanicals had rather optimistically hoped! Much nineteenth-century lighting was concerned with special effects and lighting the set and it was Appia who insisted that the lighting, rather than enhancing the bland flatness of the painted set, should create depth and shadow and provide an environment of light in which the actor should move. Another avant-garde theatre practitioner to investigate the artistic use of lighting was the poet and playwright Alfred Jarry (1873-1907) who attempted to counteract the tendency towards greater Naturalism in the theatre of his time by insisting that the actors should be as wooden and far from life as possible. In his essay 'On the Uselessness of Theatre in the Theatre' he began by proclaiming that two 'notoriously horrible things must be removed from the stage: sets and actors'. Instead he proposed that actors should be like puppets, wearing masks that are lit from below by footlights which 'illumine the actor's body along the hypotenuse of a right-angled triangle, the actor's body forming one of the sides of the right angle' (*Selected Works*, p. 72). Jarry goes on to examine the effect of the footlights as if they were the eyes of the audience, although he suggests that they should be thought of as a 'single point of light situated at an indefinite distance, as if it were *behind* the audience'. In order to underline the potential that Jarry saw in the developing art of lighting he states that actors should usually wear masks on which the play of light is particularly effective: 'With the old style of actor, masked only in a thinly applied make-up, each facial expression is raised to a power by colour and particularly by relief, and then to cubes and higher power by LIGHTING' (p. 72). Jarry does not make easy reading, partly because his ideas are presented in a highly idiosyncratic style and partly because he is writing in the context of modes of production which have died out. The footlights have gradually been rejected as a common means of ensuring that actors are well lit, mainly because of the changes in theatre forms which we have traced in this chapter. However, many of Jarry's ideas repay careful consideration for, like Appia, he saw the importance of creating a total environment and recognised that drama was shaped by very much more than the playtext.

When we consider what was attempted and achieved by playwrights, actor-managers and directors with new lighting facilities it is not surprising that a body of theoretical writing on the subject began to emerge. The new dimension in stage plays from the mid-nineteenth century onwards is recognisable both in popular melodramas and in the more serious, socially conscious plays of Tom Robertson, Ibsen or Strindberg. An example of the popular play built around scenic and lighting effects is Boucicault's *The Corsican Brothers* (1852) which was staged first by Charles Kean and later revived by Irving. In both cases the famous leading actor played the part of both brothers and a whole series of visions, appearances and disappearances and spectacular scenes were achieved by the use of machinery, gauzes and lighting. In Irving's production 'sink and rise' scenery enabled the audience to see the vision one brother had of the other while the 'Corsican trap' provided means whereby a ghost's head appeared slowly through the floor on one side of the stage and then the spectre gradually glided across the stage, rising from the ground. Thousands of feet of gas piping, thirty gas men, ninety carpenters, fifteen property men and tons of salt to create a snow scene were used in this production and it must have provided a nightmare for those concerned with continuity.

Ibsen certainly took advantage of the theatre's new technical capabilities and his plays *Brand* and *When We Dead Awaken* both call for spectacular mountain scenery with swirling clouds, snow or glaciers. But the plays of his middle period which are the most frequently performed today made more subtle use of visual impact, particularly of the quality of light. The stage directions at the opening of these plays invariably refer to the light: *Ghosts* opens in 'a gloomy fjord landscape veiled by rain', *The Wild Duck* with 'brilliantly lit lamps and a glowing coal fire', the first scene of *Rosmersholm* takes place at sunset whereas *The Lady from the Sea* begins on 'a brilliantly clear summer morning'. *Hedda Gabler* also begins in 'morning light' but it is quite clearly specified that the sun 'shines in through the French windows'. The same technique of directing light with some precision enabled Ibsen to create perhaps his most moving lighting effect: the moment when the sun rises and streams in through the window on the dying Oswald at the end of *Ghosts* as he cries 'the sun, the sun'. Ibsen's work contains many other examples of effects made possible by hidden sources of light; where he stipulates that lamps light the interiors in which so many of his plays are set he was relying on the supplementary light from hidden lanterns to light the actors adequately and he used light as a powerful image as well as a source of greater realism.

In subsequent years finely controlled electric lighting has become one of the most important aspects of all live theatrical performances. Joan Littlewood working with Theatre Workshop and Charles Chiltern in the 1960s used a series of illuminating signboards on to which terrifying statistics flashed in *O What a Lovely War*, thus providing an ironic background to the sometimes comic action. Devices of this kind together with the idea of creating a uniquely shaped environment for the performers have been the result of much creative experiment, particularly in the rock/pop field and since the impact of film and television these concepts have been seen as more appropriate employment for the theatre's technical resources than the simulation of 'real' interiors or landscapes.

Stage-lighting — a Practical Guide

We have implied that the first decision the director makes is to establish focuses for the audience's attention and the actor/audience relationship. His next task is to shape the focused areas in order to provide the desired visual and psychological effects. He will probably try to achieve five things; he will wish to make the action visible; he may wish to interpret the apparent natural source of light; he may wish to convey a mood; he may wish to direct the particular focus of the audience's attention; he may wish to make his characters stand out from their background; he may wish to create special 'effects'.

In order to achieve these goals he has a number of variable resources available to him.

(1) He can use either 'flood' or 'spot' lanterns.
(2) He can vary the intensity of these lights by choosing lanterns of different power or by limiting the power through the use of a 'dimmer'.
(3) He can vary the distance of the throw of the lanterns.
(4) He can vary the vertical angle of the lanterns.
(5) He can vary the horizontal angle of the lanterns.
(6) He can introduce colour into the light by using filters.
(7) He can put modifying elements into his lamps to alter the shape and size of the light beam.

We recognise that many students find stage-lighting a daunting prospect. What we have tried to do is to break the topic down into its elements and provide a working schedule and system so that the student will know what he might try to achieve through lighting and how to organise his efforts and those of others. Figure 1 shows a very simplified breakdown of a stage-lighting system. What it shows is the

Figure 1: Lighting Systems

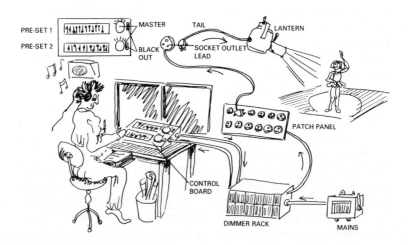

mains electricity current being tapped and directed to the dimmer racks. It is then controlled through the lighting board and led through to the patch panel and thence on to the lantern itself. The dimmer racks contain individual units called thyristors correspondent to the number of channels which the lighting board has. These, in effect, allow the amount of current passing through them to be reduced. Each theatre will have a set maximum voltage or amount of current available. In a very small theatre this might be as little as 60 volts. Each dimmer will take a proportion of that current. Some will only control 1,000 watts (1 kilowatt or 1K), others will control 4,000 watts (4K).

Lanterns

There are basically two sorts of lantern, *floods* which give a very wide spread of light and spots which have a focusing reflector behind the bulb and a lens in front which combine to give a comparatively narrow beam angle. Floodlights can be used in two forms, either as a single lamp (see Figure 2) or as a batten of lights (see Figure 3) which can be ganged together to provide a strip giving general stage cover, to act as footlights or to light the cyclorama. By 'ganging' we mean that lamps are joined to the same lighting circuit. In the case of the magazine batten this usually means that every third lamp is in circuit, so that the first bulb, the fourth bulb and the seventh bulb will all go on or off together, as will the second, fifth and eighth, and so on. There are also two sorts of spotlights, the *profile* spot which has a hard edge to the beam (Figure 4) and the *fresnel* spot (Figure 5) which has a soft edge created by the use of a stepped lens or by having shutters with a zig-zag pattern along the edge.

The use of floodlights is to give a wide cover of light. This can be for sheer visibility, to give a colour 'wash' to create a particular atmosphere or to ensure the possibility of an overall cover of light. Their disadvantage is that they have to be used at a point quite near to the stage for the beam angle is so wide that it is likely to light areas which should remain dark and to throw unwanted shadows. Floods can never be used as 'area' lights, cutting off one part of the stage from another. Spotlights can be used for all the other lighting purposes which we discuss below. The profile has a slightly limited value in that it gives a very theatrically defined area of light, but it is extremely flexible in that the beam can be modified in a number of ways. The fresnel spot, because of the soft edge of its beam, is a lamp which also allows specific areas to be lit, but provides the possibility of a more

Figure 2: Pattern 137 Flood

Figure 3: 'S' Type Magazine Batten

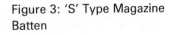
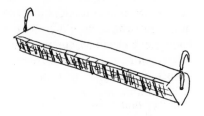

Figure 4: Pattern 23 Profile Spot

Figure 5: Pattern 123 Fresnel Spot with Barn Door

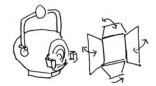

even pattern of light over the stage. Rather confusingly there are nowadays lamps which can be used either as soft-edged or as profile spots. They are called 'bi-focal' and usually they have two sets of shutters, one with straight edges, one with zig-zag edges and depending on which set is used the beam will be soft or hard edged.

Light Intensity

Lanterns in middle-scale theatres tend to be either 500 watts or 1 kilowatt in strength, though sometimes 2-kilowatt lamps will be found. Both floods and spots will be of one of these strengths but floods of the batten type are likely to take 150-watt bulbs, though when connected up each circuit of three will take 450 watts. Very simply, the higher the wattage the stronger the light. There is however the possibility of varying the intensity of all of the lamps by limiting the electricity supply to them through the use of a dimmer.

There are four other factors which have to be borne in mind when considering intensity. First, the distance of the spectator from the scene will affect the perceived intensity of the light. Secondly, some surfaces are more reflective than others and therefore, for instance, a matt brown surface will need a stronger light than gloss yellow, and even some faces are more reflective than others. Thirdly, our perception of light is relative — a torch can appear very strong on an otherwise unlit stage, whereas a couple of floods in a theatre which is badly blacked-out will seem to give little sense of illumination. Lastly, light intensity is reduced when a colour filter is placed in front of the beam.

Distance of Throw

The distance of throw affects two major factors — the intensity of light and the spread of light. In the case of a spotlight which has a beam angle of 20 degrees, the pool of light from 10 feet will be approximately $3\frac{1}{2}$ feet in diameter if the lamp is directed vertically downwards, at 20 feet it is 7 feet and so on. More usually the lamp will be angled, so at an angle of 45 degrees the spread at ground level will be rather more than 4 feet from a distance of 10 feet.

Vertical Angle

A lantern can be angled at any angle along a vertical axis to provide a variety of effects. The effect of the angle is to define areas of light and areas of shadow, so a light from below the actor will create shadows which extend upwards and from above they will be downwards. These shadows all appear on the actor's face and on any surface which the light would reach if he were not in the way. It is usually accepted that the most natural and efficient angle for lighting the actor is 45 degrees.

If the light source is below the actor the shadows created will make the face look unnatural, though the rather frightening product may be exploited for its melodramatic effect. On occasions it may be used as amplification of a natural light such as a fire or a candle or to give the natural effect of, say, reflected light off grass or water. The most common use of lighting from below is through use of footlights. Until quite recently all theatres had a row of magazine battens placed along the front of the stage to light the actors. A vestige of the days when stages were lit by candles, their use was superseded by lamps placed in the auditorium which are known as 'front of house' lights. However footlights can still be useful for giving a colour wash to the scene or to simulate the appearance of a Victorian or early twentieth-century production.

Lighting from an angle of 180 degrees to the vertical with the lantern at the level of the actor's eyes has very limited value. Its effect is to flatten features and to throw shadows on to surfaces at the rear of the stage. Very occasionally it might be used to give a colour wash.

It must be remembered that lighting may also be directed from behind the actor. The purpose of this direction is to make the actor stand out from his surroundings and the most useful angle is again 45 degrees. Care must be taken to ensure that backlighting is not so focused that it dazzles the audience.

Horizontal Angle

The problems and benefits deriving from the various horizontal angling are similar to those associated with vertical angling and against the most efficient and naturalistic angle is 45 degrees. The danger when angles become greater than this is that actors will put each other in shadow, but this can be obviated by increasing the vertical angle of the lamp.

Colour

Light is coloured by introducing sheets of coloured material in front of the lamp's lens. Different companies produce various transparent plastics to achieve this purpose, but what they all do is to subtract light of other wavelengths than those of the colour being used. Light is measured in *Angstrom* and if we shine a white light on to a spectrum it is broken up into the rainbow of colours of red, orange, yellow, green, blue-green, blue and violet, with red at 7,000 Angstrom and violet at 4,000 Angstrom.

The primary colours in light are red, blue and green, so if we place a red, a blue and a green filter in front of the same lamp no light will pass through. On the other hand if we shine a lantern with a blue filter, one with a red filter and one with a green filter on to the same white surface they will appear white. If we look at Figure 6 we see that a mixture of two of the primary colours provides the secondary colours of blue-green, yellow and magenta.

The two methods of mixing colour mentioned above are 'subtractive' and 'additive'. The latter of these two methods is commonly used in the theatre for it is less wasteful of light and by varying the amount of electricity going through the various filters by controlling the dimmers, different tones can be created so that the lighting has more flexibility.

The relationship between coloured light and coloured surfaces is necessarily subtractive. For instance a red surface is perceived as red

Figure 6: Additive Colour Mixing

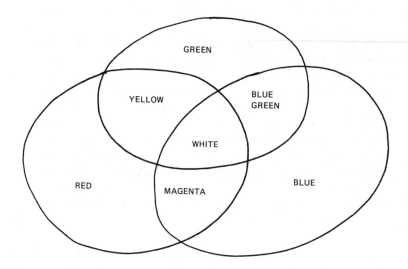

because it is able to reflect the red wavelengths and absorb all other wavelengths. If there are no red wavelengths, as in blue-green light, a red object will be perceived as black.

There are dozens of different coloured filters available which through various subtractive or additive computations provide an almost infinite range of possibilities and it is impossible to identify them all. The designer must make his own experiments. However three rules of thumb might be useful. Normally only pale shades should be used, otherwise some bizarre effects will be created. A warm colour can be balanced by a cold colour on the same area to give the possibility of different atmospheres. There must be sufficient wavelengths of the appropriate colour to allow an object to be perceived in the colour it appears under white light.

Shaping the Light

In addition to changing the colour of the light we can change its shape. Our reasons for doing this might be that we wish to define a particular area or that we wish to give the impression of light passing through a particular external object such a a tree or a window.

In order to change the shape and size of the light beam on a floodlight it is possible to fit a hood. On a fresnel we can use *barndoors* which are fixtures with four hinged flaps which slide into the front of the lanterns. The flaps make it possible to cut off the edges of the light beam. In order to modify a profile or bi-focal lantern we can use shutters if they are fitted, round or square gobbos, which are metal plates which slide into the lamp in a slit between the bulb and the lens, or an iris diaphragm which again slides into the same position, but is composed of leaves of metal which can be opened or closed to produce a varying sized round hole for the light to pass through.

The perception of light as though it were passed through some obstacle can be achieved by using another form of gobbo which is made of thin metal and cut out to create the light and shadow of the imagined obstacle. There is a wide range of designs available which includes trees, clouds, windows and so on. The effect is to give a shadow impression and the illusion of the object being off-stage.

Special Effects

In addition to these comparatively simple devices there are also available many appliances which create 'special effects'. There are special effects systems which produce moving clouds, rain, snow,

Figure 7: Gobbo and Effect

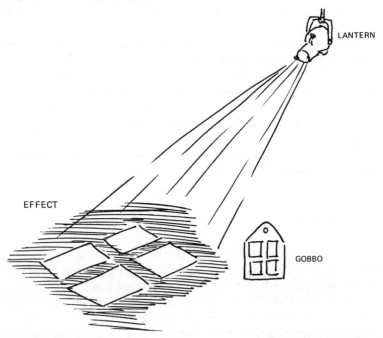

moons, suns, stars, lightning, water, ripples, flames, sea waves, smoke, almost any effect the director could wish for. The great danger is that the illusion they create is incomplete and it distracts from the drama. Perhaps if the play is very bad the audience can be entertained by machinery, but by and large special effects are more distracting than artistically enhancing.

One piece of equipment that can be useful, however, is the Linnebach projector. It is a modified Rank Strand Pattern 223 lantern which will project a shadowing of whatever shape is required on to a cyclorama or gauze, by which means a location can cheaply and easily be represented. Back projection through a wide-angled projector can also be a cheap and easy way of creating a setting.

Lighting the Performance

The aim of stage lighting is to enhance the communication of the performance. Ideally it should be so discreet that the audience is unaware of it. There are six main objectives which the designer may have.

(1) Visibility of the performer and set.
(2) The naturalness of the stage world.
(3) A psychological 'atmosphere'.
(4) The division of the stage into areas.
(5) Toning and emphasis of the lighting.
(6) Special effects.

These objectives have been converted in practical terms into:

(1) Acting area lights.
(2) Motivational lights.
(3) Rim lights.
(4) Fill-in lights.
(5) Specials.
(6) Special effects.

Acting Area Lights

The purpose of these lights in the first instance is to give an even spread of light over the stage. This should be achieved by lighting separate but overlapping areas of the stage so that individual areas can be lit independently and there can be variations of lighting intensity over the stage space. On a proscenium stage each area should be lit by a pair of spotlights, each angled at 45 degrees in both the horizontal and vertical planes, directed towards the actor from the audience's viewpoint. Figure 8 demonstrates how this might be done. In 'theatre in the round', as there are spectators on all four sides there should be four lamps to each area (Figure 9). A thrust stage with audience on three sides may be lit from just three directions, though to achieve the greatest definition of the actor it is necessary to light from four directions.

Motivational Lights

Motivational light is that which represents the ostensible natural or realistic source of light. There are two elements — the source itself,

Figure 8: Pairing of Lanterns

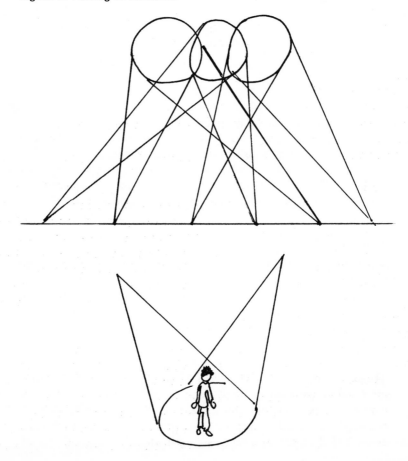

Figure 9: Acting Area Lighting for Theatre in the Round

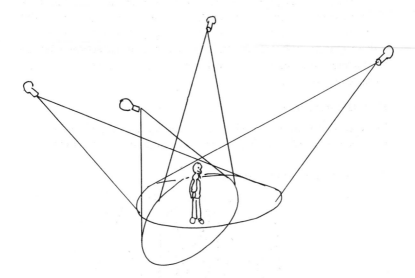

the *motivating* light, and the simulated effect, the *motivated* light. In a naturalistic play this lighting is the key (it is sometimes called *key* lighting) to the shape of the lighting design. It will provide the main focus of light and act as a motivating factor for the stage action in that people naturally orientate to light sources such as a fire, or a lamp, or a window. The realistic light source will provide the rationale for the modulation of the lighting colour and intensity over the scene.

Rim Lights

Rim lights are those which give a rim of light around the actor. Placed either to the side or behind the actor they have the effect of separating him from his surroundings. Rim lighting can be achieved with floods, but the better lantern is a large fresnel. If sufficient power and lanterns are available there should be a rim light to each lighting area.

Fill Lights

The purpose of fill lights is to permit a balance of light over the acting area. Sometimes when there is limited equipment it will be needed to compensate for a lack of acting area spots, in which case floods or battens will be used to give a light spread or colour wash over the scene.

Specials

A *special* light is one which is used for a particular purpose in the performance over and above the objectives already mentioned. A special light might be a follow-spot or a narrow angle spot which will only illuminate someone's head, or a single side light used for dramatic purposes, in fact any lantern which has a discrete function.

Special Effects

This category will include any of the projections and effects we mentioned earlier.

The Lighting Schedule

Stage 1. The lighting designer is obliged to come into a play's rehearsal schedule at a very early stage, for his ideas about how to light the play must concur with the director's and designer's objectives. It is usual for a *production meeting* to be held before rehearsals begin in earnest at which the director will present his artistic intentions and those responsible for non-acting elements of the production will agree their own interpretation and strategies. Subsequently the lighting designer must attend occasional rehearsals and hold conferences with the designer and director for almost certainly there will be modifications to the initial staging plans; the final lighting scheme must take these into account.

Stage 2. When the production has reached the point at which the design and staging have been defined, the lighting designer will start to plot his lighting. He will first establish how many lamps he has available, how many dimmers he has to control these lamps and what the potential lighting positions are. He will then plot his lighting on a ground plan of the stage which has marked on it the available socket outlets with their numbers.

The plan of a proscenium stage might look like the diagram in Figure 10. The numbers refer to the socket outlets which lead back to the control room where there are plugs with the same numbering attached to the leads which have their origin at the socket outlets. The word *dips* refers to socket outlets which are placed in the floor of the stage. They are commonly used for taking power to lanterns on stands at the side of the stage.

Near to the point where the leads from the socket outlets come into the control room there is usually a panel of lighting sockets which are

Figure 10: Ground Plan of Theatre

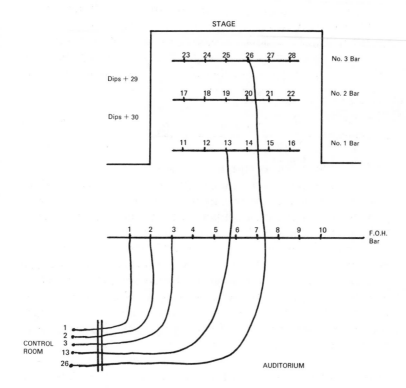

numbered and whose numbering refers to the dimmer circuit which controls them. The panel of sockets is called a *patch panel,* so called because it is where the leads from the theatre are *patched into* the dimmer circuits.

The initial lighting plot will define five elements, which lanterns are being used, where they will be hung, which circuits they will use, where they can be directed and which dimmer circuit they are to be connected to.

All of the above decisions will be written down on a layout schedule. Whilst each lighting designer will have his own way of setting down the schedule the one shown in Figure 11 identifies all of the elements which have to be organised. In the examples patt. 223 and patt. 23 refer to a 1-kilowatt fresnel and a 500-watt profile spot produced by Rank Strand.

Figure 11: Layout Schedule

Production Theatre:	A Doll's House The Gulbenkian				Sheet 1	
Position	Circuit	Lantern	Dimmer Circuit	Setting	Colour	Ganged with
example: F.O.H.	1	patt. 223	2	D.R.	50	6
or: Bar 1	12	patt. 23	15	R.D.	3	16

The column titled *setting* refers to where the lamp is directed. It is possible to divide the stage up into the conventional system shown (Figure 12) or into the more exact areas which the lighting designer may define for himself in accordance with the space he is using for his needs (Figure 13).

In Figure 12 we have marked an area 'No Man's Land'. This is an idea we get from the lighting designer Frederick Bentham, who found it useful to think in terms of a narrow unlit area just in short of either the cyclorama or the up-stage scenery. Attempts to light that area from the front will cause shadows and probably bring excessive light on to the scenery in the case of there being a set, or diminish the colour or projected effect in the case of a cyclorama. Up-stage scenery will be adequately lit by reflected lighting from the lights focused on areas down stage of it. If it is very brightly lit it will steal focus from the actors.

The numbers we use under the column 'colour' refer to Rank Strand's colour charts. Other firms have their own numbers.

The term 'ganged with' refers to the use of more than one lantern on a single dimmer circuit. It must be remembered that dimmer circuits have a specific electrical power capacity. In most small theatres this capacity will be either 1 or 2 kilowatts. If it is 2 kilowatts the lighting designer may choose to 'gang' four 500-watt lanterns or two 1-kilowatt lanterns together. In so doing of course he is denying himself the possibility of using the lanterns separately.

The positioning of lanterns is not a hit or miss matter. Each position can be calculated by drawing a plan of the stage in section and measuring the desired or necessary distance of throw and angle (see Figure 14).

Figure 12: Stage Areas (a)

NO MAN'S LAND				
UP RIGHT (U.R.)	UP RIGHT CENTRE (U.R.C.)	UP CENTRE (U.C.)	UP LEFT CENTRE (U.L.C.)	UP LEFT (U.L.)
RIGHT (R.)	RIGHT OF CENTRE (R.C.)	CENTRE (C.)	LEFT OF CENTRE (L.C.)	LEFT (L.)
DOWN RIGHT (D.R.)	DOWN RIGHT CENTRE (D.R.C.)	DOWN CENTRE (D.C.)	DOWN LEFT CENTRE (D.L.C.)	DOWN LEFT (D.C.)

Figure 13: Stage Areas (b)

XVI	XVII	XVIII	XIX	XX
XI	XII	XIII	XIV	XV
VI	VII	VIII	IX	X
I	II	III	IV	V

Stage 3. The full layout is planned out showing the lamps figuratively and the colours. There is a convention for representing lanterns created by Richard Pilbrow and stencils for the convention can be bought. The purpose of this second plan is to give instant and easy reference for the person who does the lighting *rig*, that is actually hangs the lights in position, making the wiring connections. The symbols for some of the lanterns in common use are given in Figures 15 and 16.

Figure 14: Cross-section of a Lighting Plan

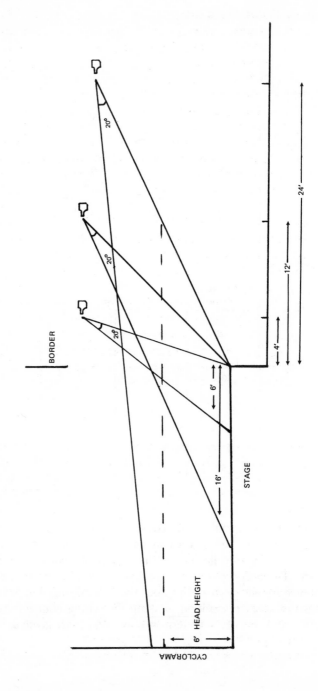

Figure 15: Lantern Symbols

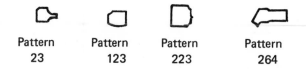

| Pattern | Pattern | Pattern | Pattern |
| 23 | 123 | 223 | 264 |

Stage 4. The lanterns are now rigged into position. Colour filters and gobbos are put in and the lamps are focused on the desired areas.

Stage 5. Each lighting cue is taken in turn and the *state* of the lighting is established. By *state* we mean the lighting intensity controlled by the dimmer. Dimmers are usually graded from 1 to 10 with 1 the least and 10 the maximum amount of light intensity.

A state sheet is next established for each cue (Figure 17). The sheet is made out to include all of the theatre's circuits and the dimmer position is then written in under each lamp in use during a particular state. If there is a blank it means that that lamp is not in use.

When all of the states have been established it is necessary to establish: (1) the exact cues; (2) the sort of change from one state to another. It may be a black-out followed by a 10-second fade-in or whatever. All of this information is then transposed on to the final cue plot.

In most modern theatres dimmer circuits have a number of pre-sets, each controlled by a master dimmer and black-out switch. Every cue can thus be set up on one pre-set and then all of the required lamps are brought in or out together. The next cue is set up on the pre-set below and so on, dependent on the number of pre-sets. As each state has been finished with another can be set up. With this system the lighting operator should never be rushed with his cues and should be able to move from one state to another smoothly and quickly.

Stage 6. The final stage is the technical rehearsal. The purpose of the technical rehearsal is to go through all of the technical elements of the performance one after the other in sequence in order to establish their order, timing and efficiency. The lighting operator will go through his cues and the focus, intensity and colour of the lights will be checked against the costume, setting and placing of the actors.

What we have provided in this discussion is a working format. It is

Figure 16: Lighting Rig

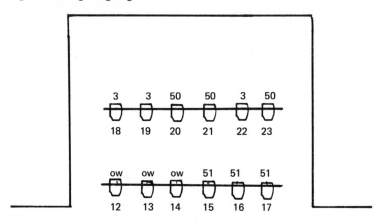

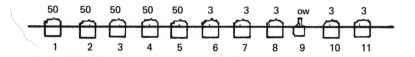

Colour numbers 50/3/51 refer to Rank Strand numbering.

not a bible and each director will want to create his own special sort of experience for his audience, but we believe that he should do this through a decision to reject the conventional methods rather than from ignorance of them. We will end this section with quotations from Brecht and Artaud in which they state their own very different beliefs concerning lighting.

There is a point in showing the lighting apparatus openly, as it is one of the means of preventing an unwanted element of illusion; it scarcely disturbs the necessary concentration. If we light the actors and their performances in such a way that the lights themselves are within the spectator's field of vision we destroy part of his illusion of being present at a spontaneous, transitory, authentic, un-rehearsed event. He sees that arrangements have been made to show something; something is being repeated here under special

Figure 17: State Sheet

Production: A Doll's House
Theatre: The Gulbenkian

Cue Number: 10

1	2	3	4	5	6	7	8	9	10
7	7	7	6	8	3				3
11	**12**	**13**	**14**	**15**	**16**	**17**	**18**	**19**	**20**
					4	4	5	5	
21	**22**	**23**	**24**	**25**	**26**	**27**	**28**	**29**	**30·**
31	**32**	**33**	**34**	**35**	**36**	**37**	**38**	**39**	**40**
					8	8	8	8	

Figure 18: Cue Sheet

Production: A Doll's House

Q No.	Page	Cue	Description	Time	1	2	3	4	5
1.			Pre-set		4		4		
2.	1.	Nora enters	In with light switch		9		8	4	

conditions, for instance in a very bright light. Displaying the actual lights is meant to be a counter to the old fashioned theatre's efforts to hide them. No one would expect the lighting to be hidden at a sporting event, a boxing match for instance. (Appendix to 'Short Description of a New Technique of Acting' in Willett, *Brecht on Theatre*, p. 141)

As we saw earlier, Brecht rebelled not only against the conventional theatre, but the technically complex theatre, arguing, 'What was the good ... of the finest lighting equipment if it lit nothing but childish and twisted representations of the world' ('On Experimental Theatre' in Willett, *Brecht on Theatre*, p. 133).

In writing about a production of *Mother Courage* Brecht said, 'Our lighting was white and even and as brilliant as our equipment allowed. This enabled us to get rid of any remnants of "atmosphere" such as would have given the incidents a slightly romantic flavour' (ibid., pp. 217-18).

Artaud, in his 'First Manifesto of the Theatre of Cruelty', wrote:

> The lighting equipment currently in use in the theatre is no longer adequate. The particular action of light on the mind comes into play, we must discover oscillating light effects, new ways of diffusing lighting in waves, sheet lighting like a flight of fire-arrows. The colour scale of the equipment currently in use must be revised from start to finish. Fineness, density and opacity factors must be re-introduced into lighting, so as to produce special tonal properties, sensations of heat, cold, anger, fear and so on. (*The Theatre and its Double*, p. 74)

The two directors make our point. Brecht's theatre was one in which both audience and performer learned from the simulated occurrences in the play. Artaud's theatre was one in which the emotional experience was totally absorbing. Their lighting ideas were to serve these objectives. Lighting is no different from characterisation or staging in that it must serve to reveal the meaning and style of the performance.

Project Work

All aspects of theatre design are now recognised as highly skilled arts which demand specialist training but the following suggestions are intended to provide valuable starting points for an exploration of this field.

(1) Consider the various locations in which the action of *Macbeth* takes place and study the stage directions (mainly entrances and exits) with which each scene opens. Devise a staging that satisfies

these demands. Compare your solutions with the designs of Craig, Hawes Craven and any contemporary production (see illustrations of designs for *Hamlet* in Ch. 12).

(2) Discuss the beliefs that might be common to an audience attending a modern performance of *Macbeth*. Conceive costume designs for the Witches which in your view satisfy both Shakespeare's text and the likely response of such an audience.

(3) Examine carefully the stage directions and setting details in Strindberg's *Miss Julie* and suggest reasons why the playwright makes specific demands.

(4) Construct a scale model of a theatre stage known to you using thick card, balsa wood, timber or scrap material and then build a design for a production of *Romeo and Juliet* or *West Side Story* which would remain virtually unchanged throughout the performance.

(5) Using two single spotlights in a darkened studio explore the range of effects that may be achieved by altering the angle, focus, spread and colour of the lanterns in relation to two actors. View the actors from positions corresponding with an audience in a variety of theatre forms such as proscenium staging or In the Round. Still only employing two lights work on Macbeth's first encounter with the weird sisters. Watch the effect of light on fabrics and faces and observe the nature of the shadows they create.

REFERENCES AND PLAYS

A. Playtexts

Beckett, Samuel (1955) *Waiting for Godot*, Faber, London
Brecht, Bertolt (1980) 'In the Jungle of Cities' in *Collected Plays*,
    trans. J. Willett, Methuen, London, vol. 1, part IV
_____ (1980) 'The Seven Deadly Sins' in *Collected Plays*,
    Methuen, London vol. 2, part III
Chekhov, Anton (1980) *The Seagull* in *Five Plays*, trans. R.
    Hingley, Oxford University Press, Oxford
Chekhov, Anton (1952) *The Seagull Produced by Stanislavsky*,
    Dobson, London
Chiltern, Charles and Littlewood, Joan (1965) *O What a Lovely
    War*, Methuen, London
Genet, Jean (1960) *The Blacks*, Faber, London
Handke, Peter (1977) *Offending the Audience*, Methuen, London
Ibsen, Henrik (1980) *Plays 1-4*, trans. Michael Meyer, Methuen,
    London
Pinter, Harold (1960) *The Caretaker*, Methuen, London
Sartre, Jean Paul (1970) *In Camera. Three European Plays*,
    Penguin, Harmondsworth.
Weiss, Peter (1965) *The Marat/Sade*, Calder and Boyars, London

B. Secondary Sources

Artaud, Antonin (1958) *The Theatre and its Double*, Grove, New
    York
_____ (1968) *Collected Works*, trans. V. Corti, Calder and Boyars,
    London
Bablet, Dennis (1980) *Edward Gordon Craig*, Methuen, London
Braun, Edward (1979) *The Theatre of Meyerhold*, Methuen,
    London
Brecht, Bertolt (1973) 'Emphasis on Sport' in J. Willett (ed.),
    Brecht on Theatre, Methuen, London
Brook, Peter (1968) *The Empty Space*, MacGibbon and Kee,
    London

Cole, Toby (ed.) (1960) *Playwrights on Playwriting*, Hill and
    Wang, New York
_____ and Krich Chinoy, Helen (1963) *Directors on Directing*,
    rev. edn, Bobbs-Merrill, New York
Craig, Edward Gordon (1905) *The Art of the Theatre*, Theatre
    Arts Books, New York; T.N. Foulis, London
Esslin, M. (1976) *Artaud*, Fontana, London
Grotowski, J. (1969) *Towards a Poor Theatre*, Methuen, London
Jarry, Alfred (1980) *Selected Works*, ed. Roger Shattuck and
    S.W. Taylor, Methuen, London
Joseph, Stephen (1968) *New Theatre Forms*, Pitman, London
McGrath, John (1981) *A Good Night Out*, Methuen, London
Mennen, Richard (1976) 'Grotowski's Paratheatrical Projects', *The
    Drama Review, 19*(4)
Potter, Robert (1975) *The English Morality Play*, Routledge and
    Kegan Paul, London and Boston
Schmuckle, H.U. (1979) 'Erwin Piscator and the Stage' in *Erwin
    Piscator 1893-1966*, catalogue of Piscator's exhibition in 1979
Southern, R. (1962) *The Seven Ages of the Theatre*, Faber,
    London
Stanislavsky, Konstantin (1929) *My Life in Art*, Theatre Arts,
    Boston
Willett, John (1964) *Brecht on Theatre*, Methuen, London
_____ (1977) *The Theatre of Bertolt Brecht*, Methuen, London
_____ (1978) *The Theatre of Erwin Piscator*, Methuen, London
Williams, Raymond (1976) *Keywords*, Oxford University Press,
    London

FURTHER READING

Baker, Hendrik (1980) *Stage Management and Theatrecraft*, Garnet Miller, London

Bentham, Frederick (1978) *The Art of Stage Lighting*, Pitman, London

Cassin-Scott, Jack (1980) *Costumes and Settings for Historic Plays*, Batsford, London, vols. 1-5

Corson, Richard (1981) *Stage Make-up*, Prentice-Hall, Englewood Cliffs, New Jersey

Gillette, A.S. and Gillette, J. Michael (1981) *Stage Scenery: Its Construction and Rigging*, Harper and Row, London and New York

Motley (1964) *Designing and Making Stage Costumes*, Studio Vista, London

Pickering, Kenneth, Horrocks, Bill and Male, David (1976) *Investigating Drama*, Allen and Unwin, London

Pilbrow, Richard (1970) *Stage Lighting* Studio Vista, London

Reid, Francis (1978) *The Stage Lighting Handbook*, Pitman, London

Stern, Lawrence (1974) *Stage Management*, Allyn and Bacon, London and Boston

Styan, J.L. (1982) *Modern Drama in Theory and Practice*, Cambridge University Press, Cambridge

Welker, David (1969) *Theatrical Set Design: The Basic Techniques*, Allyn and Bacon, London and Boston

_____ (1977) *Stagecraft*, Allyn and Bacon, London and Boston

BIBLIOGRAPHIES

Cheshire, David (1979) *Bibliography of Theatre and Stage
  Design*, British Theatre Institute, London
Pickering, Kenneth and Redington, Christine (1980) *Select
  Bibliography of Drama and Education*, British Theatre
  Institute, London. Lists sources for lighting, design, stage
  management and costume.

A useful bibliography of sources for all aspects of theatre may
also be found in *The Oxford Companion to the Theatre.*

PART II

ACTING PROBLEMS

6 ACTORS, ACTING AND BEHAVING

Actors and Acting

It is usually thought that the idea of an actor began with the Greek poet and dramatist Thespis, who around 534 BC had a solo performer separate himself from the chorus in a *dithyramb*. The individual was a chorus leader, but he represented a distinct response to the matters of the drama distinguishable from that of the chorus or of himself. He represented, embodied and personalised a set of values and attitudes. Whilst it is likely that performers in other rituals had done something similar before, the Thespian theory identifies the essential characteristics of a single impersonating actor and an audience.

Though we can define the role of actor itself, its esteem and place in society has vacillated enormously. It has been variously described as 'immoral' and 'insane', 'holy' and 'sublime'. It has been associated with both mysticism and dishonesty, seen by some as a job and by others as a spiritual medium. Its associations with the drama and theatre have also varied: often the script, the ideology, or the poetry of the play, or even the set have attempted to supersede it as the audience's dominant concern.

What then is the nature of this role and activity which we are about to explore? It is well known that to act is to do, but the idea of acting has connotations of *performance* and unless we believe that all behaviour is theatrical, such an all-embracing definition is not very helpful.

We should like to put that possibility temporarily to one side and assume that we can at least start our investigation with the behaviour of people in theatres rather than wherever they happen to be and that actors are those people, about whom there is an agreement that they are to be watched. A simple definition of actors might maintain that they are people who appear before audiences pretending to be someone other than themselves. The last few hundred years of our own theatrical history have tended to reinforce this idea. In spite of evolving beliefs concerning the determinants of human behaviour and each new generation's objections to its elders' dominant theatrical forms, it is versions of human *impersonation* which have

99

provided the actors with their basic tasks and audiences with their satisfactions. However, if we consider the full range of possibilities demonstrated in primitive and traditional theatrical forms, human impersonation represents only a small part of potential acting demands. Acting may involve being a spirit, or a table, an alter ego or an archetype, or anything imaginable.

This world of infinite possibilities does none the less contain three factors which provide us with constant points of reference and sources of comparison. The first two are related to the necessarily dyadic nature of the performing actor, for he is always perceivable as both himself and as the thing which he represents. In effect there is a continuum. At one end is the actor almost entirely as a performed version of himself and, at the other, the actor as almost completely identified with his character and his character's experiences. The film industry's star system provides examples of the first and the improvised dramas of directors like Mike Leigh provide examples of the second. However there is no law. Improvisors often just project themselves and stars like Rod Steiger almost become their characters. What usually happens, of course, is that the two worlds of the actor and character fluctuate somewhat randomly in our attention. The most obvious example of this is when an actor makes a mistake. By, say, forgetting his lines, he draws attention to his own world and breaks the illusion of the fictive world.

The actress Fanny Kemble made the point about double existence most poignantly when she wrote:

> The curious part about acting, to me, is the sort of double process which the mind carries on at once, the combined operation of one's faculties, so to speak, in diametrically opposite directions ... in that very last scene of *Mrs Beverley*, when I was half dead with crying in the midst of the *real* grief, created by an entirely *unreal* cause, I perceived that my tears were falling like rain all over my silk dress and spoiling it. (quoted in Archer, 'Masks or Faces?', p. 185)

The imperative to *display* is the third factor. Whether the actor is playing himself or Hamlet his major obligations as actor are those of presenting and communicating. He must search for behavioural signs which say those things which are to be perceived and then display them in ways that make them perceivable.

Perhaps the earliest writing on acting which still holds some authority today is Diderot's article 'The Paradox of Acting', written at the end of the eighteenth century. The paradox which he identifies is that to move an audience the actor must remain unmoved himself. The conclusion he drew from his analysis of this paradox was that the actor must discipline himself and learn techniques to control involvement with his part.

On the face of it this is convincing, but taken too far the actor as passionless robot would not seem compatible with our own pleasurable experiences in the theatre. Diderot also wrote, 'An actor who has only sense and judgement is cold' (p. xi) which leaves us where we started. However Diderot continued, 'one who has only verve and sensibility is crazy. It is a peculiar combination of good sense and warmth which creates the sublime person; and on the stage as in life he who shows more than he feels makes one laugh instead of affecting one. Therefore never try to go beyond the feeling that you have; try to find the true point' (ibid.). An argument not very far from that put by Shakespeare, 'In the very torrent, tempest, and as I may say whirlwind of your passions, you must acquire and beget a temperance, that may give it smoothness.' (*Hamlet*, Act III Scene 2).

It is likely that the reason for Diderot's hard line was that he was trying to write a new, more democratic, drama and that he found the exaggerated acting techniques of actors trained for classical drama incompatible with his own pieces. Moreoever the demand for a logical and uninterrupted flow between behavioural cause and effect had become the major acting principle. Stimulus and reponse are expected to have a perceivable and necessary relatedness within the conventions of the performance, and it is largely from this relatedness that we derive meaning in the theatre. The principle is a pre-condition of any discussion of the actor/character dualism for, whichever of them predominates, Diderot's point about laughter is still valid; in fact it is something often exploited by comedians.

Diderot's discussion is concerned with the source and behavioural logic of emotion; his main stricture seems to be against allowing the actor's own emotion full licence. He is not saying that actors allow those real emotions which they are feeling, like stage-fright or triumph, full rein, but that they simulate and indulge in emotionalism for its own sake. He is criticising the actor for performing not himself nor a character, but some additional being which has an independent emotional life whose rationale is the manipulation of the audience's emotions through the exploitation of their gullibility, and the actor's capacity for intense and infectious emotionalism.

This emotionalism for its own sake, which in our day is associated with the idea of 'ham' acting, has been derided by almost all theatre writers, particularly those influenced by Naturalism. It is its artificiality, perhaps an offence against an informal agreement to be consistent, that seems to offend. The rather bizarre logic seems to be that whilst we accept that all that the actor does is artifice, we feel cheated if this artifice is not part of an organic and conventionally acceptable system of artifice.

The theatrical evolution in which Diderot was playing a part was towards an *ordinariness* of acting style. By ordinariness we mean style which is as similar to everyday life as is acceptably within the expectations of a theatre audience. As theatre has moved away from its roots in early Christian or pagan ritual there has been a strand in its development which has gradually evolved towards ordinariness. The development probably began with the idea of *impersonation* as opposed to *personification*, or the representation of qualities or powers in human form. It has its most obvious presence today in film and television drama. Our own times have been influenced by a culmination of this evolution in Naturalism at the turn of the last century.

Whilst such writers as Zola and Strindberg gave Naturalism a particular aesthetic rationale it was its interpretation as acting which provided the most persistent and comprehensive artistic model. In effect, naturalistic acting came to mean acting as though behaving in real life and, whilst such a definition begs a host of questions, what it does identify is that acting behaviour should be subject to those influences and motivations which stimulate people's everyday behaviour. The obligation is for the actor to merge more fully with the behaviour of his character, forgoing the pleasure of simply revealing his own virtuosity. The aim was to de-theatricalise the theatre event, partly through eliminating the actor himself as a distinguishable being.

Theatre today is dominated by these principles. The training of actors focuses on bringing greater plasticity and control to their imagining, bodies and voices, in order that they be better able to impersonate. Acting consists of implementing this plasticity in a particular way and the idea of 'character' has come to be the inevitable behavioural outcome. The question is not so much 'how' would the character behave, but 'why' does it behave. The blankness of the empty space has its complement in the stillness of the unmotivated character.

The logical outcome from this manner of working might be that audiences are completely taken in and actors complete their performances with the same personality costs and benefits as those intended by the playwright for their character. In fact neither of these effects comes about. Normally the audience clap and the actors go home with their personalities modified only by the success or failure of the show. The curtain-call and the applause terminate the performance and the illusion. Nevertheless many of these performances are very convincing. That degree of reality often referred to as verisimilitude, particularly when related to an immediate and captivating set of problems, has had irrevocable effects similar to those that occur in real life. For example, an early performance of Odet's *Waiting for Lefty* both simulated and caused political action during the New York cab strike of 1935.

The idea of 'reality' in the theatre is a vexed issue. The suggestion so far is that it accrues from the actors aping real life, but many writers have argued that this is superficial and that artistic reality is a *distillation* from existence given aesthetic form. There is an interesting discussion of this in Michel Saint-Denis' book *Theatre — The Rediscovery of Style*. He writes:

On the one hand we have the deep realism which studies and expresses the nature of things, the meaning of human life, what happens behind and below appearances; and on the other, we have the realism that is satisfied with the representation of the external, the superficial realism which was called at the beginning of the present century 'naturalism'. (p. 50)

The conclusion he draws is that the necessary feature of acting for plays representing the more profound reality is 'style'. The assumption which the idea of style in the theatre makes is that theatre is not life, but a special medium through which a *transposition* of life is expressed. The meaning of 'style' is elusive, yet the word is in common use; we speak of athletes or clothing or butlers having style, but what precisely do we mean by this and how do we act it? Saint-Denis interprets it as 'the essence of the thing'. Quoting Buffon, who wrote, 'Le style, c'est l'homme même,' he concludes that 'good manners, proper training, elegance, a sense of period ... revelation of personality — all these things are inherent in style (p. 61) and that style can be defined as 'the perceptible form that is taken by reality in revealing to us its true and inner character', making for 'sincerity, simplicity ... clarity of meaning' (ibid.).

Now this advice could be almost as valuable and appropriate to a prospective débutante or Guards officer as to an actor. The implication is that specific theatre styles embody particular *codes of behaviour*, just as do specific social groups, and a similar demand to clearly *perform* this behaviour is made in each instance.

The principal difference as we see it is that whilst the officer or débutante is obliged to work within a conventional social structure, the actor has to work within a special literary form. His behaviour should be compatible with, and dependent upon, the text and its structure. Saint-Denis' advice becomes precise:

> You must not hurry or jump upon the character. You should not hurry to get on the stage and try to act, physically and emotionally, too soon. Psychological and emotional understanding of a character should come through familiarity with the text, not from outside it. You must know how to wait, how to refuse, so as to remain free. You must be like a glove, open and flexible, but flat, and remaining flat at the beginning. Then by degrees the text, the imagination, the associations roused by the text penetrate you and bring you to life. Ways are prepared for the character to creep slowly and animate the glove, the glove which is you, with your blood, with your nerves, with your breathing system, your voice, with the light of your own lucid control switching on and off. The whole complex machinery is at work; it has been put into action by the text. (p. 69)

In effect the text's imperatives are not as clear-cut as this seems to suggest. Whilst it is true that, say, Shakespearian verse does tend to insist on a certain framework of performance, the 'style' of presentation can vary, but remain legitimate; production of his plays by the Comédie Française and the National Theatre may be different, but equally valid. So if we take as given that the text makes its own persistent demands, the 'style' of presentation is the behavioural code or sign system employed to reveal it. An actor wishing to work with a company having a particular style is obliged to know, and be able to present, the appropriate sign system.

In traditional theatres these sign systems are codified. Places, costumes, gestures, masks, etc. all have particular meanings which will communicate to an audience which understands the code. In a form such as Japanese Noh it seems perfectly possible for the same style to be persistent, notwithstanding the particular fiction being played, because the fiction must be endowed with a very particular cultural perception in order that the culture is reflected and thus reinforced. However in a culture that is fluid, in which theatre has the object of confronting *new* problems and finding *new* artistic and material solutions, it is difficult to see the necessity of such consistency.

Elsewhere in his book Saint-Denis uses the term 'ensemblier', by which he means 'an artist who aims at unity of general effect' (p. 92). The implication is that style, whilst necessarily appertaining to theatre, can be a function of a common agreement between a group of actors concerning their particular behavioural code. Thus the very different styles which we have mentioned earlier can be compatible with contemporary theatre companies which set out to create and develop their own theatre language and their own meaning. Style itself derives from the economic, organic and consistent employment of that language. We can argue therefore that Theatre Workshop under Joan Littlewood had style, as did the Living Theatre and the Berliner Ensemble. Whilst each group had different objectives they had the common task of creating a particular sort of communication. A style then is a common language stemming from a particular theatrical intention.

On the face of it the Naturalists' dedication to the representation of real life is at odds with the idea of style. However if we look to the writing of Stanislavsky, the major proponent and populariser of naturalism in acting, we find that this is not necessarily the case. His major maxim is that interpretive behaviour must stem from the central idea of a play, or to use his own term, the *super-objective*:

> In a play the whole stream of individual, minor objectives, all the imaginative thoughts, feelings and actions of an actor, should converge to carry out the *super-objective* of the plot. The common bond must be so strong that even the most insignificant detail, if not related to the *super-objective*, will stand out as superfluous or wrong. (*An Actor Prepares*, p. 271)

Like Saint-Denis, Stanislavsky gives primacy to the original text. However it is unlikely that given the same text and possibly the same theatre and actors they would achieve a very similar presentation. For Stanislavsky, interpretation of the core of the play meant the discovery and presentation of the characters' motivations rather than the transcendental significance of the play's action. The display which they would choose and its codification would probably be dissimilar and thus the meaning would be different.

In our introduction we made the point that everything on the stage is a sign. All sensible matter is likely to be read by the observer. Given that the actor knows what meaning he wishes to communicate, his task is to shape his behaviour so that it conveys that meaning with clarity and in keeping with the overall style of his company in their interpretation of a fiction.

So far in our discusssion we have been considering 'acting' as something which is done by 'actors' in 'theatres'. The impulse to act, however, and perhaps the pleasure which we derive from watching acting, is pervasive in all human behaviour. The duality of the actor and the character and the requirement to display consistently, are problems which we all continually confront.

Acting and Behaving

Display

As all public behaviour is by definition observable it is a form of communication. Others will see the behaviour and attempt to interpret it. They will then adapt their own behaviour in relation to the meaning they have perceived. A simple example will illustrate the point. If A goes into a room which he expects to be empty but sees the back of another person, B, sitting in a chair, he will search for an interpretation of that presence. If A eventually recognises B he will seek indications as to the reason for his presence. If B turns round, A will read his demeanour in terms of his state of mind and B's response to himself. Given that B was unaware of A's potential entrance it is likely that he will demonstrate three sorts of communicatory behaviour. His first behaviour may be *mechanical.* He is concerned with the successful completion of a task and not with expressing anything about it or himself. The second category of behaviour may well be that of *unconscious gesture.* B may well jump up, start to perspire, jerk his head and so on without willing these behaviours. Thirdly, when he appreciates the situation he will *consciously control* his behaviour, perhaps by standing up and offering a friendly hand.

We have identified three forms of behaviour: (a) mechanical; (b) expressive and unconscious; and (c) expressive and conscious.

Michael Argyle (see *Bodily Communication*) uses the terms *sign* and *signal* to differentiate between the latter two. He acknowledges that, as distinct from mechanical behaviour, they refer to 'the behaviour ... of one organism that is received by the sense organs of a second organism and affects its behaviour' (p. 5). Signs are simply 'behavioural responses' whereas signals are 'goal-directed' (ibid.). In our example B's startled gestures were *signs* and his handshake was a *signal.*

The nice differentiation which is suggested here is misleading. Behaviour which in one case will be a sign in another will be a signal and apparently mechanical behaviour may well be signal behaviour. B may well have been pretending to read a book whilst in fact the book is hiding a revolver. The startled behaviour (probably without the sweating) may well have been a controlled simulation to persuade A to behave in certain desired sorts of ways and thus be a signal rather than a sign.

Whatever may happen between A and B the likelihood is that in some measure each of them will 'act'. The learned, controlled and communicatory nature of non-verbal communication has been explored by Desmond Morris who differentiates between *actions* and *gestures* whilst recognising the communicatory capacity of each (see *Manwatching*). He breaks the 'actions' into four sub-categories, 'inborn', 'discovered', 'trained' and 'mixed'. The most obvious 'inborn' action is sucking, but the category includes smiling and crying. He argues that these latter provide the communicatory base from which much adult behaviour is a refinement. Smiling is a response to security and crying to insecurity. The game of 'peek-a-boo' which we play with babies is therefore a basic communication game. As adults, we learn to manipulate this inborn behaviour so that we laugh to ease tense situations or feign crying in order to gain sympathy.

'Discovered' actions are those which we absorb from our culture; we learn to cross our arms, or look down our noses, or toss our heads, or stroke our chins. Morris argues that these actions are generally not *consciously* learned, but if they are they become *trained* actions and within this category he places such actions as shaking hands, whistling and winking, as well as the more skilful actions of sporting activities, or craft work, or social etiquette. *Mixed* actions are those which would appear to be partly learned and partly absorbed. There are, of course, problems in this categorisation. If we take social etiquette as an example, for a person brought up in a clear behavioural culture, as for instance within the royal family or in an aboriginal village, it is likely that the behaviour will be absorbed. However, as with Eliza Doolittle, the behaviour may only be mastered by rigorous training.

Key features of acting are 'imitation' and 'mimicry' and the ability to imitate is critical to most learning processes. Imitation also provides one of Morris's categories of *gestural* behaviour, though in truth all gesture is to some degree imitation. Morris uses gesture to mean something similar to Argyle's sign and signal. He differentiates between 'primary' and 'secondary' gesture by asking whether the gesture would be carried out by someone who was alone i.e. whether it has the intention of communicating. Primary gesture has no such conscious intention; secondary gesture does intend to communicate.

A major principle behind most secondary gestures is that they involve imitation and learning through mimicry. Morris identifies four gestural forms which he specifically calls 'mimic gestures'. They include 'social mimicry' or 'putting on a face', which takes place when a person attempts to display himself in an appearance which he feels most appropriate or more appropriate than his spontaneous inclination. Though bored, we may sometimes perform an 'interested' disguise or mask. The second category is called 'theatrical mimicry', which embraces those forms or character or mood mimicry which intend to amuse. Whilst the behaviour readily associates with formal theatre it must also include informal occasions provided by story-telling or joke-sharing. Story-telling and informal play-acting tend to include numerous examples of the third category, partial mimicry. This term refers to those gestures which indicate phenomena without there being any likelihood of the appearance being confused with the reality. The fist gun, arm waving to represent a bird in flight, the swerving flattened hand as an aeroplane or fluttering fingers as rain, are all examples of this form of mimicry. The final form is vacuum mimicry in which, as Morris says, 'the action takes place in the absence of the object to which it is related' (p. 29). The examples he gives are the cupped hand holding an imaginary glass which can indicate either that one is thirsty or inviting someone else to have a drink, depending on other associated gestures, and the somewhat similar gestures concerning eating. This gestural mode can be further refined to the point at which only the most significant recognisable element is represented, and the gesture becomes what Morris called schematic. We find it difficult to differentiate between these latter forms, but it can readily be seen that context can oblige us to inhibit communication. The gesture for 'Do you want a drink?' in the context of a crowded public house will be more complete than when performed during a board meeting. A more universal interpretation is given by Morris who cites the signs for cattle in different cultures as his example. In almost all cases the reduction is to an indication of horns through various means.

The language of gesture can become almost completely abstract. Each culture has its own system of symbolic gestures for communicating ideas not obviously associated with the gesture. We circle our finger against the temple to suggest that someone is crazy. We tap our foreheads with both sets of fingers to indicate impatience, footballers raise their arms in a particular way to indicate disappointment and so on. The abstraction is perhaps most obvious in the consciously devised gestural systems of 'technical' gestures, or those which appertain to specific tasks where verbal communication is difficult. Water skiers, crane-operators and traffic policemen all employ such systems.

It would seem that communicatory or display behaviour pervades all human public behaviour and the concomitant implication, that therefore all humans must be able to imitate and learn code systems in order to gain most of their satisfactions, is equally true. The range and urgency of this behaviour suggest that to behave is to act. Our ability to display is fundamental to our ability to get through life as a social animal.

The Actor and the Spectator

All of our discussion so far has assumed one necessary facility, that of being able to choose to distance oneself from the immediacy of action. The facility has the associated features that we are able to appear with qualities other than those by which people know us, and that we are able to objectify and control these qualities.

In our introduction to this book we discussed Peter Brook's idea of the 'empty space' which one person might occupy whilst another watches, accepting that this was a reasonable representation of the theatrical event. The actor/spectator relationship is a special kind of double act in which each role can only exist in the presence of the other. Remove one and the other loses his rationale. It has been argued that this is not just a theatrical issue and some social psychologists believe that a person must contain within himself both of these roles in order to function in society. G.H. Mead concludes that a *self* includes a subjective 'I' who continuously carries out behaviour defined, monitored and modified by a second, objective and spectating 'Me' (see G.H. Mead, *Mind, Self and Society*).

Mead argues that it is only through the existence of our dual capacities that we can communicate with, and be a part of, a social world. Without them communication would be impossible, for if when we speak we do not know what we are saying we cannot possibly know what we are talking about. The implication is drawn that not only do we hear ourselves, but we also respond to ourselves, talking and replying, just as someone else might talk and reply to us. This internal dialogue is inspired and refreshed by external feedback which is interpreted by the 'Me' who gives continual instruction to the 'I'. Thus when we go to someone with a request, the 'Me' reads the responses of that person and instructs the 'I' to behave in accordance with the perceived success or failure of the encounter. If things do not go well the 'Me' reads negative signs and modifies the 'I's' behaviour accordingly. Our behaviour then is a function of this ongoing process and it is determined at least in part by the particular interaction in which we are involved.

If we look further into this possibility then the whole issue of personality is raised. Mead argues that the self is a developing construct drawn from all of the interactions which it has perceived. As we have seen, the 'Me' can respond objectively and takes attitudes towards the 'I', but the question arises from whence these attitudes are derived. For Mead the answer lies in our capacity to take upon ourselves others' attitudes, so what happens is that we identify as fully as possible with the attitudes of others and as a result of this process are able to decide whether or not to modify our behaviour, and in what way. It is as though we watch ourselves through the perceptions of others which we borrow for the occasion. Through this process of identification with others we are able to find our role in society or within any group of which we become members.

It would seem that the actor/spectator duality is a functional part of a person's make-up. Mead regards the capacity which it provides as the greatest single feature which separates man from other animals. The dramaturgical implications are enormous. What is being said is that we consciously create our own behaviour and that this behaviour will differ according to the role or according to the extent to which our wants are being achieved or what strategies we are employing. This process is one of performing, and the theatrical experience is thus functional to our social survival. Theatricality is once more seen to be a necessary part of human activity.

'Being' as 'Acting'

The person who has explored this territory of personal presentation most thoroughly is Erving Goffman, who significantly draws most of his terminology from the theatre. His basic thesis is that each of us is always in some sort of role, but that the role is not our complete selves. We have, in addition, the controlling self which endows all of the roles with particular characteristics. He states: 'Behind many masks and many characters, each performer tends to wear a single look, a naked unsocialised look, a look of concentration, a look of one who is privately engaged in a difficult, a treacherous task' (*The Presentation of Self in Everyday Life*, p. 228).

The task is to negotiate satisfactorily and perform the myriad rituals and multiplicity of roles which social existence demands, in order that we survive socially and physiologically. This task is bedevilled by a need to sustain a recognisable self, persistent in these roles; a self which is itself a construct drawn from the behaviour of admired models, themselves subject to the vagaries of changing perceptions and attitudes. These many problems would be difficult enough in a constant world, but the individual is continually being presented with new information, new ideas and new problems which he may feel the requirement to adapt to and accommodate.

It must also be borne in mind that the feedback, accommodation and modification of behaviour which an individual undergoes in the course of an encounter are simultaneously being undergone by those with whom he is interacting. The idea of an encounter carries with it the principle that people enter into it with the intention of gaining something from it, with the concomitant possibility of failing to achieve this. The drama ensues from our doubts and anxieties about the outcome. In using the term 'drama' here we are employing it in both the sense of something dramatic and in its association with theatre, for according to some social psychologists the behaviour of people entering into an encounter is stage-managed or 'presented' in much the same way that the performance of a play is presented. Goffman elaborates on the point. He says, 'The self then is not an organic thing that has specific location, whose fundamental fate is to be born, to mature and to die; it is a dramatic effect arising diffusely from a scene that is presented' (p. 245).

The details of this interpretation of affairs are comprehensive. Goffman gives examples of the various staging aids which the individual employs to support the performance, dividing them into 'setting' and 'personal front'. Setting involves furniture, décor and the general physical layout of the environment. This may be very elaborately organised in the case of, say, a VIP reception lounge or a police interview room, or it may be hastily got together to accommodate an unusual or unexpected sort of encounter. Obvious and humorous examples will arise if someone important arrives to conduct formal business in a home when the place has been organised for informal pleasure. Interactants may have to adapt to a new and inappropriate environment, so they will improvise with features available and employ spatial distances to reinforce different stages of the interaction. A 'borrowing money encounter' can be carried out on the tennis court or in bed rather than in a bank manager's office, but it will involve similar behavioural signs.

Within the idea of 'personal front' come all those elements through which we design our appearance for the occasion. Some are formal and relate very clearly to social status. Within this category would come any uniform of office or rank and associated properties like a baton or a whistle. Others are less precise, but the suggestion is that we organise our clothes and our properties as part of presentational strategies. Other features such as sex and age, shape, posture, speech patterns, facial expressions and all the body signs which we continually emit are all available as material for our 'appearance'.

It is perhaps best to separate the ideas of personal front into two categories, *manner* and *appearance*. The latter refers to what Goffman calls the individual's 'temporary ritual state'. Thus we will adopt a certain appearance to conform with our desired image as a senior civil servant, or a sportsman, or a teenage rebel. At the same time we will also adopt a manner which informs others what role we expect to play in an encounter. So someone appearing as a senior civil servant may present a manner of meekness in order to suit his purpose in a particular situation. A known autocrat may go to great lengths to appear democratic on television, or a tramp may use strategies to suggest authority when confronted by a police officer.

We have suggested that a person is at least two entities. He is a 'self', anxious to maintain credibility and respect, and he performs a vast variety of roles within a succession of encounters. Any study of human behaviour or any attempt to create or interpret behaviours must bear in mind the possibilities, the purposes and the pitfalls endemic to the self, the role and the encounter itself.

Little has been said so far about the encounter as separately identifiable from the people who take part in it. The critical features of an encounter are that it is perceptible, it has shape, with a beginning and an end, and that persons taking part in it usually give it a common definition. The most obvious examples of this tend to be known as rituals. Weddings, funerals, public meetings, receptions, interviews are all more or less rituals in that the roles are clearly defined and separated, the codes of conduct, even the language, are constrained towards a certain conformity, and a general outcome can be anticipated. Expectations from the rituals are precise and they are recognised. Behaviour within them falls into known patterns which cultures go to some trouble to perpetuate. At their most formal they are sacred, and inappropriate behaviour would be shocking, perhaps bringing disgrace and punishment to the offender. However, the least formal of them, such as a casual conversation between strangers, tend to fit into a known pattern with participants choosing known roles. This is not to say that all casual conversations will be the same, but that interactants will choose from a finite number of modes of mutual behaviour which might come within a category of 'encounters between strangers'. There is an initial uncertainty until the participants either separate, or find a shared definition of the situation. If they take the latter choice then they will quickly accept unwritten rules of tact and role behaviour. Of course they may fail and such playwrights as Pinter or Mike Leigh frequently explore the behaviour of characters constantly on the threshold of encounters, but unable to define a satisfactory ritual.

We have seen that both the self and the role are always at risk, but it is important to remember that the encounter itself can also be jeopardised. If the self cracks up and shows its weakness or inappropriateness, or the role is not sustained, then the encounter is threatened. A drunken priest doesn't only lose face himself, but damages the wedding. The effects can be worse. A drunken anaesthetist may not only upset a surgical operation encounter, he may also kill the protagonist.

It is the potential discrediting of self and role that generates the greatest fear in social life and the greatest drama on the stage. It is the very stuff of both comedy and the thriller. Goffman associates the discredit with the ideas of 'face' and 'front'; discredit stemming from loss of these through what he calls 'incidents' or those dramaturgical errors which result in the audience seeing the man behind the mask. Examples of such incidents would include unmeant gestures perceived by the wrong person, inopportune intrusions, social *faux pas* and unbridled emotion of the sort which we associate with 'scenes'.

Of course objective perception of these incidents may not necessarily be one of shock or embarrassment. Anyone uncommitted to the encounter, particularly if they disapprove of the encounter's purpose and meaning, will probably be amused. It is funny for the objective observer when the party line or the strategy or the performance fails. We are likely to laugh if the music conductor lets his baton fly out of his hand, or a model breaks her high heel on the cat-walk. The oldest gag is for someone to get caught with his trousers down.

If we are to accept the ideas of Goffman then it would appear that most human behaviour is acting, and an inability to act would severely inhibit the capacity of a person to operate in society. In order to act, an actor has to draw on the facility he has, relating it to the particulars of a context or scene. Audience pleasure stems from vicariously participating in the characters' social risks without suffering the outcomes.

Motivation

We saw earlier that the idea of motivation has dominated one fairly persistent strand of the theatrical form. However it is the particulars of the motivation, especially if we see plays as microcosmic parables of human behaviour, which then become the issue. It may be quite valid to superimpose a social interactionist model on most of the artistic theories and practices of the twentieth century, but what will be revealed is that the theorists choose their own interpretations of the dominant motivating factors in human concerns.

The predominance of Stanislavsky's acting theories in the West has resulted in there being an emphasis on the *behavioural* interpretation of human affairs which stresses the importance of the past on our current behaviour. The American 'method' school and much improvisational theatre, both claiming roots in Stanislavsky's work, are associated with characters' introspections and those past experiences which have shaped their personalities and motivate their behaviour. Each character carries round a rag-bag of formative experiences. Only recently has there been a shift away from this position and a *cybernetic* model has been employed. The essence of the cybernetic model is that people are constantly receiving feedback from their behaviour and subsequently use the feedback to modify their behaviour in order to achieve their goals in life. The method actor plays 'motivation' and the cybernetic actor plays 'intentions'.

The most interesting analogy which we have come across which discusses the difference between the behavioural and cybernetic models is one in which the writer (Robert Cohen, *Acting Power*, pp. 33-4) considers the situation of a man being chased by a bear and running towards a hut. The 'motivational' interpretation of this is that the man is being caused to run by the bear, but the 'intention' interpretation is that the man is running to safety. The implications are that if the man thinks more about the bear than the safety he may well not get there and that for the actor such a formula would be enervating.

The principle of behaviour as tactical or strategic obliges the actor to look at his speech and other behaviour as something which he is carefully monitoring in order to achieve his goal in any encounter and which he will modify in the light of his success or failure. Other characters become obstacles or resources in our drive towards particular ends and they have to be cajoled, bullied or otherwise persuaded to assist in the achievement of our satisfactions.

The principle of emotion being the outcome from success or failure in the latter enterprise again follows logically from the principle of 'intention' and it is difficult to give an actor any better method of finding a source for the display of emotion. Even Stanislavsky's belief that emotion should stem from a detailed rediscovery of the path up to the expression of emotion as comprehensible through our own similar experiences accords with this theory. He wrote, 'Never seek to be jealous, or to make love, or to suffer, for its own sake. All such feelings are the result of something that has gone before. Of the thing that goes before you should think as hard as you can. As for the result, it will produce itself' (*An Actor Prepares*, p. 41). Emotion in all cases will be the logical outcome from a sequence of events and through identification with these events the actor can find the appropriate presentation of emotion.

Tactical emotion is another matter. As we have seen, in real life people do play emotional games displaying emotions in order that they can be read and the reader behave in a desired manner. For the actor the problem is similar. My character wants to make the other character feel pity, therefore I will cry. If we add the interactionist model discussed earlier a chain has been started. I cry for pity, you give me pity. I take advantage of your pity and blame you for what has happened, you defend yourself by getting angry and I leave home, which was the long-term objective for which I needed justification.

As actors, if we use the idea of 'motivation' we have to ask 'why' a character is doing something. If we use the idea of 'intention' we also have to ask 'what for'. If we use the idea of strategy we have to categorise the strategy and say what it is, discussing it in terms of feedback from interacting characters. Inherent in both attitudes is the belief that people want things and their behavioural practices are concerned with the satisfaction of these wants. In terms of acting theory this means that the actor draws on his own experiences of his own wants and transposes the particulars to those of a fictional other.

So far our discussion has suggested that the instinct for acting is in all humans. Fashionable views of the major influences on human behaviour will change, but the audience's pleasure is in watching behaviour similar to their own. In watching a play they are able to analyse behaviour. The actor/character is a social negotiator, the play a social model.

It would be incorrect to accept this as a full analysis of acting, for it is only in the social dramas of the last hundred years or so that the 'social' content of a performance has been dominant. If we turn to traditional dramatic forms in primitive cultures the actor takes on a quite different role. He 'transcends' his own humanity, frequently becoming 'possessed'. Possession works on a number of different levels giving rise to varying intensities of behaviour. At its most superficial it can be seen in the behaviour of someone completely absorbed by a role, whose actions are automatic and unselfcensored. The sergeant-major on parade or a demagogue in full spate provide examples of a role becoming *autonomic*. At its most profound it is the conduct of a *shaman* using his body as a medium for communication between the natural and supernatural worlds. In theatre itself the behaviour is most readily associated with the wearing of masks and the consequent effect on performance.

The role of *shaman* illustrates the nature of 'possession' behaviour most clearly. Browman and Schwartz define the term as referring to 'those persons who mediate relationships between man and the supernatural and intervene in specific cases of misfortune and illness to determine a cause and administer a cure' (D.L. Browman and R.A. Schwarz, *Spirits, Shamans and Stars*, p. 6).

The process of becoming a *shaman* is associated with ecstatic experience of trances, dreams and visions and with the direct teaching of shamanistic techniques, language, tribal myths and so on by senior *shamans*. The experience of an Australian aboriginal shamanistic initiation is described by Lommel:

At sunset the shaman's soul meets somewhere the shadow of a dead ancestor. The shadow asks the soul whether it shall go with it. The shaman's soul answers yes ... Then they go on together, either at once into the kingdom of the dead or to a place in this world at which the spirits of the dead have gathered ... The spirits begin to sing and dance ... When the dance is over the spirits release the shaman's soul and his helping spirit brings it back to his body. When the shaman wakes, his experiences with the spirits seem to him like a dream. From now on he thinks of nothing but the dances which he has seen and his soul keeps going back to the spirits to learn more and more about the dances. (A. Lommel, *Shamanism: The Beginning of Art*, pp. 138-9)

The association between shamanism and the wearing of masks is very common. The most frequently cited example is that of the Balinese festivals at which the ancestral gods are entertained and honoured. Occasionally at the rituals one of the human subjects will go into a trance and in that state will speak as though he were a god, giving answers to questions which the living put to him.

A comprehensive account of shamanishi use of masks is given by F.E. Williams in his *The Drama of the Orokolo*. Williams describes the *hevehe* ritual cycle of the Elema tribe in New Guinea. This cycle, which takes many years to complete, includes a month-long dance of the masks. Each mask is a spirit with a name; the person wearing the mask is considered to be moved to dance, not by his own will, but by that of the spirit. There is a clear parallel to be drawn between such behaviour and the behaviour in our own society of people with clearly defined roles who have submitted themselves completely to those roles. Film of Nazi rallies, experience of charismatic politicians or religious leaders demonstrate how people can allow a mask to take over the responsibility for the logic of their behaviour. Williams notes that in the *hevehe* dances the dancer is aware of himself, but is not in control of his dance. He can thus be described as a conscious medium for his spirit, operating with two distinct kinds of logic. The same seems to be true of our charismatic figures. They can both observe their own charisma and submit to it like a medium.

The most common way for a person to become possessed by random and unsolicited thoughts is through dreaming, but access to this level of consciousness is frequently achieved through meditation or the taking of drugs. Its association with shamanism has been noted by Johnson in his book *Riding the Ox Home*. He quotes the Red

Indian *shaman* Lame Deer:

> We Sioux believe that there is something within us that controls us, something like a second person almost. We call it *nagi*, what other people might call soul, spirit or essence. One can't see it, feel it, or taste it, but that time on the hill ... I know it was inside of me. Then I felt the power surge through me like a flood. (John Fire Lame Deer and Richard Erdoes, *Lame Deer Seeker of Visions*, p. 16, quoted in *Riding the Ox Home*, p. 32)

There is considerable evidence to support the theory that through meditation, drugs or hypnosis people are able to tap deep forces within themselves, reaching a state of consciousness and behaviour more profound and engaging than is common. Whilst earlier discussion has been of the actor superimposing upon himself perceived social practices, the possibility now arises of him making himself available to forces within himself, transcending his normal appearance. It has been argued (see R. Schechner, *Essays on Performance Theory* and J. Grotowski, *Towards a Poor Theatre*) that it is this level of behaviour which provides the most vital attraction of theatre and that our actors are potentially our *shamans*. Certainly the idea of 'presence' does lead to the possibility of an actor being in a heightened state of being which we can share with him and thereby derive vicarious ecstasy.

Energy

A simple explanation of the power of someone in an ecstatic state stimulated by any means is that they are able to release 'energy' which is perceivable and exciting. Yoga and other meditative practices have the objective of controlling energy, freeing the body from tensions and the mind from negative influences. It is written in the sixth chapter of the *Bhagavad Gita*, 'When the mind of the Yogi is in harmony ... all restless desires gone, then he is a Yukta, one in God' (p. 70). Iyengar (*Light on Yoga*, p. 21) confirms this, adding the energy factor, saying that Yoga is 'the method by which the restless mind is calmed and the energy directed into constructive channels'. Similar sorts of arguments are put for the practice of T'ai Chi Ch'uan which is a Taoist form of exercise based on the principles of the I-Ching:

> Movements are also performed with all parts of the body in unison

and harmony to constitute a concerted act — all parts of the body are manoeuvered ... forgetting all worldly worries and attaining a heavenly state of serenity. (Y.T. Liu, *Tai-Chi-Ch'uan, Health Exercise; For Advanced Pupils,* quoted in Wen-Shen Huang, *Fundamentals of Tai Chi Chu'an,* pp. 40-1)

The principal identifying characteristics of both T'ai Chi and Yoga are those of absorption and the economic focus of energy in a very particular desired direction. These are two qualities which are associated with both acting and general aesthetic theory.

The economic use of energy is closely akin to the idea of 'grace' and we would like to end this part of our discussion by making reference to a simplified model of aesthetic appeal which was formulated by Ray Birdwhistell:

We have been running trajectories on dancing and other arts described as graceful behaviour.

Note B and A as trajectories of an arm or leg or body. A is a smooth curve; B is the zigzag line. The sizes of these zigzags are unimportant. It is the shape of the movement with which I am concerned. A and B express the same trajectory. However, ultimately trajectory A shows minimal variation of adjustment within the scope of the trajectory. In A there is a minimum of messages being reacted to in process. This is 'grace'. In B multiple messages are being introduced into the system and there is the zigzag. The things we call graceful are always multi-message acts in which the secondary messages are minimised, and where the role of the whole is maximised. (Lecture at Macy Foundation Conference on Group Processes, 1957, quoted in Schechner, *Essays on Performance Theory,* p. 133)

The model applied to acting would suggest that the actor must have a clear focus for his energy, eliminating behaviour not necessary to the expression of the play's meaning and himself as a performing 'presence'.

Acting as Risk-taking

Our earlier suggestion was that 'acting' is taking part in rehearsed 'encounters', the outcome of which will not normally have any irrevocable effects. The concept of rituals however almost necessarily contains the notion of actual change. Many rituals are concerned with movement from one state to another. Christenings, circumcision, the Bar Mitzvah, weddings, funerals and so on actually change the status or body of some of the participants. Again the shamanistic activities seek to change the state of affairs within a culture or for an individual.

It would be possible to dismiss these latter potentially theatrical practices as belonging to a separate category of human affairs if it weren't for the fact that some of our experiences in the theatre are essentially 'ecstatic' and that some directors have the purpose of bringing about that sort of profound change which we have discussed. Just as there has been an evolutionary line towards 'Naturalism' in acting, there has been one which has been concerned with committing the audience to an emotional or ecstatic experience out of which they will emerge changed.

Aristotle wrote that tragedy is an 'imitation of an action' which 'through pity and fear' effects 'the proper purgation of these emotions' (*Poetics*, VI.2). Whilst there is some controversy about the precise meaning of this, Aristotle certainly seems to suggest that the audience, through its emotional commitment to the action of the play, is emotionally changed. For Antonin Artaud this belief became a principle. His theatre was to be like a 'plague' which would make links between the 'real world' and the world of the spirit and the unconscious. The 'theatre of cruelty' which he envisaged aimed to involve the spectator completely and change him through the depth of the theatrical experience. He wrote, 'The spectator who comes to our theatre knows that he is taking part in a true action involving not his mind but his very senses and flesh' (*The Theatre and its Double*, p. 45).

The actor's role in this form of essentially subjective theatre has been elaborated by Grotowski, who speaks of a 'holy' actor who 'through his art, climbs upon the stake and performs an act of self-sacrifice' (*Towards a Poor Theatre*, p. 43). He is to act as though in 'an elevated spiritual state' (p. 18). The audience should have 'genuine spiritual needs', wishing 'through confrontation with the performance' to analyse themselves. Grotowski writes, 'Each challenge from the actor, each of his magical acts (which the audience is incapable of reproducing) becomes something great ... something close to ecstasy' (p. 41).

Many other theatre directors have worked towards this transcendental experience. In America the Living Theatre sought not to create an 'enactment', but an 'act itself'. Julian Beck stated, 'We would not reproduce something but we would always ourselves be experiencing it not anew at all but something else each time ('Containment is the Enemy', p. 25). One of his actors, Saul Gottlieb, explains his own experience: 'What the actor goes through ... is not illusionary. You go through a very real experience ... we're not acting a role. We are becoming a part of ourselves, we are developing a part of ourselves' ('The Last Discussion', pp. 50-1).

A very explicit account of the sort of acting experience which we are identifying is in John Heilpern's *Conference of the Birds*, in which he describes the experiences of Peter Brook's company in northern Africa. In detailing a performance of the play which gives the book its title he wrote:

> And the show began.
> On top of the walls which surrounded the courtyard and from the forest behind the concrete stage, the actors appeared as half-human birds, and called to each other, gathering for a journey.
> The crowd erupted as if they were at a bullfight! ... Actors, Stanislavsky's kings and rulers of the stage, sprang to life sweeping the excited audience along with them ... the group hit back in the urgency of performing and gave the show every last ounce of energy they had left ... there was the unique and individual colour of a real group, sensing each other out, playing with danger and care, care for each other, but performing as one. It isn't a matter of fine acting performances ... It's more a question of heart. That in an empty space, a group of performers simply and openly show themselves for what they are, and hope to be. (pp. 298-9)

The performance subsequently lost its power and the actors lost their nerve, 'The old routines and familiar images' returned and 'Invisible barriers and safety nets came up' (ibid.).

In this final discussion we have tried to identify the most elusive of acting's characteristics. They appear in part in the subjective and emotional quality of both the actors' performances and the audiences' experiences, but they also associate with the sheer risks which the actors take and the skill with which these are overcome.

The actor takes on the appeal of both acrobat and *shaman* and the meaning he offers is experiential rather than intellectual. He 'dares' and the audience shares his daring. The product is a far more intense experience than that ensuing from a character's risk taking. It is immediate and the penalties are great. Theatrical encounter itself may be put in jeopardy. The person, as actor, as character, is at risk and if he fails the occasion fails on every level.

Summary

In this chapter we have attempted to provide an acting 'poetic', a rationale for the evident satisfaction which people gain from acting and from watching actors. It has been suggested that the actor has potentially mystical powers to be a vehicle for deep personal and cultural drives and the source of a profound spiritual communion. It has also been suggested that he may be a source of more objective experience and that through committing himself to the logical behaviour of a character he allows us to analyse our own lives. To an extent we have defined alternatives: acting as subjective experience and acting as objective experience. The actor must prepare himself to provide both.

7 MIND AND BODY

The Actor Himself

Peter Brook's 'empty space' once again provides us with a starting point. The first need of the actor is to free himself from unnecessary tensions in order to carry out the imperatives of his task. When he begins to work on a part he must accept what the playwright gives him rather than superimpose something which he thinks the playwright ought to have written to conform with his own inclinations. When he performs the part he must respond spontaneously to stimuli from the stage and theatre environment. When he begins to work on himself his aim must be to get rid of any physical or psychological blockage which inhibits his freedom to direct his own energy as he wishes.

Such a process is not the preserve of acting. An analogous task might be that of shot-putting in which the athlete attempts to co-ordinate the power from different muscle groups, channelling it to one very specific part of the body so that maximum effort focuses on one point. Lack of co-ordination, unnecessary muscular tension or lack of focused concentration on the objective will impair the end result. In the shot-putter we can trace a clear energy line which starts with the brain and ends where the shot reaches the end of its journey. It is worth noting that the end result is not just a function of muscular efficiency, but it also depends on the mental stimulus to the release of energy and the putter's expectations. If the energy focus stops at the hand the result will be less than if the focus is sixty feet away. This is one of the principles upon which karate is based. In striking a blow the energy is focused on the other side of the object, not on the object itself.

Freeing the body is, for most people, a very difficult process. The food we eat, the clothes we wear, the persona we present, the tasks we perform and the pressures we confront all serve to destroy natural posture and relaxation. Rather than being available to the dictates of our will our behaviour is shaped by our indigestion, our self-consciousness, our unnecessary muscular tensions and the pressures of past and future rather than the present. The result is that our voices are badly produced, our speech lacks clarity, our joints are stiff, our backbones are misshapen and we throw off undirected energy.

Whilst this is a problem for everyone, for the actor it prevents him from doing his job. All of the exercises and discussion which follow aim at *release*. The exercises are eclectic; they are drawn from Oriental practices, from Russian, American and British teachers and from our own experience. In spite of this they do combine with a single focus on freeing the actor's body, his voice and his imagination. We believe that this freedom is necessary for any actor, whether he is in a West End farce or a Noh play in Tokyo. There is a departure point when the freedom is employed in particular directions to create special styles of performance, but that cannot be our concern. It can only be the concern of the director working towards his own objectives.

The two Oriental practices which we draw from are T'ai Chi and Yoga. Whilst the exercises we give can stand alone, the reader may find it helpful to take up one or other of the practices as part of his daily training. Yoga is well known as a form of exercise, but the word is believed to mean 'yoked' together with the Divine, so it is thus a *state*, and the exercises are therefore techniques for achieving the state. There are many variants and the one we choose is *Hatha-Yoga*, whose particular aim is said to be *nadi suddhi* or the 'vitalisation of the body'. Its two major components are postures (*asanas*) and controlled respiration (*prānayama*), both of which have obvious validity in the training of actors.

T'ai Chi Chuan has been described as 'walking meditation'. It is an ancient Chinese art which aims to harmonise the body and mind and is based on the principles of the *I-Ching* or *Book of Changes*. Its basic physical aspect is a succession of exercises called a 'form' which are joined together to create a sequence which can last up to half an hour. We borrow two words from the T'ai Chi vocabulary, 'Chi' and 'Tan T'ien'. 'Chi' is energy and the 'Tan T'ien' is the point just below the navel which is believed should be the *centre* from which *Chi* should be deployed.

Meditation

We suggested in the previous section that there is a clear relationship between meditation and acting. In terms of training the actor meditation has five potential benefits: it aids relaxation; it aids breathing; it helps in a 'centring process'; it encourages an ability to concentrate; and it is a medium for the release of the imagination. The qualities engendered are all interdependent and derive from the basic practice of what has been called 'emptying', which really means a commitment to an uninhibited and unselfconscious present. The process as a whole is concerned with establishing a free relationship between mind and body, cutting out distracting influences. We focus on the thing itself rather than think 'about' the thing.

There are numerous meditation techniques, many associated with philosophies or religions; the one which we are going to suggest borrows from the teaching of Jose Silva, from the practice of T'ai Chi and from Yoga.

Practice 1 Phase 1. First ensure that you are in a comfortable, but upright, posture. Whilst many people practise the technique anywhere they happen to be, it is helpful to the beginner to establish a system. It is best to have an uncluttered space without noise or the likelihood of interruption. You can sit in any of the positions we associate with Yoga, the lotus, half-lotus or 'tailor's' position, depending on which is most comfortable and permits the back to be straight without putting strain on the base of the spine. Alternatively the kneeling position used by the Japanese achieves both comfort and a straight spine. The hands can be rested on the knees with the tips of the forefingers and thumbs touching lightly.

Figure 1: Sitting Positions

(a) 'Tailor's position'.

(b) Japanese sitting position.

Practice 1 Phase 2. Having relaxed into position, gradually become aware of your own breathing. First allow yourself the sensation of permitting breath into the body, pausing momentarily and then permitting it to leave the body. Breathing is an involuntary activity, but we can inhibit it for a while. By giving breath our assent we release tension in the solar plexus. A momentary pause in the breathing allows us to feel the very gentle energy which can become the origin of speech or movement. In your mind follow the breath down the body to the Tan T'ien. As you exhale sense the breath moving down the belly, through the genitals to the coccyx, then up the backbone, over the skull, down the sides of the face to the roof of the mouth, where it meets the tongue and the cycle begins again. Be aware of the stomach moving out during inhalation and in during exhalation, but allow this to happen rather than force it.

For the actor, breath control is critical. Through control of his breath he is able to control his voice and his emotions. He must be able to overcome the effects of nervousness and he must have the breath reserves to provide energy for vocalisation and to permit him to communicate in the theatre.

The idea of allowing the breath to circulate round the body is a *biofeedback* technique which aims to take energy to the body and relax it. Biofeedback is a comparatively new medical practice which makes use of our ability to monitor and control our own physiological activity. It is this capacity which is employed in autosuggestion, in the idea of the placebo and in acting itself. In order to act well we must be in partial control of our physiology.

Practise 1 Phase 3. When you feel completely relaxed and are breathing deeply and easily, mentally count down from three to one, counting on an exhalation and simultaneously creating a picture of the number three times, allowing the picture to be seen in the middle eye, the space between the two eyes at the bridge of the nose. When you have completed this process you will be at a deeper level of consciousness. You may go to deeper levels by counting from twenty-five to one or even using a larger number, allowing your consciousness to sink as you count. Whilst at these deeper levels you may allow your mind to focus on particular problems or merely permit your imagination to have full rein. For some people the initial experience is frightening. Images are suddenly released, some of which may be unpleasant. Try to make sure that you are fully calm before you begin the exercise and count down slowly. This should inhibit the rush of images which might otherwise occur.

In order to come out of level one, count backwards from one to five, sensing as you do it a gradual coming to the surface. When you come out you will be feeling relaxed, comfortable and at ease with both yourself and the world.

Meditation as an aid to acting may be used for bringing together different elements of a part or characterisation or as preparation for rehearsal or performance. In the latter instance the aim is to calm the mind and rid it of that clutter which inhibits us from fully concentrating on what we are doing. If a company meditates together, a focus will be brought to the work which thus becomes more creative and efficient. Initial attempts at meditation will probably last for a few minutes, but regular practice will extend the span to half an hour or more and the benefits you derive will be increasingly noticeable.

The Actor's Body

Centring

We have already introduced the idea of the Tan T'ien as the energy centre of the body. It is also our centre of gravity and the approximate point to which the diaphragm contracts when we breathe in. It is the point around which the body balances and which acts as the source of breath and voice control. Most Oriental religions associate it with mystical and physiological powers. It is seen as the seat of the 'abdominal brain' and the core of the sympathetic nervous system.

The term 'centring' in our discussion is used to refer to the process whereby the actor first eases tension away from his centre and then uses the centre as an origin for movement and speech. It becomes a point of concentration, a centre of balance and a core of relaxation.

The term has also been used to refer to a method of bringing together the body's various rhythms. Robert Benedetti in his book *The Actor at Work* argues that each individual must contact these rhythms and harmonise them in order to provide a core harmony for his personality and the energy origin for activity. The heart, the lungs, the digestive organs, the excretory process and the sexual rhythms for men plus the menstrual cycle and child-bearing rhythms for women must be brought into synchrony. Whilst we do not disagree with Benedetti, the breaking down process required to get to the individual centre is difficult if not dangerous and needs to be handled with minute and knowledgeable care.

The following practices all aim to help you to centre your body. The first is taken from T'ai Chi, the others from traditional mime training. One of the main causes of our not working from our centre is anxiety-related tension. Whilst the exercises will be helpful, there is a need for you to find your own causes of anxiety and overcome them.

We also include some partner exercises because one of the essential needs in acting is to work with your partner's centre and allow him to work with yours.

Practice 2. Carry out a deep breathing exercise by breathing from the centre and stretching the body upwards and downwards away from the centre along a vertical axis. Focus your attention on your centre. Use a point of concentration — perhaps a picture of your diaphragm raising and lowering as you breathe. Stand with feet together, one arm stretched upwards and the other downwards, with palms facing away from the centre of the body, breathe in and then as you breathe out turn the palms and with a relaxed movement bring the top hand to the top of the head and the lower hand to a little above the navel whilst bending the knees through about 45 degrees. Breathing out, turn the palms and return to the first position whilst stretching the legs (see Figure 2(a)). Keep a fluid movement and change the direction of the hands. Repeat the exercise eight times with each hand uppermost.

Again keeping the movement fluid, bring the top hand down to the navel where it meets the lower hand. Push both hands down on an inhalation, move them in a rounded movement back up to the lower chest whilst bending the knees and breathing out. Then press down and breathe in whilst straightening the legs. The movement of the hands must be gentle with wrists relaxed. Imagine as they come up that they are curling round a very fragile ball. The movement downwards should be a very gentle press. The exercise can be repeated eight times (see Figure 2(b)).

Practice 3 Phase 1. Tilts. In these exercises the body must be kept in a straight line so there must be some tension in the middle of the body to make this possible.

Standing in an aligned position with heels about an inch apart and toes some three inches apart, tilt forward, keeping the legs, pelvis, orso and head in line. Go back to vertical and then tilt backwards. Return to vertical and tilt to one side, back to vertical and then tilt to

Figure 2: Positions for Practice 2

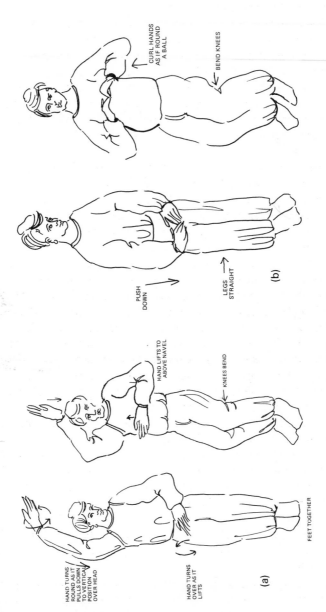

CURL HANDS AS IF ROUND A BALL

BEND KNEES

PUSH DOWN

LEGS STRAIGHT

(b)

HAND LIFTS TO ABOVE NAVEL

KNEES BEND

HANDS TURNS ROUND AS IT PULLS DOWN TO VERTICAL POSITION OVER HEAD

HAND TURNS OVER AS IT LIFTS

FEET TOGETHER

(a)

the other side. When you have mastered each phase in this exercise try moving round in a circle. As you relax and become more centred and confident you will find that the circle becomes larger.

Figure 3: Tilts

(a) Forward tilt.   (b) Backward tilt.   (c) Sideways tilt.

Practice 3 Phase 2. Open Tilts 1.   Stand with feet about fifteen inches apart. Pointing to the left toe, use the left leg as a fulcrum and lean to the left so that your body, head and right leg form a straight line. As you lean you will be obliged to point the foot of the aligned leg. Repeat to the other side (see Figure 4(a)).

Open Tilts 2.   Stand with one foot about fifteen inches in front of the other with both feet facing forward. Using the front leg as a fulcrum lean forward and come up on to the toe of the rear foot. Establish a straight line down through the head and trunk and rear leg. Come back to centre and lean backwards, using the rear leg as a fulcrum and pointing the toes of the front foot. You will be obliged to bend the rear knee. Repeat backward and forward leans a number of times aiming for balance, relaxation and a straight line. You will probably need a partner to help you to know whether you are establishing the straight line.

Figure 4: Tilts

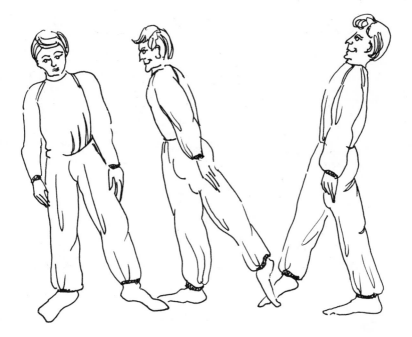

(a) Tilt to side.   (b) Forward tilt.   (c) Backward tilt.

Figure 5: Fulcrum Tilts

(a) Forward.

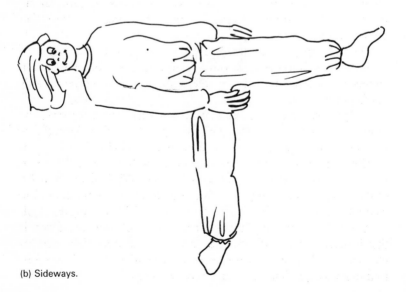

(b) Sideways.

Fulcrum Tilts.   In this exercise you lean forward pivoting on the front leg bringing the body into a horizontal position at 90 degrees to the supporting leg. This exercise can also be done sideways.

Practice 4 Phase 1. Partner Trust Falls.   Stand in an aligned position with your partner about two feet in front of you. Centre your breathing and close your eyes. Whilst maintaining tension in the body and thus remaining straight, lean forward and allow yourself to fall. Your partner breaks your fall by catching your shoulders and then gently pushes you back (see Figure 6(a)). Repeat a number of times until you feel confident and relaxed. Reverse roles and then do the exercise by falling backwards. You can vary the distance through which each partner falls, becoming more daring as you relax.

It is essential that there is a bond of trust between partners. Do not over-expose your partner. Some people find the exercise extremely difficult. Increase the distance they fall very slowly. You may find that in exceptional cases it will take many months before some actors can perform the exercise without suffering anxiety.

Practice 4 Phase 2. Partner Support.   Stand about two feet from your partner and hold hands or wrists. Relax and synchronise your breathing, then both of you lean back as far as you can whilst maintaining balance into an inverted 'A' position (Figure 7(a)). Next allow your pelvises to drop and bring your heads forward, easing down into a 'C' position. Hold the position whilst breathing easily and then reverse the process.

There are many other possibilities for this sort of exercise. It is useful to build into the work verbal games such as word association games or one-word stories when both partners are reasonably confident.

The physical centre in any joint physical activity is quite simply the point around which you work whilst using minimum strength. Partly a function of the individual's own balance, it is also derived from sensitivity to your partner's balance. The implications to be drawn from the idea of a centre are very considerable. Whilst it may be just a spatial matter, in a scene it becomes the point of orientation of the characters in terms of the dramatic tensions which are being exposed.

A useful working hypothesis for the origin of dramatic action is that it derives from a disturbance in the equilibrium of the various elements, the balance is disturbed with the result that the deharmonised parts seek to find new centres or balances.

Figure 6: Falls

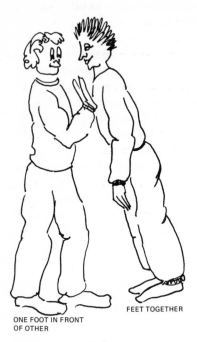

ONE FOOT IN FRONT
OF OTHER

FEET TOGETHER

(a) Forward trust fall.

(b) Backward fall.

Figure 7: Inverted 'A' and 'C' Positions

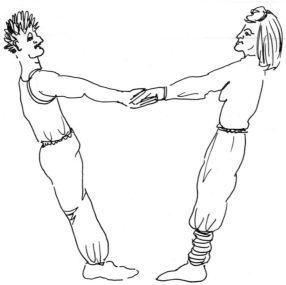

(a) The inverted 'A'.

(b) The 'C'.

Mutual balance on the stage has relevance to two dimensions of the actor's work, that of his own behaviour as part of a constantly shifting stage sculpture, an element in a kinetic form, and his behaviour as the character interacting with his fictional environment. He has to be sensitive to the movements and energies of his fellow actors and also base his character's behaviours on the motivations and energies which he derives from the script. In both instances the centre must provide the pivot and point of origin of the behaviour, otherwise the elements separate in the perceiver's mind and exist uniquely rather than as part of an organic and dynamic flow of meaning.

Posturing and Alignment

The centre is both an energy centre and a physical centre. One's posture should take cognisance of the fact by not putting the muscles and nerves under unnecessary tension, thus impairing the economic use of energy and the efficiency of the energy centre. The function of good posture is to relieve the body from unnecessary effort to remain upright, allowing the skeleton to do its job of holding us together in a balanced way so that the force of gravity acts vertically down through the skeletal structure, which is aligned to make this possible. Most of us, over the years, destroy this alignment and develop habitual muscular tensions. Obvious examples would include the effects from wearing high heeled shoes which oblige people to tilt the pelvis and then to complement this with compensatory tilting of the shoulders. Continual reading with the head down will push the upper back out and demand compensation in the pelvis. The result is that we develop tensions, use up energy unnecessarily and shift our centre away from the middle of our body and are not able to react quickly or efficiently. We have all experienced the sensation of the nervous centre in the upper back at the pivot point of the neck when surprise or anger makes us respond by tensing up in that region and pulling the head back, thus constricting the muscles, the blood flow and the nervous system. This area has been called by Frederick Alexander the 'hump' and he sees it as the source of pain, stress symptoms and cardiac malfunction. By excessive or badly employed muscle tension this hump often gradually develops through age until in some people it becomes the apparent centre of their personality, and actions appear to originate at that point (W. Barlow, *The Alexander Principle*).

Before going on to the following exercises a few cautionary points must be made. First, bad posture is likely to be partly a result of learning by imitation from parents and therefore deeply structured in behaviour patterns and in the personality. Secondly, it may stem from behaviour perhaps developed during the growing process, as for instance in the case of a child who grows rapidly to be much taller than his peers or a girl with a small frame who develops a large bust. Thirdly, posture is not neutral. In many instances we develop the way we move and stand to accord with images which we aspire to, and subsequently hold sacred. Posture is also a function of deep-seated psychological factors, a result of protective or display strategies. It can be readily seen therefore that we should proceed with caution. People are likely to be jealous of their posture no matter how bad. Perhaps most important, they will have grown to find it comfortable and will consequently find a position of good posture initially uncomfortable. It is therefore necessary to develop the work slowly, emphasising the qualities of good posture rather than the deficiencies of the old habit.

Figure 8 gives examples of four fairly common bad postures, plus one which shows the body in alignment.

Figure 8: Posture — (a) in Correct Alignment

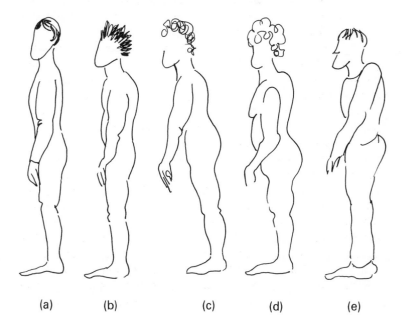

(a)   (b)   (c)   (d)   (e)

When the body is in alignment the pelvis is flattened, the back straight with only a slight convex curve at the base, the abdomen is flat, the neck is straight, the crown of the head is the uppermost point and the chin is level. The arms and shoulders are relaxed with the palms of the hands facing the body. The knees are slightly relaxed so that the joints are not locked and they are in line with the toes. The toes should be flat with the body's weight evenly distributed over the feet.

Before discussing particular exercises to help posture we would like to make four points which apply to all the exercises in this book.

(1) A vital part of an actor's training is the development of his sensation memory and his physical imagining. When you perform each exercise observe carefully the sensations which you experience, sense what is happening to you and develop the ability to recall the sensations. As an actor you will be continually expected to remember all sorts of sensations: you must train your memory to enable you to do this, and you must also train yourself to be aware of what your body is doing.

(2) An actor is essentially part of a group. He must be spontaneous in his responses to others and he must be prepared to give of himself to others. We therefore make as many of our exercises 'partner' activities as possible in an effort to build trust, responsibility and confidence.

(3) It is easy to treat acting exercises just as fun. Whilst we do not wish to imply that they are not pleasurable it is important that they are done with care and a sense of focused purpose. All work must be given the reverence due to acting itself, otherwise the actor will be unworthy of his task.

(4) People vary enormously in their physical confidence. Some people will take to these exercises easily, others will be afraid, all will be able to do them in the end if they persevere. Initial failure will result from tension, from lack of confidence and from working away from the centre, not from natural ineptitude.

Practice 5 Phase 1. The purpose of this phase is to stretch the back and ease tension away from the large muscle groups which are situated there (see Figure 9). It has been argued that the back is the source of aggressive attitudes, whilst the front of the torso is the source of friendly and loving behaviour. This point will be discussed later (see p. 203), but it is certain that easing the back relieves a multitude of tensions.

Stand back to back with a partner of about the same height and weight and link arms (see Figure 10(a)). Keeping as much contact with your partner as possible, establish a mutual deep breathing rhythm. When you are both relaxed and in good communion bend your knees and place your buttocks under his. Allow his buttocks to ease into the small of your back. Closing his eyes, he now allows his weight to come over towards you whilst you lean forward until you are supporting him. Your back will be horizontal to the ground, his legs will trail down and his head relax back. It will take a few moments before your partner feels fully confident. When you sense him to be relaxed, slowly ease your arms away from his and put your hands just above your own knees in order to strengthen your support (see Figure 10(b)). Again wait for maximum relaxation and then move your back gently up and down, incorporating a slight rocking action. The

Figure 9: View of Back Muscles

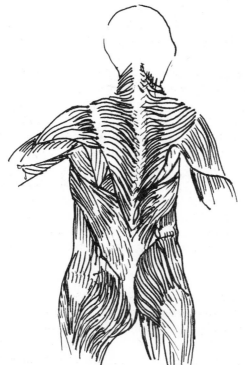

Figure 10: Easing the Back

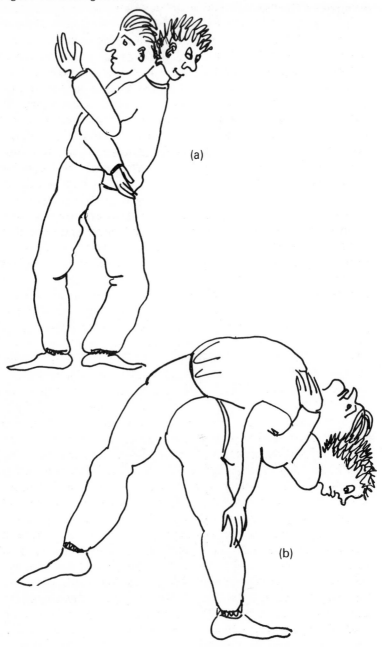

(a)

(b)

result will be a gentle back massage which relaxes the back and helps to lengthen the muscles. After a couple of minutes reverse roles.

This exercise also acts as a trust exercise and it is essential that your partner comes to no harm. For people with little physical confidence it may be necessary to have a third person standing by and holding or simply touching the supported person in order to help and reassure him. Supporting is quite hard work, but well within the average person's capacity provided he works through his skeleton and uses his powerful thigh muscles. Some people may have to be reassured that they can act as support, so go into the exercise slowly. You may not get the full pleasure and benefit from the exercise until you have done it on a few occasions. Once you have, try to remember the sensation of ease and lightness.

Practice 5 Phase 2. This phase has the objective of relaxing your partner. He should lie down on a mat or blanket and get into a comfortable, aligned position. Ensure that he is warm. Next ease his neck by first moving the head gently in all possible directions. When you feel that it is you who is moving the head without your partner's assistance cup your hands on either side of the head and just pull it gently into alignment (Figure 11(a)). The head should be gradually pulled along the axis of the back making sure that the chin does not lift. Next massage the fingers, hand and one arm, lifting the arm at the elbow to check that it is relaxed. Lift the whole arm and ease it back over the head until it touches the ground. Check for relaxation. Return it to the side and then repeat the process with the other arm. Go to the left leg and bend it towards the body (Figure 11(b)). Shake it gently whilst holding the foot and the knee. Bend the foot out and back. Check the whole leg for relaxation. Place it back on the ground and then repeat the process with the other arm. Repeat the process with the other leg and then with both legs together. Next, with the legs straight, push them back as far as you can towards the body (Figure 11 (c)). It is essential to do this slowly otherwise counter tensions will be initiated in your partner's back. Having returned the legs to the ground separate them and, moving in towards your partner, hold each leg above the knees under your arms and gradually lift. You should lift his pelvis and lower back off the ground and with the objective of stretching and relaxing the back you should shake the legs and pelvis. Gently replace the legs to the ground. Lightly pull the legs to get alignment back and repeat the aligning process with the head. Your partner should now be relaxed and lying in alignment.

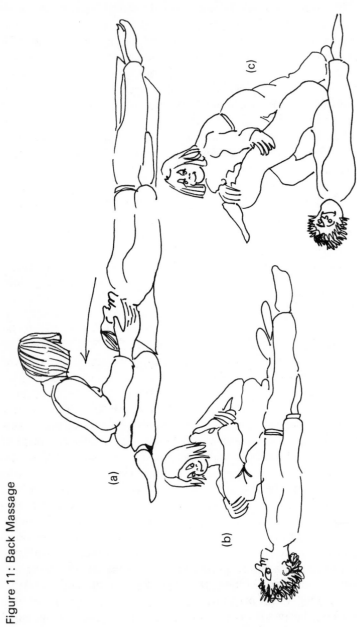

Figure 11: Back Massage

Practice 5 Phase 3. This exercise is not necessarily a development from the previous one, but preparation should include some stretching and relaxing exercises. Lying down in the aligned position, focus on your breathing. Sense that each inhalation brings with it warm energy to all parts of the body. Feel it flowing all over you. With each exhalation enjoy the sense of tension flowing out of your body. Allow the breathing to become deeper, but do not force it to do so. As you relax the breathing will ease and become deeper.

Once you feel confident that your breathing is easy, on each inhalation take the breath to a part of the body and allow that part to contract and then release as you exhale. Go through the body, to the face, the eyes, the tongue, the neck, the upper chest, the abdomen, the arms and hands, the buttocks, the knees and the feet. As a last exercise try lifting the whole body on your heels and shoulders so that it arches up and relaxes back on to the floor (see Figure 12).

Figure 12: Position for Practice 5 Phase 3

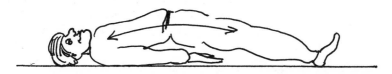

As you lie there relaxed, allow a sense of the breath easing into the muscle fibres. Take your mind to various muscle groups and sense the fibres easing away from each other until you can feel the space between them. Sense your body becoming lighter. The skin is wasting away from your flesh, the muscles from the bones. Take your mind inside your skeleton. As you move inside the bone it expands and becomes thinner and like membrane which lightly flaps. Your whole body begins to float away. The sensation is one of flying and lightness. Think light and warm. Float yourself off somewhere you associate with good memories. Land and gradually bring your body back together, feeling a gentle layering of the parts so that you finish feeling as though composed of layers of silk. Gradually allow yourself to waken up. You will feel rather dazed and very peaceful so take time before standing up. Remember the sensation which you have experienced.

This last exercise may be done at the beginning or the end of a workshop. We will frequently come back to it as a neutral starting point for voice and other physical work. It is very useful preparation for meditation, but it has the problem that if you practise it on your own you are likely to fall asleep.

Practice 5 Phase 4. This is a series of exercises which help with alignment. The more regularly you do them the easier and more beneficial they become.

Part 1. Having warmed the body up stand in an aligned position with the feet slightly apart, focus on your breathing with a feeling of permitting the breath in or out and sensing that the energy for this comes from the Tan T'ien. With each incoming breath feel the body stretching both upwards and downwards in the vertical plane from the middle. As you breathe out allow the body to relax into its new position. You will find that you gradually improve your posture, but do not focus on this, think only of expanding away from your centre.

Part 2. Standing in your improved posture focus your mind on the point at which your vertebrae reach the skull. Take a sense of lightness to that point and allow your head to loll forward. Now gradually

Figure 13: Positions for Practice 5 Phase 4

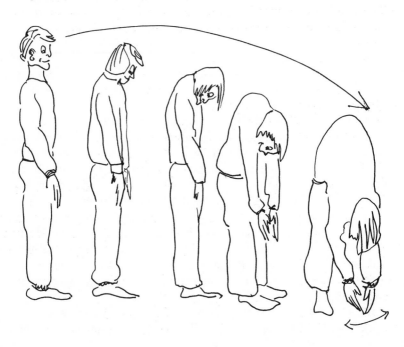

move your mental focus down the spine one vertebra at a time until your torso is hanging from the flat bone at the bottom of the spine. Think of the process bringing warmth gradually to the back. As you hang, enjoy the weight of your head and arms, let your knees sag slightly and allow your hand to brush the floor. Enjoy the relaxed sensation for a while and then reverse the process, pulling the head and torso up slowly one vertebra at a time and then finally easing the head up to a balanced position. Repeat the exercise two or three times, always doing it slowly, but developing a fluid movement rather than the jerky one which you will probably start with.

Part 3. Whilst there are only two true pivot points in the back, the points where the backbone meets the skull and the pelvis, it is possible to think of other points, because of the flexibility of the spine. This next exercise asks you to focus on all of these points. In effect we are doing an exercise similar to Part 2, but breaking it up into parts.

With the body in alignment, lower the eyes. Having established their position, lower the head, pivoting downward from the hollow point in the back of the skull. Establish that position and then lower the neck, pivoting from the 'hump'. Check that position and collapse the shoulders and chest. You will find the pivot point quite easily if you maintain a firm stomach. Again establish the position and drop

Figure 14: Spine Exercise in Parts

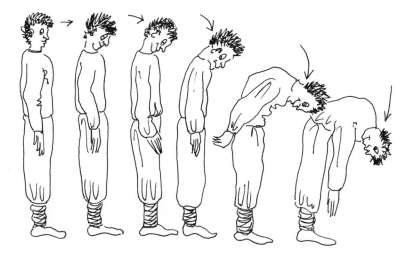

from the waist with the pivot point at the flat bone at the base of the spine. Now let the pelvis go, simultaneously allowing the knees to sag and thus the thighs to open out. Now reverse the process stage by stage. Repeat the whole cycle three or four times, making sure that you are established and relaxed at each point.

Part 4. This is a similar exercise to Part 3, but it is done dynamically so that you complete a full undulation of the body. Start with the head centred, take it down to the chest, allow the chest to collapse, the trunk to rotate downwards and the pelvis to move back with the knees moving forwards. Continue until the head reaches nearly to the knees. Push the knees forward, then the pelvis and allow the upper spine to uncurl, bringing the head up last and then repeat, using a shoulder rotation to bring the head forward initially and to return it to position.

Many Yoga exercises can be used to aid posture and all Yoga is concerned with relaxation and the centring process. The following two exercises are particularly useful.

Part 5. The Sarvangasana Cycle.

(1) Lie on a blanket or mat with arms by the side and legs straight. With minimum effort raise the legs on an exhalation until they are vertical. (If you have very weak stomach muscles you may have to bend the knees as you bring the legs up. If this is the case it is essential to work on your stomach muscles and probably to lose weight.) Note that the head is straight. Try to stretch the shoulders away from the neck (Figure 15(a)).

Breathe in again and as you exhale raise the legs further, lifting the back and hips off the ground. Move your hands to support the back and continue the movement until the legs and back are perpendicular. At this point only the back of the head, the neck, the shoulders and the upper arms are touching the floor and the breastbone is pressing against the chin (Figure 15(b)). Stretch up vertically and your body will be in a straight line. Gradually you will become accustomed to this position and breathing will become easy. Try to maintain the position for about five minutes, focusing on relaxing the muscles whilst remaining perpendicular. Relax from the centre.

(2) Slowly lower the legs towards the floor beyond your head, keeping your back and legs straight. Once they reach the floor stretch your arms out towards your feet. Walk your feet as far away as possible whilst stretching the spine. Now move your arms to the floor

Figure 15: The Sarvangasana Cycle

(a)   (b)   (c)

behind your back and interlock the fingers, allowing your little fingers to rest on the floor. This final movement will give an extra stretch to the back. Hold this position for two or three minutes (see Figure 15(c)).

(3) First bring the arms up to support the back then bend the knees, allow the back to relax and walk the knees in until they are on either side of the head. Gradually relax, focus on easy breathing and enjoy the restful position.

(4) Stretch the legs out again, lower the spine and hips whilst moving your arms back to your sides, leaving the legs as far behind as possible. Keeping the legs straight, bring them slowly to the ground.

Part 6. The Headstand (Sirsasana). This is quite an advanced exercise and shouldn't be attempted until you are confident in Sarvangasana, but it is excellent for the spine, relieves fatigue and isn't as difficult as at first seems.

Kneel on the floor with a thick blanket or mat just in front of you. Rest the crown of your head on the ground. Make two other points of a triangle with your hands placed shoulder width apart, straighten the legs, walk your toes towards your head and, on an exhalation, lift both legs until they are in the position shown in Figure 16(a). Make sure that your weight is on the crown of your head. Slowly straighten your legs until you are vertical, the reverse position of the standing posture, with head, back, trunk, pelvis, legs and feet all in line (Figure 16(b)).

Relax into the position and hold it as long as you can. Initially it is best to practise near to a wall, ideally in the corner of a room, or with a partner, to prevent you from being anxious about toppling over. At first you will only hold the position for a very short time, but as you grow in confidence and relax into it you will find that you can easily hold the position for five or ten minutes. Come out of the position slowly and rest a little before standing up. This posture is carried out traditionally with the head cupped in the hands and the forearms on the floor (Figure 16(c)). Whilst this is the method you should aim for, it is slightly more difficult than the triangular position.

Figure 16: The Headstand (Sirsasana)

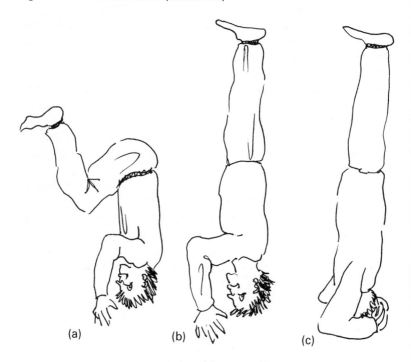

(a)   (b)   (c)

So far we have discussed exercises which will help focus the concentration and develop good posture and breathing. These are basic exercises to be repeated and perfected. We would like to introduce two further fundamental exercises, one of which is elementary to voice production and the other which is a warm-up exercise suitable for any workshop, performance or rehearsal.

Basic Vocal Exercise

Practice 6. First of all go through Practice 5 Phase 4 Part 1. It is helpful when people are stressed or tired to incorporate a simple self-hypnosis exercise into this practice. There is no need to be afraid of the idea of self-hypnosis. At this level we are only speaking of developing a relaxed and concentrated state of mind. There are no dangers attached to the exercise.

With each exhalation bring the word 'calm' into your mind, placing it between the eyes. Allow the breath to take on the sound and shape of the vowel sound 'ahh'. Sense the sound beginning at the centre of the body and easing up until it comes out through the point where the picture of the word is being created. (For a detailed discussion of the rationale behind this exercise see the section on voice.) As you relax, allow the sound to develop into a sigh and enjoy the relief sensation which this provides. Now introduce a 'hh' sound before the 'ahh'. The effect of this is to ensure that the throat is open. Focus on using minimum effort to produce the sound. You should attempt to relieve tension in the face, skull and neck by allowing the sound to act as a mental massage. Place it in different areas and allow it to act as a relaxer of tension. Now vocalise the sound. The initial focus must be to use minimum energy to produce the sound.

Gradually increase the energy and focus the sound on the middle eye. This increase must be very gradual or the sound will drop back into the pharynx. As you continue the exercise allow the jaw to relax and open the mouth upwards until there is a clear flow of sound up from the pit of the stomach and out into the atmosphere (see Figure 17). This part of the exercise may now be repeated, using the 'ee' sound focusing the sound on the middle of the hard palate.

Figure 17: Vocal Exercise

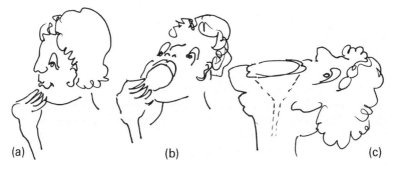

(a)   (b)   (c)

Whilst it is certain that actors should warm up before any activity, the nature of the work will vary according to the content and objectives of the rehearsal or workshop. However in terms of body and voice we have found the following warm-up a splendid utility system and many actors use it before performing. The exercise can be performed after the previous voice exercise and the 'ah' or an 'ah-oo-mmm' sound can be incorporated into the exercise with each exhalation.

Practice 7. Surya Namaskars. This exercise is a series of six Yoga postures which are joined together in what is known as the sun salutation or Surya Namaskars. It is the most comprehensive and economical set of exercises that we have encountered in terms of encouraging the blood flow throughout the body and warming up the major joints and muscle groups. It also works as a centring exercise. The exercise can be repeated up to twenty times, though to begin with five will probably be enough. Start gradually, but the speed at which you do the exercise can be as fast as is compatible with an even flow of movement and controlled breathing. Practise each element separately at first, imprinting the sensation; learn the sequence and then make sure that you can co-ordinate your breathing.

(1) Stand in an aligned position with palms together. Establish the deep breathing rhythm.

(2) Whilst breathing in, reach back above and behind your head with your hands, allowing your back to arch and your head to go back. As you attain the posture allow a slight pause before you breathe out.

(3) Breathing out, bring your hands back down the centre of your body through the first position, bending at the waist until the hands reach the ground. Pull your forehead in to your knees. Have as much of your hands as possible on the ground whilst keeping your legs straight.

(4) Whilst you breathe in, keeping your hands and one foot in place, reach out behind you with the other foot. Look up and bend your back as much as you can by dropping your hips.

(5) Breathing out, take the second foot back and straighten both legs. Keep your heels on the ground, drop your head and look up towards your groin. Arms and legs must be straight. The spine should be stretched. Take another breath in whilst in this position.

(6) Breathing out slowly and leaving your feet and hands in position, bring your knees to the ground and, by leaving your pelvis as

high as possible, ease your body along the ground, first brushing it with your nose, then chin, then chest, until you have to drop your pelvis. Bring your head up and look as high as possible. Your hips will just be touching the ground.

Figure 18: Surya Namaskars

(7) As you breathe in bring your head up and look back, straighten the arms and legs. Your weight will be supported on your hands and toes, with the hips just off the ground.

(8) Breathe out as you lift your hips in the air and return to the position in (5).

(9) Breathing in, bring the leg forward which you originally took back in (4) and assume the position in (4). The forward legs should be between the hands.

(10) Breathe out as you move back to position (3), bringing the other foot in line with the first.

(11) Breathe in as you take your hands off the ground and move back to position (1).

(12) Breathe out and then begin the cycle again as you take your next breath in.

Many of you will have been inculcated with the grunt and groan attitude to exercise. The attitude is wholly inappropriate to the exercises we suggest. They must be done with concentration, you must work from the centre, you must control your breathing and you must focus on freeing tensions. The body is always relaxed into position.

So far we have identified four essentials, relaxation, concentration, centring and posture. Their importance will pervade all your work. The exercise must be returned to and used to endow character work and acting itself with the energy necessary for your own motivation and your communication with an audience.

In the next stage of our discussion we will focus on the application of these essentials to further body work, to voice and to your work with others. Because of our belief in the critical importance of sensitivity to others and acting as the outcome from all elements of the body and mind working in synchrony with each other and with those of the people you are working with, the exercises we discuss will rarely be exclusively relevant to just one aspect of the actor's resources.

Most of the exercises demand that initial work is done on the basic breathing exercise practice and the voice and body warm-ups. It is not being suggested that all of these exercises should be carried out during any one workshop. Which you choose will be dependent on the overall content of the session and your particular theme and objectives.

All of the exercises demand an atmosphere of absolute trust and commitment. They all, in some way, expect you to reveal yourself to yourself and to others, and if there are social or physical tensions this cannot happen. The room must be warm and secure; so must relationships.

The Back

As we have suggested, the spine is a critical element in the central nervous system and the back contains large muscle groups which tend to become centres of tension. We have already noted a number of practices which will benefit the spine, but the following are specifically designed to help the back whilst incorporating partner and voice work.

Practice 8 Phase 1. Stand with feet apart. Imagine that you are balancing a bowl of soup in your right hand. Curl it in and towards your body and then continue the movement so that your elbow comes up and you are forced to lean slightly to the left. Keeping the soup unspilled, take the cup as far over to the left as possible across your body, then, leaning back, take it as far behind you as possible, finally returning it to its original position. Transfer it to the other hand and repeat the process in the other direction. Repeat the exercise a number of times, trying to extend the range of movement on each repetition. The movements should be fluid and the body balanced. Always use a centring exercise before you start.

Practice 8 Phase 2. Reclining Forward Fold, with Partner. Stand back to back with your partner, linking arms. With eyes closed focus on your breathing until you have established an easy mutual rhythm. Begin to touch the 'ah' sound together, maintaining the same rhythm. Try to focus the sound on the small of your back. You will find that you can sense each other's sound vibrations and a warm feeling will develop in your back (see Figure 19(a)).

Now gradually sit down with your partner by pressing against each other whilst bending and walking the legs forward (Figure 19(b)). Maintain the sound synchrony. Once you are in position on the ground (Figure 19(c)) one of you bends forward whilst the other is pulled up on to his back. Find the comfortable position (Figure 19(d)) for this. It is best if your partner is of a similar size to yourself. Stay in this position for about half a minute and then rock back so that the roles are reversed (Figure 19(e)). Maintain the sound. After half a dozen repetitions of the exercise come back to the middle position and stand up with your partner. Initially you may find it difficult to establish an easy movement into the reclined position. You will find it easiest if both partners bend their knees whilst getting into position and then straighten them once the position is established.

Practice 8 Phase 3. The Body Roll. This exercise is demanding and must not be carried out shortly after eating, or vomiting is likely. It is a 'roll' exercise similar to the head and hip rolls which we discuss later and acts also as a centring exercise in which the actor is finding his own centre and releasing himself to his body's various functions and rhythms.

First establish your breathing. Stand with feet well apart. Curl down the vertebrae, slowly relaxing the body as you curl. Allow your torso to hang from the base of the spine. Now roll your torso to one side, then to the back and then on to the other side. Check for relaxation. Roll round in the opposite direction. The hands, arms, shoulders and neck must be relaxed and any tension may cause muscle strain. Easy breathing must be maintained. Breathe in while the head is going back and out when it is coming forward. Allow a breathing cycle between repetitions.

Figure 19: Reclining Forward Fold, with Partner

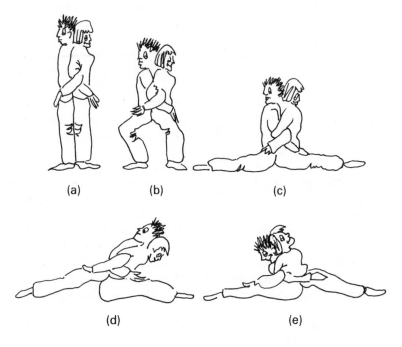

(a)   (b)   (c)

(d)   (e)

The exercise is difficult for two sorts of reasons. First, it demands considerable relaxation and centring, otherwise you are likely to fall over. Secondly, you wil feel physically and psychologically exposed as you roll back, leaving the front of your body vulnerable to attack. This insecurity is balanced when you are hanging forward protecting yourself. Initially don't repeat the exercise in the same direction. Only do a couple of repetitions at first and gradually build the number up.

In discussing this exercise and the other rolls Richard Schechner in his article in R.P. Brawn's *Actor Training I* emphasises the 'association' possibilities stemming from them. By this he means that once the exercise can be accomplished easily, because of the mastery of one's fears and a total commitment to one's body there is a freeing of the imagination and 'associated' images will come into the mind. Follow these images, allowing them to develop. You will probably have choices in that more than one image will present itself initially. Make a clear choice. Sometimes the images will be frightening. Occasionally take the risk and follow them.

Practice 9. The Double Shoulder Stand
(1) This is the Yoga posture (Salamba Sarvangasana) discussed earlier, but modified to emphasise partner work. It should be carried out on a soft surface. First one partner gets into the shoulder stand. The other then goes into the plough a short distance away. Then, by using the hands they shuffle in until both backs are touching. They next raise their legs up into the shoulder stand. Arms are then interlocked. Make sure that heads and necks are straight and torsos are vertical. Again establish a neutral breathing rhythm and then touch sound. This time try the 'ah' sound first and then allow this sound to slide into an 'mm' sound. What you will get is an 'ah-oo-mm' sound similar to the Yoga mantra 'om'.

(2) Once you are both relaxed and breathing in harmony each take one leg down behind you at the same time, both partners moving the same leg. Bring that leg up and lower the other. Establish an easy mutual rhythm whilst raising and lowering the legs.

(3) Now try lowering both legs into the plough. Once you are both in position push up with the toes and roll the hips together. Maintain the breathing and sound. Next walk your legs in a clockwise direction and then back in an anti-clockwise direction, holding each extreme position for a few moments. Come out of the position slowly.

Figure 20: The Double Shoulder Stand

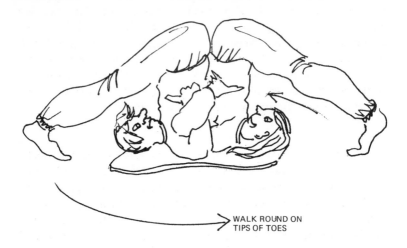

WALK ROUND ON
TIPS OF TOES

The Head and Neck

The head can be rotated from the point high in the back where we identified the 'hump' earlier. The point of rotation is the vertebra which is most obtrusive in the area and it can be found easily by bending the head forward.

Practice 10 Phase 1. After establishing breathing and posture, slowly turn your head to the right as far as possible. Focus on relaxing the neck. Make the movement as slow as possible and follow an imaginary object, perhaps a fly or an aeroplane in the distance. Keep your shoulders facing the front. Repeat the movement right round to the left, again taking your head round as far as possible, slowly return to centre. Now follow an object slowly down to the top of your chest, then back over your head as far as possible and then back to centre. Repeat.

Practice 10 Phase 2. With head initially centred allow the chin to drop to the chest, now rotate the head round as far to the left, the back and the right as possible, finishing the movement with the chin on the chest. Repeat in the opposite direction. Repeat the cycle three or four times.

Practice 10 Phase 3. The Head Roll. Stand in a relaxed position with feet a little apart. With your eyes closed allow your head to drop forward. Use minimum energy to allow the head to move to one side, then minimum energy to allow it to flop back, then to the other side and lastly back to the middle with the chin resting on the chest. Repeat in the opposite direction. The roll can be repeated three or four times in any one direction without dizziness occurring. Breathing should be deep and the rhythm of the cycle will vary. As with the body roll allow associations to develop and let the rhythm of the movement synchronise with them.

The Pelvis

The pelvic area provides a centre for considerable energy blocks which inhibit people's movements and reveal psychic inhibitions. Both the anus and the genitals are areas which we tend to protect and are led to be ashamed of, or associate with essentially private or smutty activities. The exercises which follow have to be presented carefully, for people will either be afraid of them or find the sexual associations so powerful that they will not take them seriously. Whilst it is true that we have the persistent aim of freeing actors from their own hang-ups, an initially clinical approach is probably best, so these exercises should be done in the order that they appear.

Practice 11 Phase 1. Place the hands on the hips, as in Figure 21(a). Press the pelvis back as far as you can. Change the position of the hands (Figure 21(b)) and press the pelvis forwards as far as possible. Try to isolate the movement in the pelvis keeping the knees and torso in position. Repeat a number of times focusing on relaxing the thighs and buttocks in order to make the movement possible.

Practice 11 Phase 2. Imagine that your pelvis has a torch fastened to either side at the front. Set the pelvis back and shine the twin torches to the ground as near to you as possible. Explore the floor with the lights. Now focus the lights on the ceiling and explore that. Explore the room at every level. The same process can be carried out with imaginary torches fastened to each buttock.

Practice 11 Phase 3. The Hip Roll. First relax the head and back. Get into the hanging position identified in the body roll. Come up to vertical, sustaining a relaxed quality in the pelvis. Start to move the pelvis gradually and carefully in a circular motion. Imagine that you are pushing something away from you in all directions as the pelvis

Figure 21: Position for Practice 11 Phase 1

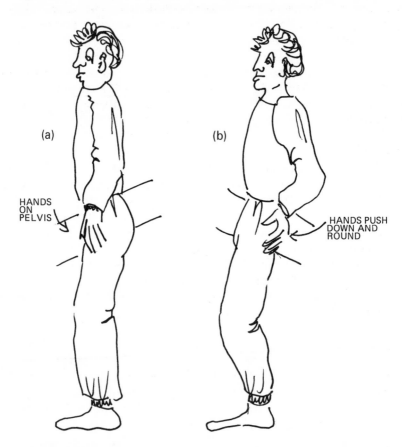

(a)

(b)

HANDS
ON
PELVIS

HANDS PUSH
DOWN AND
ROUND

rotates. Gradually ease into a rhythm of movement, keeping your eyes closed and allowing the associations to come.

Practice 11 Phase 4. Stand facing a partner. Find a mutual breathing rhythm, synchronise the hip rotation. Whilst maintaining the hip movement, keeping your eyes constantly on your partner's eyes, share your associations, taking it in turn to give each other a vocalised image.

The Arms and Shoulders

We have found that most students have problems with tension in their shoulders and in their hands. The results are strangled speech, inhibited action and the perennial problem for inexperienced actors of having unusable energy in their hands and consequently not knowing what to do with them. The following exercise encourages a sense of lightness which helps to relax both arms and shoulders.

Practice 12 Phase 1. Go through the posture exercise (Practice 2, Phase 4, Part 1). Standing in good alignment and, with eyes closed, focus the mind on the right arm: endow it with a sense of lightness. After a few seconds, if you are fully concentrated, your arm will begin to rise as though lifted by a cushion of air. The success of the exercise depends on the focus of your concentration. Finely focused, the arm will rise up to shoulder level and above. Allow the arm to return to your side. This may be difficult and you may have to gently press your arm down. Now transfer your focus to the other arm and repeat the process.

Figure 22: Practice 12

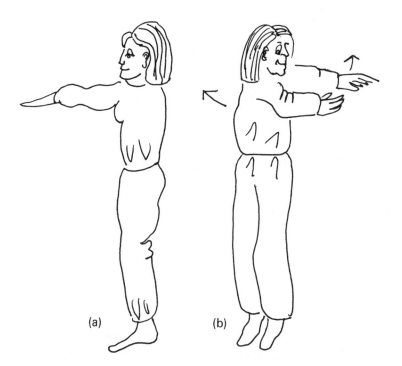

(a)   (b)

Practice 12 Phase 2. With both arms hanging lightly, allow them to rise gently in front of you until they are parallel with the ground. Simultaneously go up on to your toes. Now rotate the head and spine to the right, taking the arms round as far as they can go (see Figure 22(a)). Return to the middle position, lower the feet and then repeat the exercise to the other side. Bring the same sensation which you received from the earlier exercise and you will find that you sustain balance and at the end feel light and relaxed. Breathe in slowly as you rise up, out as you rotate, and then in as you return to centre, finally breathing out as you come to rest. This second phase should follow on immediately from the first. It is important in both phases to establish an easy breathing rhythm which develops into the 'purr' sound focus before starting the exercises themselves.

The Legs and Feet

The legs are probably the least abused parts of the human body, but none the less they need strengthening and the muscles and tendons need to be stretched. The following exercises should help to achieve these results.

Practice 13 Phase 1. One Leg Balance. Stand about four feet away from your partner. As you breathe out stretch forward and grasp each other's wrists. Bring your torsos parallel to the ground whilst sliding your hands up each other's arms and lifting one leg so that it gets into line with the torso. If you look into each other's eyes it will cause your spine to curve slightly. Hold the pose whilst establishing a mutual deep breathing rhythm. The exercise is of particular benefit to the inner legs and ankles. Start by balancing on the same leg, then alternate, maintaining a shared breathing cycle synchronised with the movement. This sort of exercise, once it has been mastered, should be given an extra dimension. Vocal exercises can be added or sound sharing (see Practice 26) or image release with partners (see Practice 24) or one of the narrative games (see Practice 37) or simple dialogue. An 'I want it' scene or an argument will make demands on your ability to remain relaxed.

Practice 13 Phase 2. The Chair. Stand back to back with your partner. Let your bodies sink down together whilst pressing against each other's backs and walk your legs out until they are bent at right angles. Make sure that your backs are in contact over a maximum area. Try to walk round together in a complete circle.

Figure 23: Practice 13

Again, once the exercise has been mastered give it an additional purpose. Try the following:

(1) Harmonise your breathing whilst standing up, then begin to touch sound, perhaps an 'ahh' or the 'ah-oo-mm', and move into the final position whilst retaining the sound harmony. The sound can be varied. Move the sound around your backs, feeling the vibrations at various areas of contact. Allow your arms to hang.

(2) Improvise a scene which might happen in such a posture, at an art gallery, in a train, in the park. Set the exercise up so that hand movements are necessary. This creates additional, but possible, problems of balance.

Practice 14. Warm the feet and ankles up by circling the ankle, going up on the toes, walking on the outsides of the feet, on the ball of the foot and the heels. Shake them out, spread them, wiggle your toes. An amusing and rather tender exercise is to allow one of your feet to notice and then court the other one. Improvise from their first meeting and take it through whatever outcome you wish. The work can be extended to character work. Create improvisations in which your brain is in your feet. The notion can be applied to any part of the body.

It may be found surprising that we have given so much emphasis to the importance of physical release and competence. The British theatre tends to be dominated by words and directors prefer to cast according to 'type'. 'Elocution' still has authority in some drama schools and with many school-teacher/directors. Nevertheless the development of much European and American theatre is towards the primacy of the actor as an expressive physical presence. Unless this presence is subject to his control he will severely limit his range of both parts and acting styles. We agree with the British actor Clive Swift, who wrote, 'Acting is energy. In the theatre people pay to see energy' (*The Job of Acting*, p. 5). Only by being physically and imaginatively free can we release that energy.

Figure 24: The Chair

8 THE ACTOR'S VOICE

We have tried to stress the organic nature of the actor's work. His body, intellect and imagination must harmonise in response to the demands created by the playwright and director in order to make a joint communication with an audience. The actor's voice and speech are no exception; they must not be thought of as separate from the other elements of his behaviour. Vocal centring is akin to physical centring and both indicate a deep centre for the imagination and emotions. Muscular tension inhibits voice as well as action and desired communication. Emotional inhibition reveals itself vocally as well as physically. Voice work is fundamentally, therefore, a particular extension of the release work which we have been discussing.

Put very simply, what happens when we speak is that an impulse is sent from the motor cortex of the brain which stimulates our body to allow air to enter and leave it. This air, as breath, plays on the vocal folds, which are situated in the larynx, creating oscillations. These oscillations cause the breath to vibrate. The vibrations are amplified in the resonating cavities of the pharynx, mouth and nose and the resultant sounds are articulated by the lips and tongue to create words. Additional resonance is available through all of the hollow areas of the upper body including the skull and chest which are reached through the conduction of sound through the skeleton and through sound waves vibrating on one surface, setting up sympathetic vibrations on another. The resonators provide the *tone* of the sound whilst the *pitch* is determined by the rate of the vibration of the vocal folds.

Our focus for this discussion is on release. We believe that the aim of voice work is to free the breathing process, the passage of sound through the body, the resonating surfaces, the organs of articulation and the origins of emotion from psycho-physical inhibitions which have been placed upon it as we have grown up.

Freeing the Breath

Breathing begins with a brain signal to the diaphragm to contract. The diaphragm is a piece of muscular membrane which separates the chest from the abdomen. As a result, the diaphragm lowers and flattens out. The area around the lungs is then increased and consequently the density of the air in this area is decreased. The air inside the lungs is now more dense than that around them and it expands, pushing the lungs out to equalise the pressure. By this time the pressure inside the body is less than that outside so air enters the lungs via the trachea to restore the balance of pressure inside and outside the body. In order to allow an exhalation the diaphragm expands and moves up, increasing the density of the air around the lungs and the whole process is reversed.

It can readily be seen that the emphasis of the process is in the abdominal and lower chest areas. In order for the lungs to be filled to their maximum, the abdominal muscles and the muscles which control the lower, floating ribs (the inter-costal muscles) have to be relaxed. The view from outside the body is of the stomach coming out and the lower chest coming up when we breathe in and the reverse when we breathe out. In spite of the certainty of this statement many people actually do the very opposite: their stomachs go in as they breathe in and out as they breathe out. The effect is that they only use the upper part of their lungs, with the corollary that they attempt to expand the comparatively rigid upper chest and raise their shoulders to make up for the lack of movement in the chest. The result is a lack of breathing and thus voice control, thinness of tone and enormous upper body tension. There are three major causes of this breathing pattern; simple tension — which may be partly cosmetic (in that protruding bellies are culturally disapproved of) and partly psychological; chest and lung disorders such as asthma or bronchitis; intensive sports training, particularly swimming, where the need is for the rapid uptake of oxygen into the bloodstream. All of these causes are likely to have the interdependent problem of bad posture.

The first need is to encourage yourself to be aware of the *possibility* of breathing properly and to discover a *sense-memory* of the process. The second need is to release the muscular and postural inhibiting factors.

All voice work must be preceded by exercises which encourage relaxation. The supine exercises mentioned earlier can be used for this purpose because in the supine position it is easiest to relax the abdominal muscles. Focus must be on breathing from the centre. The following exercise incorporates both relaxation and breathing and is based on the spine fold exercise.

Practice 15. Standing with feet slightly apart centre your breathing and then gradually fold down the spine until you are hanging from its base. It is useful to use the exercise in which you visualise and breathe the vowel element of the word 'calm' as you go down. Achieve a sense of all tension draining down your back and out through your fingers. Relax into position and be aware of your breathing right down in the pit of your stomach. It might help to get a sense of a balloon expanding forwards and backwards at the bottom of your torso. Try to sense it pushing on the stomach and the back with each incoming breath. As you breathe establish the sense-memory of the experience. Repeat the breathing cycle half a dozen times. Now, in four stages, come up to the upright position, taking at least four breathing cycles at each stage and building up a sense-memory of the full experience as it goes up the body. In the upright position continue to breathe deeply whilst attempting to retain the sense-memory of the full expansion.

Figure 1: Warm-up Exercise

Practice 16. This exercise prevents the tendency towards upper chest breathing. Stand upright with your arms stretched out in front of you. Breathe out. Whilst inhaling, bring the arms down and back, and bend your knees so that you finish up in a racing dive position. Again establish a sense-memory of your breathing in the abdominal area. This exercise can now incorporate a leap to upright on the exhalation, using your centre as the original stimulus for movement. Quite vigorous and demanding, this makes a good warm-up exercise.

The next exercise is used by yogis to tune up the abdominal organs, lungs and heart as well as to increase diaphragm mobility.

Practice 17. Uddiyana Bandha. It is unwise to do this exercise if you have eaten a meal within the previous couple of hours. Stand with feet

Figure 2: Uddiyana Bandha

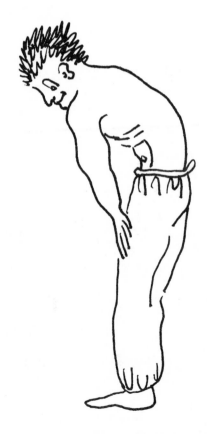

about fourteen inches apart. Stoop slightly forward bringing your chin to your chest and bending the knees a little. Put the hands on the thighs. Inhale deeply and then exhale fully so that all of the air goes from the lungs. Hold the breath. Contract the stomach and suck it in towards the spine, pulling it up under the breastbone. Hold the position for five to ten seconds and then relax the abdominal muscles and inhale slowly. Now repeat the exercise, but when you have attained the full position move your hands to your hips whilst keeping your chin on your breastbone. Working from the centre, move your belly in and out three or four times before relaxing and inhaling. This exercise can be repeated five or six times.

If you find this exercise impossible at first, lie down on your back and try to bring your belly in by expanding the rib-cage. The supine position will relax the stomach. The following exercise makes use of the sense-memory deriving from Uddiyana Bandha and applies it more particularly to a voice/breath exercise.

Practice 18. First sigh two or three times from the diaphragm. Now imagine that you are moving your diaphragm up and down. Place an object in the middle and bounce it up and down, varying the height it bounces and the rapidity of the bounce. Now let an unvoiced 'Huh' sound replace the object. Repeat the short sound five or six times and then exhale the rest of your breath in a continuous 'Huh-uu-uu-uh' sound.

Freeing the Sound

Whilst it is untrue that vocal sound stems from the belly, the sense of that happening can help the actor to find a relaxed and focused stream of sound starting there and ending at the mouth.

The major inhibiting factor at the mouth end is the face itself. The face is the most readily perceivable area for human communication. It is therefore paradoxically potentially the most revealing part of our body: pain, anguish, love, the whole range of emotions are likely to show themselves there and it is the most tightly defended part of the body for the same reasons. In order to inhibit emotional 'leaks' we find ways of clamping the dozens of muscle groups into a single posture, permitting just a few voluntary communicatory variations. We build a stiff upper lip, a firm jaw, eyes of steel and create special compositions of laughter or anger or whatever emotion we are prepared to show the world. Regional loyalties, shyness, anxiety, desire for control or superiority, severe or introverted models of behaviour all work towards making the tongue, the jaw, the soft palate and the throat inflexible and serve the destructive purpose of inhibiting vocal sound.

The Jaws

Posture itself has a profound effect on the flexibility of the jaw. It is a waste of time doing jaw release exercises if the neck is pushed forward or pulled back or the head pulled in. The first step then is to achieve a level chin with the crown of the head uppermost. This in itself will have a radical effect on some students.

The jaw is attached by a hinge joint to the rest of the skull. When it is open and relaxed it drops down and back. In order to get a sense of the jaw's action put your finger tips just inside your face from your ears and yawn. As you yawn you will feel the jaw move downward, thus opening the area at the back of your mouth. It is important to think of this particular area of expansion. Actors are often told to open their *mouths* whereas in order to make greater use of the mouth resonator they should open their *jaws*. Lessac, in his book *The Use and Training of the Human Voice*, uses the term 'structural action' to describe this process. He makes the point that the aim is not to get sound out through the mouth, but to amplify it, and suggest that we should think of a funnel with a small opening at the lips which fans out to a large opening at the back of the mouth. He created a 'structural stretch' exercise to make this possible in the belief that if this is carried out correctly the jaw will naturally relax.

Practice 19. Lessac's Structural Stretch. Lessac writes:

> Place a slice of cork about $\frac{1}{4}$ inch thick and one and a quarter inches in diameter between the upper and lower molar teeth. Now, with a large lip opening, sound the vowel 'ah' and gradually reduce the opening until you come to the vowel 'OO'. Try not to bite hard on the cork, and make the action easier by inducing a mild, comfortable yawn sensation in your cheek and lip muscles … move from the longest to the smallest lip opening pronouncing the entire series of vowels correctly … without reducing the space in the cavity.

The next stage is to remove the cork and place the tips of two fingers on the outside of the cheek between the side teeth. He explains:

> Beginning with the mouth open wide and the tongue gently touch-
> ing the inside of the lower front teeth, stretch the facial muscles
> foward so that the lips protrude softly ... gradually reduce the lip
> opening whilst running through the vowel sounds from Ah to OO.

The stretch can be practised by yawning forward, pulling the muscles
which go from the eye and cheek bones to the lips. A piece of adhesive
tape stuck to the face running from just under the eye to the top lip
will allow you a clear sense of the stretch sensation (*The Use and
Training of the Human Voice*, pp. 56-7).

This exercise is extremely useful, but we suggest that you combine
it with one which we derive from the Polish director Jerzy Grotowski.

Practice 20. Establish a good posture, checking your head and chin
positions. Hold the chin with your hand and open your mouth by
lifting the top jaw as far up as you can. Now close the mouth upwards
by pushing your lower jaw up. Again open your mouth upwards and
again push your bottom jaw up to close your mouth. At this stage your
head should be as far back as it can go. Complete the exercise by
reversing the process. This exercise should be repeated until you are
fully aware of the movement of the lower jaw. The jaw can be further
relaxed by opening and closing the mouth by using the hands on
either side of the jaw. The full exercise is completed when you breathe
out on a voiced 'ah' sound whilst opening the jaw upwards. (See
Figure 17, p. 149).

Freeing the Tongue

Whilst most people use the tip of the tongue quite enthusiastically the
rear part tends to remain immobile and have an inhibiting function on
sound. There is a tendency to pull it back in moments of anxiety, thus
constricting the cavity at the back of the mouth and imparing sound
quality.

Practice 21 Phase 1. Place the tip of the tongue against the lower teeth
and try to relax it so that it just lies flat in the bottom of the mouth.
Relax the jaw and allow the mouth to open a little. Now, whilst
keeping the tip of the tongue in position, push the middle of the
tongue forward and sense a full stretching right back to its roots. Once
you can do this easily repeat the exercise as rapidly as you can.

Practice 21 Phase 2. Keeping the tip of the tongue in position make the 'uh' sound first with the tongue down and next with it stretched forward. Alternate a number of times, first pitching the same note and then trying to go up and down a scale. Try moving from the 'huh' sound with the tongue flat to a 'hee' sound with it stretched forward.

Freeing the Soft Palate

The soft palate stretches back from the hard palate ending up in a little fleshy tail called the uvula. If the soft palate becomes lazy it will serve to deaden sound and possibly produce nasality of the sort which we associate with the Liverpool and Birmingham accents.

The two consonant sounds which we produce in the area of the soft palate and 'k' and 'g'. The former unvoiced plosive sound provides a good medium for releasing exercises.

Practice 22. Make an unvoiced 'k' sound, feeling the action at the back of your mouth. Repeat the sound rapidly. Now make the sound 'kah'. Try making it whilst breathing in as well as when breathing out. The effect of whispering as you breathe in is to dry out the throat and it gives a cold and rather unpleasant sensation. It isn't harmful, but for comfort's sake don't do the exercise more than half a dozen times. Try to remember the effect of the cold air on your soft palate and try to employ the full areas when producing the sound whilst breathing out so that it spreads over the soft palate.

Freeing the Resonators

Whilst it is true that due to the conductivity of bone almost any part of our body is a potential resonator the critical areas are the chest, the throat, the mouth, the teeth, the nose, the sinuses and the skull. Focusing on these areas in succession will provide a *resonating scale.*

The first part of the process of freeing the resonators for efficient use should have been completed. By freeing the tongue, jaw and so on we have made them available for our use and limited their potential constricting effect on the resonators. The second stage is to become aware of the areas and to start to use them consciously.

First a note about vowel sounds. A vowel sound is produced by vocalised breath passing through the mouth, which is differently shaped by movement of the jaws, lips and tongue to provide the different sounds. Whilst there is some argument about whether some sounds are truly diphthongs (double vowel sounds) we will be referring to the thirteen sounds which are found in the sentence 'Who (oo) would (ou) know (oh) ought (aw) of (o) art (ah) must (u) err (uh) and (a) then (e) take (ay) his (i) ease (ee).'

Combined Work for Chest, Mouth and Teeth

Whenever we give you a vowel sound to use we preface it with an 'h' sound. The purpose of this is to open the throat and avoid the glottal shock which may happen should you go straight to the vowel.

Practice 23. First release the neck by dropping it backwards and forwards and rotating it in each direction. Next sigh out on the 'hah' sound as you allow your head to drop back. Repeat this until the sound is free and relaxed. Now vocalise the sound as you drop your head back, making sure that your throat remains open. Feel the vibrations in your chest. Repeat, maintaining the relaxed throat. Next let your head go back whilst you say the 'hah' sound and then change to a 'huh' sound as you bring it back up. Repeat a number of times until you feel a free movement of vibrations from the chest to the mouth. Next repeat the exercise but end with the 'hee' sound so that vibrations are now moving from chest, to mouth, to teeth. The exercise can be reversed and repeated until you are making maximum use of the resonating surfaces.

The 'ee' sound is the basis of another of Lessac's exercises which he calls the 'Ybuzz'. He suggests that the front of the skull can be looked on as a kettle drum with the hard palate and teeth, the nasal bone, the sinuses and the forehead vibrating whenever sound waves strike the hard palate, no matter where you feel the specific action of the vocal tones.

Figure 3: Sound Vibrations in 'Ybuzz' Exercise

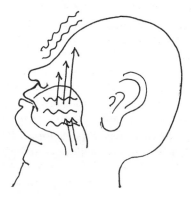

In order to achieve the 'Ybuzz' say the word 'yes', sustaining the Y-y-y. If this fails, say, 'easy', holding both the syllables. The sound should be focused on the hard palate, just above and behind the teeth ridge and it will be felt to vibrate up the front of the skull (Figure 3).

A useful exercise which brings into play all of the resonators in turn is called the 'rocket'. Devised by Raymond Rizzo, the process is to use each of the words 'mean', 'main' and 'moon', starting at the top point of the falsetto range, using the top of the skull as principal resonator and running down your range to the lowest pitch you can reach with comfort. The exercise has the objective of literally stretching the vocal folds and helps to create elasticity in the folds and gives confidence in the full vocal range.

The Sinuses

After locating the sinuses in the hollow between your nose and cheeks, first massage them slightly and then exercise them by wrinkling your nose. Now breathe out on a 'hee' sound, placing it in the front of the hard palate. Alternately wrinkle the nose and make the sound. Make sure that the back of your tongue is relaxed, for there is a tendency for it to tense up during the exercise.

Nasal Resonators

Blocking up each nostril alternately, hum through the free nostril and feel the vibration in the nose. Next hum a 'mmmeee' sound through both nostrils. Continue the exercise whilst doing the forward body roll. Wrinkle the nose and produce the 'mmmeee' sound first and then the 'mmmayay' sound, allowing the latter to spread out to the sides of the cheeks.

Freeing the Articulation

The major articulatory surfaces are the back, front and middle of the tongue together with the surfaces which they touch, the lips in various contacts with each other and the top teeth meeting the lower lip.

The Lips

Smile sideways, stretch your face and lips forwards and sideways, pull faces. Stretch your mouth by pulling out the corners with your hands. Blow through your lips making them vibrate. Play with sensations on the 'b', 'mm' and 'p' sounds, adding vowels.

The Front of the Tongue

Push the tongue out of the mouth, stretch it from side to side and up and down. Try wiggling the tip. Make the 'l' sound on the top lip rather than the hard palate. Use the 'l' sound followed by a variety of vowel sounds producing it by making contact between the tongue and top lip.

The Back of the Tongue

First release the soft palate and then produce the English sound 'ng'. After yawning with this sound, follow it with a variety of vowels. Work on the 'k' and 'g' sounds again following them with vowels.

All of these exercises may be repeated again and again in order to achieve and maintain flexibility. We provide below a list of vocal exercises which you can follow in order to work on the range of articulation problems. There is no mystery to these exercises: it is simple enough to devise your own. Bring some of the sounds, like 'bdgd' or 'bdbd' or whatever, into improvisations so that communication is through these sounds alone. Courtship scenes, quarrels, shop scenes, any scene can be used to bring life to the exercises.

(1) Alternate 'b' with 'd' using a vowel sound after the consonant, e.g. 'bah'-'dah'-'bah'-'dah' ... Reverse the process to 'dah'-'bah'.
(2) Alternate 'g' plus vowel with 'd' plus vowel and reverse.
(3) Alternate 'g' plus vowel with 'd' plus vowel with 'b' plus vowel.
(4) Alternate 'm' plus vowel with 'n' plus vowel.
(5) Alternate 'm' plus vowel with 'n' plus vowel with 'ng' plus vowel.
(6) Alternate 'p' plus vowel with 't' plus vowel.
(7) Alternate 'k' plus vowel with 't' plus vowel.
(8) Alternate 'k' plus vowel with 't' plus vowel, with 'p' plus vowel.
(9) Sustain a 'v' sound on the lips, add vowel sounds.
(10) Sustain a 'z' sound on the lips, add vowel sounds.
(11) Say tongue twisters going up and down a scale.

All of the above exercises should first be whispered and then voiced.

What we hope to have achieved so far in this discussion of voice is an understanding of the mechanics of speaking and to have provided some exercises which will help you to improve. However, there is a certain aridity in voice exercises done for their own sake. Talking is partly about opening yourself out to your own feelings and responding to those of others. This is particuarly true for the actor. Whether he is in the National Theatre or in a political drama in a cellar in Runcorn he is always in some measure a man who works in public with his body, offering it publicly and 'if this body restricts itself to demonstrating what it is — then it is not an obedient instrument capable of a performing act' (Grotwoski, *Towards a Poor Theatre*, p. 46). It is not sufficient to resonate, to breathe correctly and to be clear, there has got to be a revelation of the actor himself. He must understand what he *says* with his body and have a *need* to communicate, not borrow inflections and speak loudly. This ability and attitude will only come with continually asking the actor to commit himself totally to his task, stripping himself bare of his own barriers, the defences with which we all mask ourselves. There are no magic exercises. Those suggested earlier will help, provided that they have the clear objectives of releasing the actor himself and awakening a desire to communicate. However we would like to complete this section with a few exercises which perhaps more obviously demonstrate this purpose and which may provide the reader with a clearer example of the organic nature of his work.

Practice 24. Image Release with Partner. Stand facing your partner with hands flat and gently touching. Having decided who is to lead and who is to follow, close your eyes and breathe deeply until you harmonise your breathing. The person who is leading now starts to move his arms in any direction whilst retaining contact with his partner. He can move anywhere in the room. The objective of the exercise is to maintain physical and energy contact with your partner. It is an exercise in commitment and sharing. The exercise is very delicate and should be completed by the leading partner finally bringing his hands together, gently releasing contact with his partner. When each partner has had opportunity to lead it should be possible to carry out the exercise with neither partner being very sure about who is leading. Try it without designating a leader. The next stage of the exercise is to add speech. Again you should start with a leader and aim to forget who it is. The leader has to tell a story which is told simultaneously by his partner, so just as the movements happen at the same time, so too does the story. With practice you will find that you have no idea whose story is being told.

Practice 25. Sound Releasing. This exercise should be carried out by a group of five people, four of whom are helping the fifth to relax and find sound. First relax the fifth person by using the descriptive techniques discussed in Practice 5 Phase 3. Next get him to focus on his breathing, breathing deeply and easily from the centre; now get him to touch sound. His object is to find sounds in the centre of his body and release them. As he explores the sounds begin to move him around, lift parts of his body, lift him, move him around, shake him, lift him high. As a group you can do anything provided he comes to no harm. All the time he will be making sounds from the centre, exploring the sounds, enjoying them, releasing them. Finally place him back on the ground and let him relax, but make sure you retain contact. The exercise is extremely releasing and can be frightening. Initially the sounds will not be very loud, which doesn't matter; what matters is that they are coming from the actor's centre.

Practice 26. Sound Sharing. Sound sharing exercises are part of our basic stock-in-trade. Many exercises are used for this purpose. For this particular one sit facing your partner with one person's thighs over those of the other. Make physical contact. This may mean holding hands or allowing your cheeks to rest together. It is not important where the contact is made so long as you are both warm and comfortable. Harmonise your breathing so that one partner breathes out as the other breathes in. When this has been achieved vocalise your breath in turn with the sense of giving your partner sound. He then returns a sound, again giving it and sharing it. Keep the exercise going, working for greater sharing and an exploration of the sounds, trying to get increasingly profound expressions. The exercise can be repeated using word and image associations or sharing a story-telling experience.

Practice 27. Word Colour. Drama is essentially an experiential medium. Its meaning is dependent on the interplay of the actor's body, mind and imagination which in turn affect the bodies, minds and imaginations of the audience. It is through behavioural images rather than intellectual content that the theatre communicates and one of the actor's tasks is to release these images.

We have tried to stress the importance of sense-memory, of sensitivity and of the commitment of the imagination to the art of acting. Our final voice exercises are merely indications of what should be continually happening. They try to 'associate' the actor with the images he is communicating.

Practice 27 Phase 1. The first phase is to find ways of involving yourself with sounds. There are a number of ways of doing this. Try associating consonant sounds with instruments of the orchestra. Feel the vibrations of the instrument. Play with, taste, explore and develop consonant sounds; find emotional content in vowel sounds, working from the centre. Find images for sounds, let them develop. Create rhythm and orchestration of sounds which inspire movement; move with the sounds.

Practice 27 Phase 2. Using expressive words randomly, create a picture in your mind's eye, take the picture down to your centre and respond to it first just with sound and then with the word. Remember the word is merely the outward sign, the full meaning is derived from your association with it. Try the same exercise with less obvious words like prepositions or conjunctions. Create short strings of words, finding coherent images for them.

Practice 27 Phase 3. Work on speeches for personal images. Use something evocative to begin with, like the work of Dylan Thomas or Gerard Manley Hopkins, then move on to something more vernacular such as the poems of McGough or speeches from modern plays. The aim is to find your own centre with the images. The danger is of becoming pantomimic or mechanical. Go on to image games (see the section on imagination in Ch. 9) to renew your spontaneity. Disturb your security by saying the words whilst performing unsympathetic actions like juggling or doing fairly strenuous exercises.

Stanislavsky wrote in *An Actor Prepares*, 'Every movement you make on the stage, every word you speak, is a result of the right life of the imagination' (p. 71). What he was saying is that the actor must, through his imagination, enter into the character he is playing and the situation in which he finds himself as though events were happening spontaneously. Through his own similar experiences and vicariously understanding those of other people the actor must be able to recreate the perceptual responses of another in order to express their outward signs.

The need for the commitment of the imagination goes further than that, however. It is through the actor's imaginative experience that the audience's imaginations can be released and enriched. Joseph Chaikin argues that it is particularly true at this time, 'Because we live on a level drastically reduced from what we imagine, acting promises to represent a dynamic expression of the intense life' (*The Presence of the Actor*, p. 2). One of the actor's task is to infiltrate events with his imagination, bringing about the possibility of a deeper and more personal understanding of them.

The actor's work on his imagination is directed at developing an imaginative understanding of what it is like to be someone else, to reproduce that person and to free his own imagination from self-censorship and clichés so that his performances can have truth, freshness and vitality. There are therefore three prime concerns: (1) to expand the actor's consciousness of human experience; (2) to give him freer access to what we might call his subconscious; (3) to enable him to bring these capabilities together in analysing and performing a part.

The actor's major source of security is his lines. If all else fails he can walk on stage, say the lines he has learned, clearly, from an acting stereotype and go off. In fact that is what many amateur actors do. They make no imaginative commitment. All human beings have a few roles at their disposal. Those who are more extrovert can project these roles as caricatures with some stage authority. Teachers, lawyers, politicians all have to develop 'public authority' in order to do their job. Endow a stereotype with this authority and we have a sort of acting performance. The lines themselves, said with conviction, will get the amateur actor through. The rehearsal process for the better of these actors is concerned with 'understanding' his lines or finding out what they mean and then moving around so as not to get in the way or as a prelude or post-script to speaking. The end-product is a rehearsed recitation in which the story and theme are more or less evident. Words do not always have to be given the right intonation or psycho-social context to be understood intellectually, so the intellectual theatre-goer can achieve quite reasonable satisfaction from such an experience.

We are not suggesting that 'understanding' is unimportant — it is merely the first step. There should perhaps be a section of this book which deals with the actor's 'intellect'. There isn't, because the development of the intellect is too general a matter. However, we take it as axiomatic that the actor must understand the meaning of the play and the contribution which his character, speeches and scenes contribute to its meaning. These are the constraints within which his imagination must ultimately operate as well as act as its trigger.

Assuming that a general understanding has been achieved, the next stage in the process is for the actor to interpret this intellectual understanding through his imagination, working from the general, 'what would it be like to be such a person' to the specifics of a precise person coping spontaneously with a particular context.

The process is not as clear cut as this. Decisions about meaning and character tend to be 'pencilled-in' and later amplified or changed according to the evolution of the performance, but there has to be some constraint, otherwise the imagination wanders without purpose.

How then can we help the actor to develop the aptitude for putting himself into the shoes of another person and the capacity to apply this aptitude to specific roles? The first need is to explore, analyse and remember his own emotional and physical sensations. He must be able to recreate the specifics of pain, anxiety, fear, love, warmth, etc. from his own experience. He must therefore enter imaginatively into his own experiences. It is only through this process that he will learn to avoid what we call 'acting in general', a term which indicates the style of acting which uses vague behavioural signs to indicate emotion.

The second need is to make persistent demands on him to explore human behaviour. To observe and analyse the causal system behind what people say and do, how people hide and reveal their emotions, how and why they play strategies, how and why they modify their behaviour in different circumstances. The barriers to this process are the temptations which we have to *judge* people rather than *interpret* them, our own prejudiced perception which interprets *in our own terms* rather than those of the person we are considering, and a desire to hang on to the security which this subjective perception allows us so that we block out other possibilities. In a way the actor has to implement Jean Paul Marat's suggestion in Weiss's *The Marat-Sade* that 'The important thing is to pull yourself up by your own hair to turn yourself inside out and to see the whole world with fresh eyes.'

All improvisation work which forces the actor to go behind clichés and obliges him to observe human behaviour will assist this process. Unfortunately, actors very quickly acquire a repertoire of characters and responses which they reproduce scene after scene. They learn to adapt their own mannerisms just sufficiently to indicate another character, they play emotionally and physically 'safe'. It is up to the director to see this happening and push the actor further, rejecting his clichés.

It is very difficult in a book to provide exercises which will help this process. However an exercise which has been found to be generally helpful is to build up a very full characterisation and make it operate in the real world. Students can be asked to build up a character physically and biographically until they can give almost as good an account of it as they could of themselves. They must gain a wardrobe, hobbies, precious objects, likes, secrets, lusts, phobias, loyalties, social groups, the fullest possible range of those constraining influences which shape our behaviour. Characters can then be put into improvisation situations. Meetings can be devised between characters and some actors can play 'roles' to the others' characters; so they can be barmaid, doctor or whatever is deemed appropriate. In his own time the actor should carry out some of his daily tasks in character. He should have a bath, clean his teeth, eat a meal, get undressed in character.

The next stage is for the actor to go out into the real world in character. Let him go out to the library, to buy a magazine, to have afternoon tea, go on a train journey, ask advice, spend an afternoon in town. Again anything which is appropriate to the character. If the character's role is important he should get experience of the role if it is possible. If he is a milkman he should persuade his own milkman to let him go on a few rounds with him to get the feel of the task. He should talk, as himself, to the sort of people his character would mix with. Find out what their conversation strategies are, find the group conventions and interests. At least once during his training an actor should go through this very full exploration of character. He will probably never need to use such detail, but his imagination will have been awakened to the possible depths of individual human behaviour.

The assumption behind the approach discussed above is that we all have imaginations, but we don't necessarily use them. The exercise forces us to do so. To an extent it is very like mask work. If the basic work has been done thoroughly, you will find that automatically you sustain your character's logic, you behave quite spontaneously as the character, and intermittently he will take you over.

So far as making the actor conscious of the content of his own subconscious is concerned, the need is to free him from his own barriers, allowing him opportunity to reveal himself in a safe context, tapping the inner worlds which he has repressed. This is no simple matter. In the case of some actors, acting has become a way of hiding from themselves, the pretence is their shelter. Other people have built up impregnable barriers around them which no acting class will penetrate. In the end it is an individual matter which demands perseverance and will always cause conflict. People don't want to give up their defences and some never will.

Nevertheless virtually all of the exercises which we have suggested will help to free the actor's imagination. Simple practices like word-association games, story-telling exercises and spontaneous improvisation all help to free the actor from that self-consciousness which inhibits him. We are going to suggest just one further practice which we have found particularly useful. It is a very powerful exercise and should not be used until a group is reasonably free and working with trust and responsibility. Some students have found it extremely moving and frightening and there is a need for considerable physical contact and caring. Should a student begin to cry his partner should end his part of the exercise and simply physically comfort him. The exercise is not, however, dangerous — the crying is a release or a way of inhibiting a memory or thought.

Practice 28. The exercise is carried out in pairs. One partner lies down on his back. As there is considerable loss of body heat during the exercise make sure that the room is warm and possibly that people lying down are covered. They should be comfortable. The second partner next massages his colleague (See Practice 5 Phase 2) and then takes him through a relaxation process (see Practice 5 Phase 3).

The relaxation should end with the partner lying down being asked to imagine himself somewhere. He then says where he is. He then has to describe the place in more detail and to explain what he is doing there. What subsequently follows is that a story is evolved from that starting point. The story is nudged along and modified by the second partner who can introduce non-specific elements like 'a person behind you' or 'a blue car' which his partner has to interpret. It is important that he push his partner more deeply into the story. If he detects blocks or parts where his partner avoids an element he should take him back to that point. However if there are physical signs that the partner cannot possibly cope with them he should allow him to escape. The usual physical signs are deep furrowing between the eyes and restless head movements. If you think they are becoming too powerful, move the story on a little; you may even introduce some protection or escape.

The aim of the guiding partner is to take his partner into the story and then allow him to develop it himself. He should withdraw his own contribution as his partner becomes more fluent. At the end of the story he should take over the narrative and find a peaceful resolution or ease his partner towards finding his own. One final warning. Students doing this exercise should under no circumstances set out to take their partner into a frightening situation. Let him move towards his own situations and then try to ease him into them.

A version of this exercises which is potentially less traumatic is for one partner to pretend that he has a story in his head, and the second partner then guesses the story. The first partner allows him to be right when he feels that there is some depth to the suggestion. Initially make your partner go through quite a number of suggestions, then become less demanding so that he begins to feel that he really is reading the story which is in your head. You can work from a pattern so that you accept the third suggestion, then the second, then the first and so on.

We started this section by stressing the critical importance of the actor's imagination. Our whole chapter on acting has the single theme that the actor's first task is to explore himself and find in himself the energy and capacity to take on the form and life of another in order to communicate. By developing and tapping his imagination the actor is on the way to finding the bridge between himself, the play and the audience.

The Actor as Character

Probably the most vexed question about acting is that of how the actor goes about creating his character. Indeed the even more fundamental question of what is a character is by no means easy to answer. Plays of such diversity as *Othello, Hedda Gabler, Mother Courage, Sweeney Todd* or *South Pacific* seem to offer quite different answers.

Acting theories themselves seem to be equally diverse. The nineteenth-century critic A.C. Bradley saw Shakespeare's tragic characters as real people with a pre- and post-play life and an overriding passion. F.R. Leavis argued that Shakespeare did not invent people but 'put words together'. Stanislavsky tells us that characters must have a consistent objective, Strindberg that they must vacillate, be 'out of joint, torn between old and new ... conglomerates, made up of past and present stages of civilisation'. Some actors work from externals like a gait or a gesture. Some borrow behaviour from people they know, others work from their own personalities in the belief that they have a number of people inside them. Brecht's characters must reveal their contradictions. Grotowski's actors must use an 'inductive technique' of eliminating external effects in a search for their own 'psycho-analytical language of sounds and gestures'. The novice actor reading books on acting theory is more likely to be confused than helped.

What we propose to do is offer an acting model which will provide a starting point for the actor and give him a working analytical framework. Whilst some elements may be found to be irrelevant in playing a certain part, we believe that their possible relevance must be considered before they are dismissed.

Before describing our model we would like to suggest that there is one absolute law that the actor must recognise. He must learn to see his character from his character's own viewpoint. Brought up in a tradition of objective analysis it is difficult for us to switch perception to one of egocentricity, but in order to discover the life in your character this is necessary. You must see your character's qualities in the way that you see your own qualities, not as your critics see you. When you speak of your character's temperament, wants and behaviour, speak of them as though they were yours, not as though they were someone else's. It is not possible to act a hypocrite, but it is possible to have conflicting loyalties, hypocrisy is the imputation of others. It is difficult to be evil, but you can pursue absolute principles because you believe they override all others.

What follows is an identification of the major elements of the model. Essentially we are discussing the 'action' of the play in performance. Charles Marowitz in his book *The Act of Being* defines action simply as what a character wants:

> Not what he says he wants, but what his underlying drive compels him towards from moment to moment. This 'want' is constantly changing as a result of pressure from other characters, with other 'wants' (counter-actions) and it is the interaction between the character's actions and the actions of others which produces the conflicts in scenes ... or within the character himself. (p. 29)

Our interpretation of action is slightly wider. We see it as a product of the interaction between all those elements which have an effect on behaviour. It is the product of the numerous tensions which develop as characters pursue their individual 'wants'. There is some difference between Marowitz's 'wants' and our own. We take the view that characters are striving towards long-term goals and the 'wants' which Marowitz refers to are intermediate and immediate aims. The source of action is also the source of what is referred to as subtext, which is the motive underneath the surface verbal behaviour provided by the playwright.

Intention

The most commonly accepted character indicator is the character's 'intention'. Such an approach stems from Stanislavsky's idea of 'super-objective' which he used to describe the *logic* of a character's behaviour so that each element of it fits into a causal pattern related to his principles and goals. The idea is that each character in a play has a long-term objective which his behaviour is directed towards and which gives coherence to it. The context in which he is pursuing this goal provides a variety of obstacles which inhibit him from achieving it. The material world, his own circumstance and nature, the ambitions or goals of others, block his progress. He is thus obliged to employ strategies which will help him to overcome, circumvent or destroy the obstacles. He therefore has short-term objectives which are to overcome specific blocks in his progress towards his long-term 'super-objective'.

It is not necessarily implied that the character will ever achieve any of these objectives. It is quite likely that he will deploy successively hopeless tactics to achieve an increasingly unattainable goal. Perhaps the characters of Willy Loman in *Death of a Salesman,* or Desdemona in *Othello,* are examples of such character progression.

Whilst the idea of a long-term intention is fairly easy to grasp, the playing of short-term intentions requires the actor to be clear about *why* his character is behaving in that way. It is necessary to be clear about your character's current interpretation of his situation so you need to decide not only what he wants, but why he wants it at this time.

It must be remembered that as actor rather than as character you have the benefit of foresight. Unlike real people who perhaps largely blunder on only half aware of their objectives, an actor is in full knowledge of them at all times for he has seen how the character has progressed throughout the play. Very often the plot of a play provides evolving clarification of objectives and it is with knowledge of the final definition that earlier behaviour can be understood. A good example of this might be of the character of Nora in *A Doll's House.* Occurrences in the play's action gradually move Nora to a definition of her own needs which at the beginning of the play are so ill-defined that she appears to have quite other objectives. This example anticipates our later discussion of values, for in examining and subsequently re-defining her values, Nora discovers her objectives. A clear connection is established between values and objectives.

Given Circumstances

Again this is a term which we take from Stanislavsky. There are two elements to 'given circumstances', first the theatrical context in which the play is being performed, which includes the setting, lighting, form of staging and so on, and secondly the fictional context of the play's action. The former context does not concern us at this moment. The latter provides all of the modifying elements which influence the particular behaviour of our character. Whilst we may always be J. Smith, we will also be J. Smith up a ladder or J. Smith consoling his bank manager or whatever. Character is therefore not a stable factor, we behave according to our circumstance, what we wish to achieve from the circumstance, and how we wish to achieve this.

The possible elements of given circumstances are almost infinite. A list would have to include every factor potentially capable of influencing human behaviour. However there are some categories of circumstances which provide guidelines for the actor to work from. The list which follows is provided as a check-list and a source of acting exercises. Remember that the particular influence of a factor depends on how that factor is perceived by the character. Outside death few experiences have an influence which absolutely determines behaviour. It must also be remembered that whilst more than one of these influences is always at work, it is quite possible that one will dominate to the diminution of others.

(1) The Material World
(a) Is the scene outside or in?
(b) Is the environment known or unknown to the character?
(c) Does the environment induce feelings of security or insecurity in the character?
(d) Where are the objects and furniture?
(e) What is the climate?
(f) Are there any totemic or taboo objects with particular resonances for the individual character? What are these?
(g) What is the immediate off-stage world? Where are its accesses into the stage environment? Are there associations of freedom or restraint, fulfilment or deprivation?

(2) The Character's Psychological World
(a) What has just happened to him?
(b) Where has he just been?
(c) What was his last experience of the material environment?
(d) Is he in a hurry?
(e) How near the surface is his intention?
(f) Is he being threatened in terms of achieving his goal or in any other terms?
(g) Is he anticipating a future event soon to happen?

(3) The Character's Social or Interactional World
(a) How will the other characters potentially effect the achievement of his goal?
(b) What was the outcome of the previous encounter with the other characters?
(c) Does the character know anything about the other characters?
(d) Does the character need to be perceived to have particular qualities by the other characters? Is there conflict between one expected appearance and another?
(e) What events are taking place simultaneously with the action of the scene.

All of the factors suggested above serve as either a constraint or a resource for the character in pursuit of his goal. Some will help, some hinder. We can therefore think of behaviour in part as a response to the constraint/resource qualities in the world around us, but which category an element belongs to is determined by how the character sees it in terms of his objectives. Prison, whilst most obviously a constraint, can provide satisfaction for needs of security, or sex, or status or companionship. A limp may only be a partial constraint, for it can also serve as a resource for gaining attention or sympathy.

Constraints and Resources

In a way, defining this element we are merely interpreting given circumstances in terms of a character's perception. However, if we assume that the principal logic of a character's behaviour is defined by the objective he is working towards, the given circumstances become tools or blocks, available to help or hinder his progress. They are also there to be evaluated by the character and used or avoided according to his capabilities or needs. All objects and people are necessarily dynamic and play an active role in the play's action. Frequently they will provide essential tensions, they will determine the character's emotional state and oblige him to move in particular ways. It might be argued that emotion is derived from the satisfaction or otherwise which the character is achieving. We are happy because we are secure and successful according to our own criteria. We may cry because we are being thwarted from achieving our ends.

Our spatial patterns are also determined by our relations with people and objects in the space. In a way this is self-evident, but many actors and directors seem to create their moves with only a rudimentary acknowledgement of the potential spatial tensions which can exist between every element of the stage world. Any movement calls for a re-adjustment of these tensions. In any scene there are a finite number of tensions determined by the plot at that time, so for one character there may be a tension between him and another in that the latter represents a threat, a door which represents escape and a hammer which is on the sideboard. Directing entails manipulating the tensions between those three elements. Ibsen's plays abound with such tensions, almost every object in, say, *Hedda Gabler* having resonances far beyond its instrumental value and providing varying tensions throughout the play.

Again it must be reiterated that external circumstances and objects have only the significance that we give to them. No element is constant or neutral. We weigh up what personal resources we have and use them accordingly, either putting energy behind them and creating a forward dynamic or losing confidence and setting up our own energy blocks. The need for the actor is to decide what is in the given circumstances for his character and how it affects his use of energy.

Energy

We discussed the idea of energy earlier, but we now need to consider it in terms of its effect upon character behaviour. Essentially we need to ask whether our character is using his energy economically and dynamically in pursuit of his goal or whether he is being obliged, through the influence of internal or external forces, to block his energy. There is a physiological and anatomical dimension to this problem which we will discuss later, but in terms of action the energy factor determines at least the following elements of human behaviour:

(1) the determination with which he pursues his goal;
(2) the degree of influence which blocks have upon the dynamic of goal-striving activity;
(3) the control which the character maintains in spite of external blocks.

The questions are whether the character is centred in terms of energy and personality and whether he is positive in pursuit of his goals. The answers to the question will provide the rhythm and tempo of your character's behaviour and it will determine his predominance or otherwise in any scene.

Values

Without undermining the importance of 'intention', a highly significant feature of character behaviour is his system of values. One of the best indicators of how to behave is what your character's values are. Our hypothesis is that all people, all characters, hold some things to be sacred and others to have little value, and it is potentially possible to define a scale of 'preciousness'. This definition will determine what a character will fight for or give up easily. It will suggest his emotional life, define the way in which he conducts his negotiations and suggest the sorts of strategies he will be prepared to employ. Incidentally, of course, it provides a medium for the moral debate within a play and frequently its theme.

The essence of drama is conflict and whilst the major source of conflict tends to be derived from mutual blocking (this term should not be confused with the word commonly used to describe the process of determining moves during rehearsal) between characters the internal conflict for each character is what principles he will hold on to or give up in his efforts to stay on course for his objectives. His emotional state will depend very much on whether or not things which he holds to be sacred are either being jeopardised from outside or forced into jeopardy by the pursual of his goal. The outcome is often stagnation or even death when two equally sacred principles are in conflict and the character finds that he can give up neither. John Proctor in *The Crucible* has the principles of survival and self-respect, which become mutually incompatible. The result is that he is obliged to allow himself to be killed.

The extension of these values can often be material objects or other people. Thus a chair or a letter or a vase or a toy can have powerful value resonances. If one thinks of a dead child's doll in a Nazi concentration camp or a sole remaining wedding present in a geriatric ward or a letter which contains evidence of guilt or a valuable item in a sale of otherwise valueless furniture the point is made. Similarly an old family retainer, an unacknowledged child or someone who represents role values has wide resonances and is available for protection or, of course, rejection.

Probably highest on the list for most people of 'sacred' factors are those which they associate with their own personality. So, speech may be absolutely critical to the person who is narrowly holding on to high-class status, or the role of working-class leader. Clothing, manner of walking, gestural modes, posture may all be precious. We discussed these issues before in terms of the actor himself. Those inhibiting features which the actor himself has been obliged to over-come in his training may provide the essence of characterisation. If one studies public figures who have been in a position to modify their appearance it is interesting and informative to note how they have shaped the modifications in order to have particular appeal and therefore have a range of strategies available to them. The appearances become increasingly sacred as they reinforce public expectations, for without them the personality and the mutuality between figure and followers are in jeopardy.

It can be seen that there is a direct and complementary relationship between values and appearances. As people we attempt to maintain a consistency between the two. As actors we can use the values as a source of information about how we should contrive our appearance. This is not to say that appearances *are* the values, but that they are dependent on them. Part of the actor's task is to interpret his character's principles in external behaviour. We are evaluated and categorised by others according to their perception of our behaviour and appearance. With this in mind we organise those elements over which we have control to establish the image we desire.

Strategies

A strategy is a mode of behaviour decided upon as a way of progressing towards a goal. If we assume that that is what a character is doing, then all of his behaviour has to be seen as strategic. Of course its relation to the goal may sometimes be obscured by the immediate situation in that the character is obliged to deal with a block perhaps by blocking someone else, in order just to remain on course. He may also have, perhaps temporarily, to compromise, possibly even compromise his principles. All of the sets of behaviours which a character performs are tactical and it is normally possible to break down a character's behaviour into strategic sections in order to discover how to perform a scene.

It is a useful practice to give a name to the strategy which your character is playing, for it will provide associations from your own behaviour. 'Nobody loves me,' 'OK, I'll grovel,' 'Hard to get,' 'Dare you,' 'You're the same as me,' 'Let's have a quarrel,' 'I'm right,' 'Let's pretend' are all possible strategies, amongst a host of others. Examination of a Pinter play, particularly *The Lover* or *The Dumb Waiter*, will lead to an understanding of the rich range of human strategies which are available.

It is important to remember when you are analysing your character's strategies that they must be compatible with his values rather than your own. Whilst you yourself may frequently play the 'You don't really love me' strategy, if you are playing a tyrannical leader it is unlikely that he will employ that strategy. Whilst it is probably true that most of us will play any strategy we have in our repertoire if pushed by, say, the threat of death, we all have a purposefully limited vocabulary of strategies which are chosen to support the personality and value perception which we wish to achieve. Strategic behaviour is determined then by character in relation to given circumstances, objectives and values.

The idea of strategies has been discussed extensively in political science terms and some of the ideas drawn from a consideration of decision-making are worth noting. One theory is that in deciding on a strategy decision-makers have three perspectives to consider, the likely 'pay-off', the 'probability' of the strategy working and the subjective value associated with the decision. Any one of these can have dominance, depending on the nature of the person making the decision as well as the issue and context. The critical personality quality which determines which predominates is the placing of the decision-maker on an optimist/pessimist continuum. For the actor the important decision is the degree to which his character will take risks and the associated issue is whether the risk is blind, informed or based on past fortunate or unfortunate experiences. Is he hopeful?

One other dimension to the issue is whether a person or character is seeking to maximise from the strategy in terms of his goal/interest or whether there is a threshold of satisfaction below the maximum. In other terms, though your character is seeking a goal in his strategies, what is the threshold of satisfaction so far as his achieving a step towards this goal? Is he easily satisfied?

Character

We have left this ostensibly fundamental element until last, because to a certain extent it is defined by what seem to be secondary elements, the hypothesis being that a person or character is a pre-determined appearance striving towards a goal in the context of restraining or enabling factors. To some people this is too abstract or cynical a view and to the actor, who is principally aware of his need to have a physical and vocal appearance, it is an unsatisfactory starting point. Also to those who reject the essentially 'naturalistic' interpretation of the actor's craft it would seen quite inadequate or misleading so far as a play's statement might be concerned. Plays in which ideas dominate over action or abstract dramas in which characters are mere representations, or even narrative dramas in which the story appears to be all suggest that the model may not be valid. However we maintain a belief that even in these cases our model will provide a basic working framework and the source of dramatic interest.

In its heart drama does not deal with ideas, but ideas made concrete in terms of human interaction. The abstraction of character merely reduces the complexity of influences on behaviour, it does not obviate them. What holds our interest in a story is the plot, an element which is congruent with our notion of 'action'.

Of course if one's sole concern is with the sound of poetry or the quality of the ideas in a play, then our argument will not hold water, but the question arises as to whether such expectations could not be better served by some other medium.

We will be dealing with some more direct ways of approaching characterisation later, but we would suggest that when you are preparing your character you try to discipline yourself by working back from the intentions to the physical appearance rather than the other way about. If you work this way it will be less easy to fall into the habit of hanging speeches on to one of your pet physical caricatures.

The model is now complete. What we have tried to identify are the sources of 'action' and 'character'. Character is a function of values, intentions and desired appearance. Action is the playing of strategies to achieve and maintain these latter three elements in the context of problems ensuing from particular social and material circumstances. The actor's prime concern is to sustain coherence between his character and his character's 'action'.

What the model provides is a package of variables which are potential sources of behaviour. What it does not provide is the relative weighting of these variables. That can only be decided with respect to a particular part in a particular presentation, with a particular purpose. It may be that the fact that your character is in a dustbin must only create a metaphor and it would be quite inappropriate to show the usual behavioural responses to such a situation. It is probably unnecessary for a maid who merely announces tea to bring on anxieties about her boy-friend, but there again it might be vital to the plot or atmosphere of the play. The question must always be, 'Does my behaviour amplify the organic world and meaning of the play, or does it set up an alternative interest for the audience?'

Exercises Based on Model

The number of potential exercises is infinite and it is the responsibility of the director to devise exercises based on our model, but applied to the play which is in rehearsal. The following exercises are merely a sample which might be found useful as indicators of what might be done.

Practice 29. Playing 'Wants'. Work with a partner. One of you has a want in mind and without saying what it is try to persuade your partner to let you have it. Your partner has the task of finding strategies to counter your arguments. At no time during the scene is the article specified.

Practice 30. Playing 'Appearances'. This exercise is carried out in pairs. One of you first creates a character. Work from his values and then build a character around these. Give him a biography and a source of these values. Create a context in which the second actor is playing a role which attacks these values. The aim of the first actor is to maintain an appearance consistent with the values. The aim of the second actor is to undermine this appearance.

Practice 31. Playing Wants in Given Circumstances. Interpret the following scene or scenes, endowing each character with specific wants; he then interprets the lines in accordance with strategies which he is employing to achieve his wants. Find different given circumstances for the scenes.

Scene 1. For three characters

   A. It's over there.
   B. I'll get it.
   A. When did you arrive?
   C. It makes a great difference.
   B. Ages ago.
   C. Will you be able to do it?
   B. I love this place.
   A. Can I take that?
   B. Have you made your mind up?
   C. I understand your problem.
   B. When will Jane arrive?
   C. You're looking tired.
   A. There's one somewhere around.
   B. I really do think that it was for the best.
   C. How did it happen?
   B. Never mind about that.
   A. Should we get on?
   B. I'm just going to get something.
   C. Now.

Scene 2. For two characters

   A. Hallo.

B. So.
A. Were you able to do it?
B. Could you give me a hand with this?
A. Can't it wait?
B. There's a principle at stake.
A. Is there anything else I can do?
B. Don't sit over there.
A. I saw James.
B. Oh, yes.
A. You know why.
B. Yes.
A. How's your ...
B. I haven't had time to find out.
A. Would you rather I went?
B. Have you read this?
A. It could be different.
B. It is.
A. Can we?
B. Nothing's changed.
A. Right.
B. Ummm.

Practice 32. Composite Exercise. This exercise should be conducted over a period of about five hours. It is an attempt to bring together work on intention, given circumstances and character and is in effect a series of exercises which complement each other and build towards a final performance.

When you have worked through the scene once build in extra problems. Each of the characters has a personal problem; one character is in a hurry, the other wishes to delay as long as possible — establish the reasons; each character has a physical problem; play different intentions in different environments.

The task is to create an improvised play which includes four characters played by two actors. The play is in four scenes, each scene containing two characters. We will refer to the actors as A and B and the four characters as A1 and A2 and B1 and B2. In Scene 1 characters A1 and B1 interact; in Scene 2 characters A1 and B2 interact, in Scene 3 A2 and B2 interact and in the final scene A2 and B1.

All of the characters have long-term objectives which they sustain throughout the play. These objectives have associated values and character appearances. Each character in a scene provides a 'block' for the other.

The play's theme is that appearances must be maintained. In the case of groups of three members the third person will play two characters, each of whom acts as an audience for the others.

Working Programme

(1) Decide on the social and spatial circumstances in each of the four scenes.

(2) Decide on the character objectives and wants in each scene. There will be a consistent appearance in each scene, but each scene will demand that this appearance is modified.

(3) Establish character against the following questions:

  (a) Why do your characters want what they want?
  (b) What are their energy centres?
  (c) Ask each other's characters to complete the following phrases:
    I like to ...
    The thing I hate most ...
    When I go to bed at night ...
    If it weren't for ... I would ...
    People annoy me when ...
    Find other opening phrases for them to complete.
  (d) Test your characters' hands, voice, torso and walk in the following contexts:
    (i)   a value reinforcing situation;
    (ii) a situation in which their values are under threat, but their needs are such that they will modify them and thus their appearance;
    (iii) a situation in which their values are threatened, but they will try to reinforce them.

(4) Improvise the four scenes.

(5) Polish the improvisation in terms of (a) playing wants, (b) playing appearances, (c) clarifying the play's theme.

This exercise can be carried out using characters from a play which is being studied or rehearsed.

A Note on Playing Contradictions

The model we have presented will probably seem more consistent with the theories of Stanislavsky or the 'cybernetic' interpretation of human behaviour than with the theories of Bertolt Brecht. Brecht's theory of acting has been seen as an alternative to that of Stanislavsky. The latter's emphasis on contextual particulars and biographical detail has been contrasted with Brecht's emphasis on the alienation effect, on making the action seem strange and on preventing the audience from losing themselves in the emotions of the characters before them. Stanislavsky has been seen as presenting 'psychological' reality, while Brecht focused on social and historical reality. Stanislavsky's emphasis on the character's 'super-objective' has been thought to be in contradiction with Brecht's argument that 'the coherence of the character is in fact shown by the way in which its individual qualities contradict each other'.

The tendency to contrast the two theorists has been encouraged by the fact that where Stanislavsky maintained that the actor must constantly seek to present his character as a consistent, organic whole, Brecht insisted that the actor must always try to present the contradictions involved in the character's position and the alternatives facing him at any given moment of choice:

> When he appears on the stage, besides what he is actually doing, he will at all parts discover, specify, imply what he is not doing; that is to say he will act in such a way that the alternative emerges as clearly as possible, that his acting allows the other possibilities to be inferred. (*Brecht on Theatre*, p. 137)

The implication of Brecht's position is that we must not see individual behaviour as inevitably determined by psychological factors, but by social and historical forces which the character is free to influence in his turn.

The implication for the actor is that the presentation of a character's personal or biographical reality must sometimes be subordinated to the need to make a general point about how social forces act on people and people may act upn social forces. Angelika Horwicz, talking of her performance as Kattrin in Brecht's production of *Mother Courage*, made this point in connection with Kattrin's dumbness. She realised that to take her behavioural cue from the line 'A soldier let her have it in the mouth when she was small' would be likely to make Kattrin seem both dumb and stupid, thus destroying the rationale of her role in the play. She wrote:

> It would have been quite wrong to give an impression of retarded development. What was important was to show that intelligent people, born to happiness, can be crippled by war. Precision in portraying an individual case had to be sacrificed for the general truth. (quoted in Hayman, *Techniques of Acting*, p. 52)

This approach enabled her to play the final scene, where Kattrin wakes the sleeping town and provokes her own death, not as an emotional self-sacrifice, but as a lucid act of courage by an intelligent person determined that others should not be crippled as she had been crippled.

Uncertain interpretations of Brecht's theories have bedevilled many a production of his plays. There is a general inference that the Brechtian actor must be unemotional. This is not the case. He must be as emotional as is consistent with his character's position in the social and historical contexts, revealing their influences as the final determinants of behaviour. Brecht wanted his actors to look for the 'social gestus' in each scene and each action. This meant understanding not only the determining influences on that character but also the intentions and consequences of a given action as they related to the surrounding people and society. In *The Caucasian Chalk Circle* Azdak becomes a judge as the result of an unusual set of social and political circumstances. Once installed in office, he decides to deliver unusual judgements, favouring the poor rather than the rich and turning bourgeois class justice on its head by not seeking at all costs to preserve the established order. The actor performing the part of Azdak must convey this 'social gestus' by finding an appropriate set of physical gestures. An example of one such gesture is alluded to in the text when Azdak uses the massive book of the law, not to look up difficult cases, but as a comfortable cushion to soften the hardness of the judgement seat.

The Berliner Ensemble first came to Britain in 1953 with its production of *Mother Courage*. Accounts of the impact these performances made on Bill Gaskill the director, or Kenneth Tynan the critic, (see *Brecht in Britain*, Theatre Quarterly Publications, 1978) show how they impressed people by their use of concrete, material objects on stage, such as Mother Courage's cart. By the way in which the actors used these material elements, and were, in their turn, used by them, these performances presented an account of human beings caught up in the processes of war and business more complex than anything British theatre-goers were used to. Since 1953, the British theatre has gradually absorbed elements of the Brechtian style, in particular the tendency to present the heroic figures of the classical repertoire in an unromantic style. Tynan, in 1966, wrote of Olivier's Othello: 'I think Larry would have played Othello quite differently twenty years ago. This is an unromantic Othello — a wild animal, unheroic. This wouldn't have been possible in the pre-Brecht period'. This is quoted by Ronald Hayman in his book *Techniques of Acting*, p. 58, where he amplifies the point.

We believe that the acting model presented in this book can accommodate the Brechtian emphasis on presenting a character's contradictions and social conditions. A performance by a good Brechtian actor will be no less complex, no less concerned with the elements of strategies, values and appearances that we have identified than the actor following the Stanislavsky method. He will simply pay more attention to the broad social and political implications of his character's behaviour and he will be more aware of the contradictions involved in the way every one of us constructs his character, chooses his appearance, etc.

The Physicalisation of Character

As we suggested earlier, the first need is to establish your character's intentions, the reasons behind his wants, the sort of strategies he employs and the likely appearance which he would wish to display, before attempting actually to give him a body which moves. The desired appearance is the final indicator for the actor's choice.

In our earlier discussion of posture we suggested that it is something which is developed over the years, largely as an extension and amplification of the qualities which we wish to express. Consequently our stance, movements and gestures are profoundly associated with who we wish to appear to be. The inference for the actor is threefold. First, he can only work within his own possible physical range, so for example it is impossible for a fat actor to play a thin man: he has to go for those qualities associated with 'thinness' in order to perform a type outside his own physical range. Secondly, his own characteristic behaviour is liable to come between him and the character he is playing. He will tend to ignore indicators which impel him to behave in ways which are uncomfortable or alien to his system of values. The result can be that he will introduce behaviours which are inimical to the character he is playing. A problem we have frequently had is that some female actors' pride in appearance has made it extremely difficult for them to become slovenly. Men who cherish their good physique can also provide problems when called on to be unhealthy characters. The actor's first need is to be able to recognise his own behaviour and to understand its rationale and those elements in it which are critically supportive of the presence he wishes to provide. The third inference is that the actor must be able to take on the demeanour of another.

The Actor's Own Demeanour

All of the exercises on the actor's self will help to diminish more idiosyncratic and inefficient behaviour, but it would not be our wish, even if it were possible, to destroy the actor's own identity. Nevertheless the need remains to make him conscious of how he behaves. We will suggest a number of similar sorts of exercise which will help towards this goal. The exercises in themselves are quite interesting and enjoyable, but the need for the actor and his director is to apply the principles repeatedly to work in progress rather than being satisfied by the exercises.

Practice 33 Phase 1. The group should stand in as large a circle as possible. One member is asked to walk around the inside of the circle. As he does so the rest of the group draw his attention to peculiarities in the way he moves. As each peculiarity is noted he should exaggerate it until he finishes up as a larger-than-life version of himself. Each member of the group is subjected to the same process. All sorts of little quirks will be discovered. Someone will have one shoulder higher than the other. Some will smile only with their eyes, others will stretch their mouths sideways, others purse their lips. Some will turn their toes out, stick their bottoms out, push their chin forward, have stiff legs, walk with a roll; every element of the body's movement is potential material.

This exercise not only identifies characteristics, it also helps students to be observant and is sometimes a way of identifying sources of physical problems which the student is having. It must be carried out in a spirit of friendliness and care must be taken not to expose the most vulnerable people early on or in such a way that they feel excessively threatened. The coaching should be organised in such a way that the student being studied does not panic and sees performing himself as a clearly defined series of problems.

An important complement to this exercise is a discussion of the reasons behind the characteristic behaviour. It is essential that the student should examine these reasons, but it is equally important that he is not frightened off by the process. It may only be possible for the director to discuss the psychological and social rationale of behaviour in general terms, leaving students to draw their own private conclusions about themselves. Ideally, however, sufficient bonds of trust will be established to allow more direct and personal discussion.

A similar process can be carried out with the voice and speech. Again this is a good method of encouraging awareness in the students of the mechanism of speech and getting a sense of the voice production of both others and themselves. The success of the exercise will be at different levels. Some students will only notice accent, but others will find detailed resonating areas and rhythmic patterns and be able to associate these with general posture and movement.

Practice 33 Phase 2. Improvised scenes should now be performed with you acting out exaggerated versions of yourself. Any simple role scene will do with performers playing shop assistant/shopper, doctor/patient, parent/offspring roles or whatever. The aim of the improvisation is to sustain an exaggerated version of yourself.

Practice 33 Phase 3. This phase emphasises your ability to observe and recreate the behaviour of another. Working with a partner you first coach your partner to play a version of yourself. Teach them to walk, show them gestures, give them simple tasks to perform, put them in speech situations, until they are giving adequate performances of an exaggerated you. Next, exchange the coach and actor roles. Finally create an improvisation in which you perform each other. Take on a 'want' which you readily associate with your character and the character he wants it from. Use a situation with which you easily associate, such as the common room or the bar. The exercise is one which encourages self-awareness and develop powers of observation. Further improvisations can be created with new combinations of character and contexts. Attempts can be made to build composite characterisations using elements from different people and finding a rationale for them.

Playing a Physical Other

We would like you to think of the physicalisation of a character as giving it an *appearance.* In life there are three major determinants of physical appearance, the body we are born with, the values we have acquired and the appearance which we wish to convey in a particular encounter. Behaviour is a function of the interaction of these three elements.

We wish to stress the importance of the voluntariness of appearance in the belief that it is determined by what we feel to be precious, which is itself a function of how we interpret our interests and thus our intentions. So a person will gain contacts, friends, security, status, money, marriage, etc. from maintaining a particular appearance. If he changes that appearance he will put his interests at risk. Physicalisation is determined by our character's interests and his sources of material and personality reinforcement.

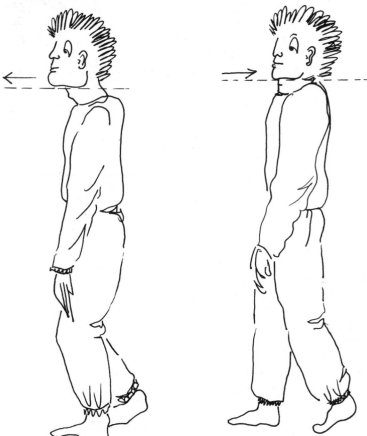

Figure 1: Head Transtations

In terms of training the actor, however, it is worth exploring physicality for its own sake. Our following discussion considers the issue from the perspectives of simple physicalisation, personality centres and mask work.

Simple Physicalisation

The following exercises aim at two things — first, developing a wider range of physical behaviour and, secondly, a sense of a total and organic physicalisation.

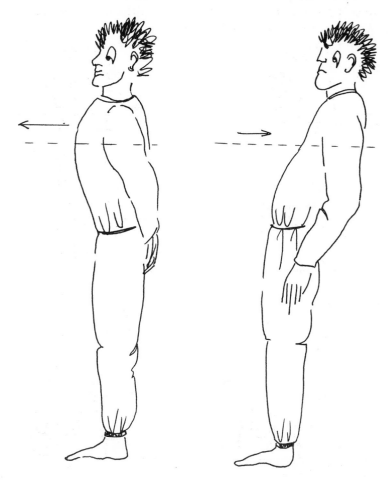

Figure 2: Chest Transtations

First do a thorough warm-up of the voice and the neck and shoulders. Include a mime exercise ('head transtation') in which the head is first pushed forward, then brought to the centre and then taken back, with the chin remaining level with the ground and the chest remaining still. Repeat the process a number of times, making sure that the chin neither raises nor lowers (see Figure 1). Next move the chest forward whilst keeping the shoulders in position so that the chest moves in front of the pelvis. Bring it back to the centre and then take the chest back so that the upper back is behind the pelvis, without letting the shoulders move forward (see Figure 2). Repeat several times.

Practice 34 Phase 1. Stand in an aligned posture. Slowly lower the head down until the chin is as low as possible, by curling down the upper part of the spine. Continue the movement so that the top section of the back-bone curves forward. Walk about the space finding a character. When you have found one try a new position for the shoulders, but keep the back bent and head down. Find a new character. Now vary the position of the head, again keeping the back bent. Try it pushed forward, pulled in, eyes up, but head down, pulled upwards, any variation that you can find. Try as many postures as you can, keeping the back bent, but changing the position of the head and shoulders. Improvise simple tasks in the various characters. Find a voice for each one. Now stand back to back with a partner. Adopt one of the character/postures. Spend a moment or two establishing the character then turn to face each other and play a scene. There is no need to pre-plan the scene. Given that you are used to improvisation there will be an initial adjustment and then the scene will flow easily. Try a second scene using one of your other character/postures.

Practice 34 Phase 2. Give yourself the back and chest of a sergeant-major. Again vary the shoulder and head positions. Try out various combinations and voices and improvise scenes.

Practice 34 Phase 3. This form of exercise can be repeated for other parts of the body. We suggest that you try various types of taut bottom, of slack bottom, of wide open eyes and of narrowed eyes, of wide smiles and of pursed smiles. Build characters up from each element, vary the elements, vary the voices, play scenes. The aim is to find the organic character.

Personality Centres

There is a tendency for the characters developed under the preceding system of exercises to move towards caricature. Don't worry about this, enjoy playing the caricatures, but be aware that they may be too big for most plays.

Another way to establish character is to work from a personality centre. We believe that almost any part of the body can be a personality centre. In his book *The Actor at Work*, Robert Benedetti, developing the research of Lowen, identifies five character structures — the head-centred, the shoulders, rounded, swayed back, the belly-centred, the rigid and the schizoid. The head-centred tends to be off-balance, almost trying to forget his body. Energy tends to be wasted in all directions. The belly-centred is heavy and calm. The rigid is the military type with a firmly rooted body and movements which tend to be mechanical and aggressive. There are two forms of the rounded-shoulder type. One is termed 'oral', when the energy centre is the head with the chest collapsed and aggressive energy blocked. The other is the 'masochistic', when the shoulders and back are rounded, giving an ape-like appearance. According to Lowen the aggressions of this type are turned in on themselves. The schizoid is unstable, awkward and lacks direction. Hands, arms and torso will tend to contradict each other and movements will be imprecise.

Try working with these body types by directing your energy in the way that they do. Allow the various centres to initiate your movements. Work through exercises, similar to the ones we discussed under simple physicalisation. Test the typing against a characterisation from a play.

A theory which we have found helpful with regard to characterisation is that the back of the body is the source of hard, aggressive and negative attitudes, whilst the front is a source of soft, open and positive attitudes. We have found this particularly useful in achieving changes in character behaviour so that it is possible to 'soften' an aggressive character by relaxing the back and using some part of the front of the body as the energy origin or vice versa.

In the material so far devoted to the actor, we have begged the question of how far the actor should abandon himself to the role he is playing so as to exist only through the persona and with the desires of the character he takes on. Although Stanislavsky sometimes contradicts himself on this issue, the view to which he returns most frequently is that the actor should abandon himself as completely as possible to the character for the duration of the performance while at the same time maintaining a broad control of his performance, for Stanislavsky was in no doubt about the distinction to be drawn between art and life. Brecht also, in a different way, demands this combination of abandon and control: he asks the actor to move his audience to tears at one moment and then to break their mood sharply at the next. Our belief is that in mask work we come close to the necessary experience of all good acting, whatever the terms that are used in its analysis. We put on the mask and find ourselves being used by it, but at the same time we retain control.

Masks and Countermasks

The most freeing and exact work on the physicalisation and vocalisation of character can come from mask work. It is not in the scope of this book to explore mask work fully, but we have found that it is so useful in releasing actors into character that we use it as a basic teaching medium rather than a form in itself.

First a note of caution. Mask work can be rather frightening, so actors wearing masks must be looked after carefully. The release can result in violent behaviour, so a director must be on hand to talk the mask down should this happen. Masks themselves must be treated with respect. They should not be played with. Actors must first get to know the mask and then to know themselves whilst wearing it before attempting to act.

Really a mask is a behavioural logic which takes over the wearer determining what he does. He inhabits the mask and it takes control.

The term 'mask' is far from specific. We can refer to a clearly defined social role as a mask. A policeman on duty, a politician at the hustings, a teacher or a taxi-driver can all be masks. Items of clothing can be masks, a military hat, a judge's wig, an academic gown, a dog collar can all dictate behaviour. Novelty toys such as false noses or spectacles or beards can all free a tentative actor into spontaneous and unselfconscious improvisation. We have found the nose/spectacles/moustache type particularly useful and make it a starting point.

Mask work should be carried out after work has been done on freeing the voice and body. The actor should then be given his mask and a mirror. He puts it on with his back to the class. Let him then play a scene with another person in a mask (we normally refer to the person in a mask as a mask). There is no need to set the scene. Just set out a couple of chairs and let the masks meet: they will interact. This exercise must be taken very seriously. The actors must be obliged to spend considerable time preparing themselves, but feel no obligation to be witty or clever.

Although masks have always been in use in the theatre, they came to be used in actor training in recent times when Jacques Copeau began his work at the Vieux Colombier in Paris in the 1920s. Michel Saint-Denis, who worked with Copeau, wrote:

> To us, a mask was a temporary instrument which we offered to the curiosity of the young actor, in the hope that it might help his concentration, strengthen his inner feelings, diminish his self-consciousness and help him to develop his powers of outward expression. (*Theatre — The Rediscovery of Style*, p. 103)

The extraordinary thing about wearing a full or half-mask is that it frees the wearer from needing to act, but simultaneously gives him an impulse to take on its traits. One of the pervasive problems with many young actors is that they act acting. Their work is superficial, but in a mask they are denied the chance to behave in such a way and their work gains considerable depth. The face and the rest of the body and voice fall into line with the indications given by the mask. The whole posture and system of gestures are harmonised behind the mask. Margaret Mead in her discussion 'Masks and Man' tells us that 'those who wear the masks are able to assume new roles, to move with a licence or a dignity, a ferocity or a frozen grace unattainable without a mask'.

Bland Masks. There are three major types of mask used in the theatre — the neutral mask, the full character mask and the half-mask. The neutral mask is also known as the 'bland' or 'universal' mask. It has no features of its own and has the effect of de-personalising the actor, obliging him to work with the very minimum of effort, all movements and gestures becoming economical and without pretence. The effect of wearing this mask is described by Bari Rolfe, who writes: 'Temporarily and without affecting his personality he [the actor] is asked to set aside his own gesture, posture, reactions, rhythms in order to prepare himself for a wider range and greater scale of character delineation to come later.'

Exercises with Bland Mask. Any exercises from everyday life may be attempted, though the mask should not be made aware of its own

Figure 3: Masks: (a) Bland Mask (b) Half-mask (c) Character Mask

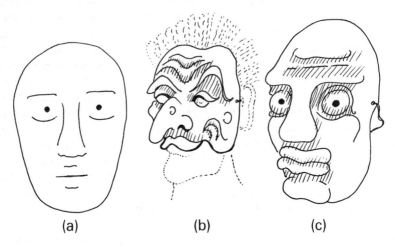

(a)   (b)   (c)

inadequacies by miming eating or drinking. Let the mask prepare itself for the day, give it occupations, let it work with others. Do an improvisation in which one mask starts an activity and two or at most three other masks join in. The aim of bland mask work is to achieve simplicity.

Character Masks. This mask is known to the French as *le masque expressif* and, as the name suggests, it has well defined features which give it a character and indicate modes of behaviour. In fact, the character and behaviour will vary according to the wearer.

Work with character masks can best be a development from bland mask work. If an actor comes straight to the character mask he will tend to work too hard and not be responsive to the mask's indications.

Exercises with Character Masks. First spend some time getting accustomed to the mask. Examine the mask, move it into different angles, talk to it, then put it on carefully whilst looking into a mirror. Improvise little scenes to yourself. Give the mask little actions to perform, let it pick something up, get a meal ready, sharpen a pencil, wash the dishes, wash its hands. Get someone to give it a present, which is wrapped up. Put a number of masks into a situation, in a bar, at the doctor's, on the Underground. Create mime scenarios for the masks, the precise nature of which will be dependent on the masks themselves.

Half-masks. The main virtues of the half-mask are that they allow speech and permit contradictory behaviour. A character mask tends not to lie, be self-consciously funny or contradict itself. The half-mask can do all of these things.

Exercises with Half-Masks. As with the other masks, go through the lengthy introductory process. A very good initial exercise is to sit the mask in front of the rest of the group who are unmasked and allow the group to ask it questions. The mask will gradually gather confidence and frequently becomes quite garrulous.

Any further improvisations can be attempted. Have masks meeting each other, create scenarios for them. The half-mask can be a very useful tool in the rehearsal process. It will aid concentration and help in the definition of character and motivation. The full mask can also be used in rehearsal. It obliges the actor to get to the emotional essence of his scenes. The danger is that he may attempt to use pantomime as a substitution for words. This should only happen if initial work has been careless. If it does, stop the masks and set the scene up again more carefully. Concentrated work will endow the acting with extraordinary sensitivity and depth which will carry over into the full performance.

Countermask Work. Of all work on character, countermask work is probably the most significant for the actor. The countermask is based on the notion that all of us carry around numerous contradictions. Whilst outwardly poised we may be inwardly terrified and reveal this terror in small gestures; whilst performing a noble deed we may be aware of our base motives and again suggest the contradiction in the minutiae of our behaviour. On another occasion the terror or the baseness may be the mask, with the other qualities acting as countermask. The contradiction and the flow between one mask as dominant and the other as subordinate is often at the core of characterisation. Pinter's *The Lover* is based on the process, much of Genet's work explores the multiple masks which we all have. Any character under threat or in a state of transition is playing both a mask and a countermask.

Exercises on Countermask Work.
(1) Play a scene with another actor in which you are saying aggressive and hostile things whilst behaving as though you were courting them. Reverse the process.

(2) Play a scene in which you smile continuously whilst telling someone off; they scowl whilst being submissive.

(3) Play the master/servant game which Keith Johnstone speaks of in his book *Impro*, in which one person is cast as master, the other as servant. The master calls the servant in to tell him off for doing something which involves him in looking intermittently in a particular direction. Whenever he looks away from the servant, the servant must make a rude gesture of some sort. If he is caught the master hits him over the head with a balloon or a rolled-up newspaper and continues the telling-off. The exercise can be developed to include a servant's servant who gets the blame and whose task is to have a polite front whilst taking every opportunity to be rude behind the original servant's back. Punishment is again the reward for being caught. Johnstone's status transformation scene is also a countermask scene. In this a person of *high status* sits next to a person of *low status.* The progression of the scene is from the *low status* person to become *high status* and vice versa.

(4) Do scenes wearing a half-mask in which you make your body a countermask to your face or your face a countermask to your body. Allow the dominance to move from one to the other.

We would like to end our discussion by quoting the actress Geraldine Page. Her statement is not definitive, but it comes as close as anything we have read to an honest description of the experience of good acting:

> Sometimes the character comes out in ways which surprise me ...
> If I do something, and a bell rings somewhere in me, and it feels right, I have a tendency to repeat what I did and find other pieces that fit in with it ... When you take the character and use the character, you wreck the fabric of the play, but you can be in control of the character without the character taking over. When the character uses you, that's when you're really cooking. You know you're in complete control, yet you get the feeling that you didn't do it. You have this beautiful feeling that you can't ruin it. (quoted in Hayman, *Techniques of Acting*, pp. 46-7)

10 THE ACTOR AS ENSEMBLIER

You will remember that the term 'ensemblier' was used in our introduction to mean 'an artist who aims at general effect'. Michel Saint-Denis amplifies the meaning of the word in describing the work of his own company: 'We set out to develop initiative, freedom and a sense of responsibility in the individual, as long as he or she was ready and able to merge his personal qualities into the ensemble' (*Theatre — The Rediscovery of Style*, p. 92).

The ensemble is the end-product of actor training. Its output is the collective communication made by actors using common conventions. To an extent the ensemble is the message. No matter what training has been carried out on voice, character and movement it only has a full purpose when it is channelled into a group communication.

What an ensemble does is to harness acting skills to its own philosophy and objectives. We have spoken at length about 'character', but there is no absolute rule about creating a character and, as Joseph Chaikin argues, 'Since there is no existing discipline to use an acting company must invent its own ... The frustration arising out of a group of people looking for an alternative way to represent the "who" is the most essential part of the development of the company' (*Presence of the Actor*, p. 15). The company will work from its own premises about the shaping forces of human behaviour; characterisation must stem from an interpretation of these, not from some golden rule.

The role of physical movement again will be determined by the ensemble's beliefs about how their theatrical communications should be made. Edward Gordon Craig argued, 'the actor must go, and in his place comes the inanimate figure — the Über-marionette' (*On the Art of the Theatre*, p. 81). George Bernard Shaw also saw great possibilities in the puppet, for it releases the audience's imagination: 'when you give us "Maria Marten" ... played by figures which cannot even stand on their legs properly ... and ... can neither change their fixed, intense facial expression ... the dramatic effect is sometimes actually greater than that produced by living performers'. He goes on to quote Shakespeare: 'The best in this sort are but shadows; and the worst are no worse if imagination mend them' and concludes, 'Shakespeare knew ... that the imagination of the audience has far more to do with the effect of a play than the movements of the actors' (private undated letter to Clunn Lewis, a Kentish puppet master). Such arguments would be anathema as working rationale to such directors as the Becks or Peter Brook. What the ensemble must decide is the role of the actor's physical presence and gesture in making its principles clear.

Even the voice has little universally valid quality. Grotowski wrote that the audience should be 'penetrated' by the actor's voice 'as if it were stereophonic'. He continues, 'The actor must exploit his voice in order to produce sounds and intonations that the spectator is incapable of reproducing or imitating' (*Towards a Poor Theatre*, p. 147). Such demands are a long way from those made by the Polish director Tadeusz Kantor in *Death Class*, in which the actors spoke 'as if they were only repeating somebody else's sentences' with the aim of creating a 'sense of the GREAT VOID'.

In spite of the impossibility of training an actor for a hypothetical ensemble, his training must include work which makes him able and willing to respond to those with whom he is working. It is a self-evident point, but one which very many actors fail to apply.

We have tried to ensure that as many of our exercises as possible have nurtured a mutual trust and sensitivity. We now include some exercises which have the specific purpose of training the actor to work off his colleagues. As with our other practices they are of a general nature, and the director must interpret them to serve his particular ends.

Practice 35. The Mirror Game.   This exercise is probably the best known in acting workshops throughout the world, but it is worth mentioning because it is invaluable in establishing or reinforcing sensitive communication between actors.

Having established partnerships, one partner imagines that he is looking into a mirror. He then makes any sort of 'underwater' movements slowly enough for his partner to ape as though he were a reflection in the mirror. The onus is on the image partner to work with sufficient precision and care for his partner to be able to follow. The exercise is one of responsibility, not competition. After a time the image/reflection roles are reversed and the final part of the exercise is to work with an imperceptible alternation of leadership. With sufficient concentration and sensitivity you will find that you reach the point at which even you do not know who is leading and who is following.

Having reached this point add an extra dimension to the exercise. One of the partners leads the movements whilst the other begins to speak. The exercise can be a story. The person leading the speech begins, 'Once upon a time', his partner must try to say the words simultaneously so that we have the situation in which one partner is leading a sequence of movements whilst the other is leading a story. Leadership roles can be exchanged. Once a good understanding has been established, as with the movement element, the speech element can imperceptibly move from one leader to another. The point will arrive at which you lose all sense of who is responsible for the story and it will just flow on.

Practice 36. Acted One Word Story.   This is another narrative exercise and we learned it from the British director Anna Scher. Working with a partner, start a story which you tell one word at a time. The story is started with the word 'we' and the second word is 'were'. The words continue and you act out the story. So if the next word is 'crawling' you both get down and crawl and so on. It is important to avoid using direct speech or the story becomes an incompatible mixture of drama and narrative.

Practice 37. Actor and Storyteller. This is a fast-moving exercise and the director should change roles fairly frequently. Working with a partner one of you is the narrator and the other an actor. The narrator tells a story and the actor has to be whatever character or object which the narrator introduces. When you change roles you continue the same story. Once actors are at ease with this exercise limits can be set. The actor may just be one character and the story can be a thriller or a love story or whatever. The scenes can be played with various qualities with the exercise perhaps being used as a warm-up or for establishing very concentrated and intense work.

Practice 38. Thank You — It's a Pleasure. This is a partner exercise. First one partner adopts any position he chooses other than simply standing. The other partner then uses the posture as though the first person were an object of some sort. He might be a tray, or a motorcycle or a fruit machine. Having used his partner the user then says, 'Thank you very much' and the person used says 'It's a pleasure.' Roles are reversed and the exercise continues. After an initially slow start, this exercise always gains enormous momentum and considerable group energy is released.

Practice 39. Blind Game 1. Gluing. Blind games are extremely useful in developing trust and sensitivity. It is important to create a calm atmosphere before introducing them.

This first exercise is rather like 'tick'. The whole class closes their eyes and then moves around the room, trying not to make physical contact with anyone else. If they do make contact they 'glue' to the other person at that point. The exercise continues until the whole class is glued together.

Practice 39. Blind Game 2. Find your Partner. The class stand in a clump at the centre of the room with their eyes closed. Each person has a partner. The director disorientates them by moving them around slightly. They then must find their way to the side of the room. When everyone is at the side each person must try to find his partner by calling out an agreed word which everyone uses, any single word will do, perhaps the name of your town. You 'claim' a partner by touching them and then identify them by listening to them say the word. Each person you touch must be identified. The game continues until everyone has found their partner, at which point everyone opens their eyes.

Practice 40. Tug-of-war. Each person in the class picks up an imaginary length of rope about three feet long. One piece at a time, all of the lengths of rope are tied together until there is one long rope. At this point, without any discussion the class forms two tug-of-war teams and has a tug-of-war.

Practice 41. Singing. The whole class should form a tight group in the centre of the room — they can sit or lie, but they must be in contact with each other and they must be comfortable. Once concentration and relaxation have been established the whole group harmonises its breathing. The director can suggest sounds to breathe out on. Return to breathing without sound. What happens next is that quite spontaneously a member of the group begins to sing the chorus or first verse of a song. As the others recognise it they join in. If they don't know the words they can hum. When the verse is completed the group returns to silence until someone else begins another song and so on. This is an excellent exercise for ending a rehearsal or a workshop for it creates a very relaxed and comradely feeling. You will probably find that the start is fairly hesitant, but soon the actors relax and the exercise develops a rhythm. Don't worry if there are quite long gaps, let the group find its own moments to start singing.

Games

Most children's games can be a useful way of developing group energy and sensitivity. The best thing to do is to use games with which your actors are familiar. One of the most beneficial parts of the experience is when the group recalls the rules from its collective memory.

Some American directors use one-to-one, or small-team, games as a way of inculcating a sense of purpose into their actors. In the belief that an actor should be playing an 'intention' and therefore be playing to 'win' or 'beat' other characters in a scene, they have actors rehearsing scenes or improvising whilst arm-wrestling or playing table-tennis or even cards. The game can be chosen for its rhythmic suitability to the scene itself. What such exercises do is to help actors to be sensitive to the feedback they are getting and subsequently demand such feedback from their fellow actors in a scene.

REFERENCES

The references have been divided into eight categories, though they are not mutually exclusive. Sometimes it has been difficult to separate Acting Theory from Acting Practice or Ritual from Interaction and so on, but the reader should have a general indication of the emphasis of the books within each category.

A. Broad Aesthetic Issues

Birdwhistell, R.L. (1971) *Kinestics and Context,* Allen Lane, London

Brook, P. (1972) *The Empty Space,* Penguin, Harmondsworth

Burns, E. (1972) *Theatricality,* Longman, London

Dodds, E.R. (1957) *The Greeks and the Irrational,* Beacon Press, Boston

Elam, K. (1980) *The Semiotics of Theatre and Drama,* Methuen, London

Fergusson, F. (ed.) (1961) *Aristotle's Poetics,* Hill and Wang, New York

Langer, S.K. (1953) *Feeling and Form,* Routledge and Kegan Paul, London

Schechner, R. (1977) *Essays on Performance Theory, 1970-1976,* Drama Book Specialists, New York

B. Theory

Archer, W. (1957) 'Masks or Faces? A Study in the Psychology of Acting' in L. Strasberg (ed.), *The Paradox of Acting and Masks and Faces,* Hill and Wang, New York

Artaud, A. (1970) *The Theatre and its Double,* Calder and Boyars, London

Bablet, D. (1981) *The Theatre of Edward Gordon Craig,* Methuen, London

Beck, J. (1969) 'Containment is the Enemy', *The Drama Review,* *13* (3) 24-5

Braun, E. (1979) *The Theatre of Meyerhold*, Methuen, London
____ (1982) *The Director and the Stage*, Methuen, London
Brecht, B. (1965) *The Messingkauf Dialogues*, Methuen, London
Cole, T. and Chinoy, H.K. (1970) *Directors on Directing*, Crown, New York
Craig, E.G. (1962) *On the Art of the Theatre*, Heinemann, London
Diderot, D. (1957) 'The Paradox of Acting' in L. Strasberg (ed.), *The Paradox of Acting and Masks and Faces*, Hill and Wang, New York
Esslin, M. (1976) *Artaud*, Fontana, London
Gottlieb, S. (1969) 'The Last Discussion', *Yale Theatre*, 2 (1), 50-1
Grotowski, J. (1969) *Towards a Poor Theatre*, Methuen, London
Hayman, R. (1969) *Techniques of Acting*, Methuen, London
____ (1977) *Artaud and After*, Oxford University Press, Oxford
Heilpern, J. (1979) *Conference of the Birds*, Penguin, Harmondsworth
Hunt, A. (1976) *Hopes for Great Happenings*, Methuen, London
Jacobs, N. and Ohlsen, P. (eds.) (1977) *Brecht in Britain*, Theatre Quarterly Publications, London
Kalter, J. (1979) *Actors on Acting*, Sterling, New York
Marowitz, C. (1978) *The Act of Being*, Secker and Warburg, London
Piscator, M.L. (1970) *The Piscator Experiment*, Southern Illinois University Press, Carbondale, Illinois
____ (1980) *The Political Theatre*, trans. H. Rorison, Methuen, London
Saint-Denis, M. (1960) *Theatre — The Rediscovery of Style*, Theatre Arts Books, New York
Seyler, A. and Haggard, S. (1945) *The Craft of Comedy*, Frederick Muller, London
Smith, A.C.H. (1972) *Orghast at Persepolis*, Methuen, London
Stanislavsky, K. (1950) *On the Art of the Stage*, Faber, London
____ (1980) *My Life in Art*, Methuen, London
Strindberg, August (1976) *Plays*, Methuen, London
Swift, Clive (1976) *The Job of Acting*, Harrap, London
Willet, J. (1977) *The Theatre of Bertolt Brecht*, Methuen, London
____ (1978) *The Theatre of Erwin Piscator*, Methuen, London

C. Practice

Barkworth, P. (1980) *About Acting*, Secker and Warburg, London

Benedetti, R.L. (1976) *Seeming, Being and Becoming*, Drama Book Specialists, New York

_____ (1981) *The Actor at Work*, 3rd edn, Prentice-Hall, Englewood Cliffs, New Jersey

Boleslavsky, R. (1978) *Acting — The First Six Lessons*, Theatre Arts Books, New York

Brown, R.P. (ed.) (1972) *Actor Training I*, Drama Book Specialists, New York

Chaikin, J. (1980) *The Presence of the Actor*, Atheneum, New York

Chekov, M. (1953) *To the Actor*, Harper and Row, New York

Cohen, R. (1978) *Acting Power*, Mayfield, Palo Alto, California

Hapgood, E.R. (ed.) (1963) *An Actor's Handbook by Constantin Stanislavsky*, Theatre Arts Books, New York

_____ (ed.) (1968) *Stanislavski's Legacy*, Theatre Arts Books, New York

Johnstone, K. (1979) *Impro*, Faber, London

King, N.R. (1981) *A Movement Approach to Acting*, Prentice-Hall, Englewood Cliffs, New Jersey

Pisk, L. (1975) *The Actor and his Body*, Harrap, London

Rizzo, R. (1975) *The Total Actor*, Odyssey Press, Indianapolis

Rolfe, B. (1977) *Behind the Mask*, Persona Books, Oakland, California

Scher, A. and Verrall, C. (1975) *100+ Ideas for Drama*, Heinemann, London

Shephard, R. (1972) *Mime: The Technique of Silence*, Vision Press, London

Spolin, V. (1963) *Improvisation for the Theatre*, Northwestern University Press, Evanston, Illinois

Stanislavsky, C. (1979) *Building a Character*, Methuen, London

_____ (1980) *An Actor Prepares*, Methuen, London

_____ (1981) *Creating a Role*, Methuen, London

D. Voice

Berry, C. (1973) *Voice and the Actor*, Harrap, London

Lessac, A. (1969) *The Use and Training of the Human Voice*, Drama Book Specialists, New York
Linklater, K. (1976) *Freeing the Natural Voice*, Drama Book Specialists, New York

E. Broad Related Issues

Barlow, W. (1973) *The Alexander Principle*, Gollancz, London
The Bhagavad Gita (1962) trans. J. Mascaro, Harmondsworth, Penguin
Brown, B.B. (1977) *Stress and the Art of Biofeedback*, Harper and Row, London
Carrington, P. (1978) *Freedom in Meditation*, Anchor, New York
Hendricks, G. and Roberts, T.B. (1977) *The Second Centering Book*, Spectrum, Prentice-Hall, Englewood Cliffs, New Jersey
Herrigel, F. (1953) *Zen in the Art of Archery*, Routledge and Kegan Paul, London
Huang, Wen-Shen (1973) *Fundamentals of Tai Chi Ch'uan*, South Sky Book Company, Hong Kong
Iyengar, B.K.S. (1976) *Light on Yoga*, Unwin, London
Johnson, W. (1982) *Riding the Ox Home*, Rider, London
Lysebeth, André Van (1978) *Yoga Self Taught*, Unwin, London
Man-ch'ing, Cheng and Smith, B.W. (1967) *Tai-Chi*, Tuttle, Rutland, Vermont
Ohashi, W. (1976) *Do it Yourself Shiatsu*, Unwin, London
Orme-Johnson, D.W., and Farrow, J.T. (1977) *Scientific Research on the Transcendental Meditation Program, Collected Papers*, Maharishi European Research University Press, Wessis, Switzerland, vol. 1
Richards, M.C. (1964) *Centering*, Wesleyan University Press, Middletown, Connecticut
Silva, J. and Miele, P. (1977) *The Silva Mind Control Method*, Simon and Schuster, New York

F. Games

Avedon, E.M. and Sutton-Smith, B. (eds.) (1971) *The Study of Games*, Wiley, New York
Barker, C. (1977) *Theatre Games*, Methuen, London

Bruner, J.S., Jolly, A. and Sylva, K. (eds.) (1976) *Play — Its Role in Development and Evolution*, Penguin, Harmondsworth

Callois, R. (1962) *Man, Play and Games*, Thames and Hudson, London

Huizinga, J. (1955) *Homo Ludens*, Beacon Press, Boston

Opie, I. and P. (1969) *Children's Games in Street and Playground*, Clarendon Press, Oxford

Winnicott, D.W. (1971) *Playing and Reality*, Tavistock, London

G. Shamanism and Ritual

La Barre, W. (1972) *The Ghost Dance*, George Allen and Unwin, London

Belo, J. (1953) *Bali; Temple Festival*, University of Washington Press, Seattle and London

_____ (1960) *Trance in Bali*, Columbia University Press, New York

Browman, D.L. and Schwarz, R.A. (1979) *Spirits, Shamans and Stars*, Mouton, The Hague

La Fontaine, J.S. (1972) *The Interpretation of Ritual*, Tavistock, London

Lame Deer, John Fire and Erdoes, R. (1972) *Lame Deer Seeker of Visions*, Simon and Schuster, New York

Lévi-Strauss, C. (1966) *The Savage Mind*, University of Chicago Press, Chicago

Lommel, A. (1967) *Shamanism: The Beginning of Art*, McGraw-Hill, New York

Mead, Margaret (1946) 'Masks and Man', *Natural History, 55* (June)

Rapaport, R.A. (1967) *Pigs for the Ancestors*, Yale University Press, New Haven and London

Williams, F.E. (1940) *The Drama of the Orokolo*, Oxford University Press, London

Winstedt, R. (1951) *The Malay Magician*, Routledge and Kegan Paul, London

H. Social Interaction

Argyle, M. (1975) *Bodily Communication*, Methuen, London

_____ (1966) *Social Interaction*, Methuen, London
_____ (1967) *The Psychology of Interpersonal Behaviour*, Penguin, Harmondsworth
Benson, L. (1974) *Images, Heroes and Self-perceptions*, Prentice-Hall, Englewood Cliffs, New Jersey, and London
Berne, E. (1970) *What Do You Say After You Say Hello?*, Grove Press, New York
Goffman, E. (1961) *Encounters*, Bobbs-Merrill, Indianapolis
_____ (1963) *Behaviour in Public Places*, Free Press, New York
_____ (1969) *The Presentation of Self in Everyday Life*, Penguin, Harmondsworth
_____ (1971) *Relations in Public*, Penguin, Harmondsworth
_____ (1975) *Frame Analysis*, Peregrine, Harmondsworth
Hall, E.T. (1970) *The Silent Language*, Doubleday, New York
Lorenz, K. (1967) *On Aggression*, Bantam, New York
Mead, G.H. (1962) *Mind, Self and Society*, ed. C.W. Morris, University of Chicago Press, Chicago, vol. 1
Morris, D. *et al.* (1979) *Gestures*, Cape, London
_____ (1978) *Manwatching*, Triad/Panther, St. Albans
Scheflen, A.E. (1972) *Body Language and Social Order*, Prentice-Hall, Englewood Cliffs, New Jersey
Sorell, W. (1973) *The Other Face*, Thames and Hudson, London
Watzlawick, P. *et al.* (1967) *Pragmatics of Human Communication*, Norton, New York
Wildeblood, J. (1973) *The Polite World. A Guide to English Manners and Deportment*, Davis Poynton, London

PART III

CONTEXTUAL ISSUES

11 STUDYING PLAYS

We have seen that the study of drama involves a careful consideration of plays as potential pieces of live theatre and that we can only gain a comprehensive and balanced view of the meaning and nature of a play when we think about it in relation to performance. It follows therefore, that although their ultimate aims may be different, the kind of 'study' in which the actor, director or student engages is largely the same, for the idea of performance must always be present. Many school and university courses employ a different method, concentrating entirely upon literary analysis of the text and students are never forced to test their ideas in the laboratory of real or possible performance. Such an approach may lead to one level of understanding but it fails to take into account many of the aspects of a play which only emerge in the theatre.

We have also discovered just how many issues can and do affect the performance of a play: factors which may include the style of acting, the nature of staging, the attitude of the audience and the topicality of the play. From a large number of such factors it is possible to discern *two* major strands. First there are those qualities indigenous to the play itself: the author's intentions discernible from the text with its characters and plot and (where these exist) in stage-directions and an author's preface. Secondly there are those qualities which the performers, playhouse and audience bring to the performance of a play. Clearly, when writing his play, the playwright may be influenced by the knowledge of who is to perform it and in what conditions, but if the play is not contemporary, we, who wish to perform the play again, are left to explore the links between the two sets of qualities we have mentioned.

To make these links, a play must be examined in the context of the theatre conditions that were current when it was first written. This leads us on to the whole question of the use of theatre history, to which we shall return in detail. Far too often, teachers assume that illustrations of Shakespeare's Globe or of medieval pageant waggons can do the same work as a modern production photograph. In fact these pieces of pictorial evidence raise as many questions as they answer, although the pursuit of such questions is often a fascinating and worthwhile task in its own right.

Social and Cultural Conditions

Before we can consider the importance of players and playhouses, we need to look at plays in the context of the social conditions and attitudes and the broader movements within the arts which existed at the time of their creation. Does this mean that a student of drama must also be a student of social and political history, the history of moral or religious beliefs and of the arts? To the extent that drama both reflects and is capable of dealing seriously with some of these issues, the answer must be 'Yes.' Drama, the most public of all the arts, always involves people; either the imaginary characters of a play or the real people who give them substance and the real people who watch. Therefore any aspect of the human condition may become the business of the dramatist, the performer or the student of drama. This does not mean however that we should begin our study of a play with comprehensive research into the history of the period in which it was written. This mistake has adversely affected drama studies in the past when, for example, students of Shakespeare have been asked to acquire an 'Elizabethan World View'. Obviously some knowledge of contemporary customs, fashions and attitudes is helpful because the dramatist peoples his play with characters who most frequently move, speak and think like his contemporaries; nevertheless an over-generalised view of a particular period is unlikely to be productive.

In establishing an appropriate method for gaining contextual information the first principle must be that the play itself will reveal what is relevant. Instead of asking, 'What information about the author and his times is necessary for a full understanding of this play?' we should initially ask two questions: (1) what can we learn about the author and the social conditions and attitudes of his times *from* this play? (2) what are the relevant issues on which we require further information? Both these questions will help us to recreate imaginatively the conditions in which the play was first written and performed: a vital process if we hope to examine its 'afterlife'. This will not provide the complete picture, because we are setting aside for a moment the history of the theatre itself, but we often fool ourselves into thinking that a play is really about one set of issues because we are bringing our current beliefs and attitudes to bear upon it when, if we examine the play in its original context, it turns out to be about something quite different.

We can illustrate our method of enquiry and the possibility of detecting social attitudes from a playtext by considering views on marriage expressed in *The Man of Mode* by the Restoration dramatist George Etherege. During the course of the play various characters make statements about marriage; here are some of them:

(a) *Shoemaker.* 'Zbud, there's never a man i' the town lives more like a gentleman with his wife than I do. I never mind her motions, she never inquires into mine, we speak to one another civilly, hate one another heartily, and because 'tis vulgar to lie and soak together, we have each of us our several settle beds.

(Act 1 Scene 1)

(b) *Dorimant.* She's a discreet maid, and I believe nothing can corrupt her but a husband.
Medley. A husband?
Dorimant. Yes, a husband, I have known many women make a difficulty of losing a maidenhead who have afterwards made none of a cuckold.

(Act 1 Scene 1)

(c) *Old Bellour.* You need not look so grum sir; a wife is no curse when she brings the blessing of a good estate with her; but an idle town flirt with a painted face, a rotten reputation and a crazy fortune ... is the devil and all.

(Act 2, Scene 1)

(d) *Harriet.* I think I might be brought to endure him, and that is all a reasonable woman should expect of a husband.

(Act 3 Scene 1)

This is only a small sample of the many references to marriage in the play, but from these two things are apparent: first the expectations of marriage, of what it will bring and its chances of success, are extremely low; secondly, this is obviously a very different scale of values from our own — for although there are now many broken marriages and marital chaos is favourite material for stand-up comics, these words would be unlikely to appear in a contemporary play, at a time when expectations of marriage are extremely high.

Now it is a reasonable supposition that the characters of Etherege's play are intended to be believable seventeenth-century people: they may have exaggerated traits but in the main the dramatist appears to be showing us a representative group of upper-class people talking, intriguing, falling in love, going to the theatre and so on. Therefore we can assume that the hardheaded things they have to say about marriage represent attitudes that were quite common in such circles. But was Etherege commenting on a particular social attitude? Further evidence from other plays of the period will help in answering the question. In his play *The Beaux Strategem* George Farquar has included a scene in which Mrs Sullen meets her sister-in-law and describes in vivid detail the shortcomings of her husband.

Dorinda. Morrow, my dear sister; are you for church this morning?

Mrs. Sullen. Anywhere to pray; for Heaven alone can help me. But I think, Dorinda, there's no form of prayer in the liturgy against bad husbands.

Dorinda. But there's a form of law in Doctors-Commons; and I swear, sister Sullen, rather than see you thus continually discontented, I would advise you to apply to that: for besides the part that I bear in your vexatious broils, as being sister to the husband, and friend to the wife, your example gives me such an impression of matrimony, that I shall be apt to condemn my person to a long vacation all its life. But supposing, madam, that you brought it to a case of separation, what can you urge against your husband? My brother is, first, the most constant man alive.

Mrs. Sullen. The most constant husband, I grant ye.

Dorinda. He never sleeps from you.

Mrs. Sullen. No, he always sleeps with me.

Dorinda. He allows you a maintenance suitable to your quality.

Mrs. Sullen. A maintenance! do you take me, madam, for an hospital child, that I must sit down, and bless my benefactors for meat, drink, and clothes? As I take it, madam, I brought your brother ten thousand pounds, out of which I might expect some pretty things, called pleasures.

Dorinda. You share in all the pleasures that the country affords.

Mrs. Sullen. Country pleasures! racks and torments! Dost think, child, that my limbs were made for leaping of ditches, and clambering over stiles? or that my parents, wisely foreseeing my future happiness in country pleasures, had early instructed me in rural accomplishments of drinking fat ale, playing at whisk, and smoking tobacco with my husband? or of spreading of plasters, brewing of diet-drinks, and stilling rosemary-water, with the good old gentlewoman my mother-in-law?

Dorinda. I'm sorry, madam, that it is not more in our power to divert you; I could wish, indeed, that our entertainments were a little more polite, or your taste a little less refined. But, pray, madam, how came the poets and philosophers, that laboured so much in hunting after pleasure, to place it at last in a country life?

Mrs. Sullen. Because they wanted money, child, to find out the pleasures of the town. Did you ever see a poet or philosopher worth ten thousand pounds? if you can show me such a man, I'll lay you fifty pounds you'll find him somewhere within the weekly bills. Not that I disapprove rural pleasures, as the poets have painted them; in their landscape, every Phillis has her Corydon, every murmuring stream, and every flowery mead, gives fresh alarms to love. Besides, you'll find, that their couples were never married: — but yonder I see my Corydon, and a sweet swain it is, Heaven knows! Come, Dorinda, don't be angry, he's my husband, and your brother; and, between both, is he not a sad brute?

Dorinda. I have nothing to say to your part of him, you're the best judge.

Mrs. Sullen. O sister, sister! if ever you marry, beware of a sullen, silent sot, one that's always musing, but never thinks. There's some diversion in a talking blockhead; and since a woman must wear chains, I would have the pleasure of hearing 'em rattle a little. Now you shall see, but take this by the way. He came home this morning at his usual hour of four, wakened me out of a sweet dream of something else, by tumbling over the tea-table, which he broke all to pieces; after his man and he had rolled about the room, like sick passengers in a storm, he comes flounce into bed, dead as a salmon into a fishmonger's basket; his feet cold as ice, his breath hot as a furnace, and his hands and his face as greasy as his flannel night-cap. O matrimony! He tosses up the clothes with a barbarous swing over his shoulders, disorders the whole economy of my bed, leaves me half naked, and my whole night's comfort is the tuneable serenade of that wakeful nightingale, his nose! Oh, the pleasure of counting the melancholy clock by a snoring husband! But now, sister, you shall see how handsomely, being a well-bred man, he will beg my pardon.

(Act 2 Scene 1)

Mrs. Sullen's observations seem to confirm the views on matrimony expressed by the characters in *The Man of Mode*, and a study of other plays from the period provides an understanding of the attitudes to marriage among fashionable classes of the late seventeenth century. To modern eyes their marriages seem more like business transactions or essays in diplomacy and the titles of many of the plays of the period show a concern for and interest in marriages of convenience, marriages of old men to young women, infidelity and other sources of tension. Such plays as *The Country Wife* (Wycherley), *The Provoked Wife* (Vanbrugh), *The Provoked Husband* (Vanbrugh and Cibber), *The Tender Husband* (Steele), *A Bold Stroke for a Wife* (Centlevre), *The Careless Husband* (Cibber) all reveal a fascination, if not obsession, amongst Restoration dramatists with the nature of marriage.

Other features of the context in which seventeenth- and early eighteenth-century dramatists were writing may be discovered by a consideration of the action and activities of the main characters in any one of the plays mentioned. The most striking feature is that few of them ever appear to work in the modern sense; they enjoy infinite leisure, considerable fortunes and complete mastery of their time. They are able to devote most of their energy to love affairs, fashion, entertainment and gossip, they revel in scandal and move only in titled and court circles; they despise the country and glory in the elegance of the town; they travel in sedan chairs and inhabit gracious and spacious houses.

Such matters written about on so wide a scale indicate the nature of the audience for whom the plays were intended: a comparatively small, aristocratic circle revolving around the court which gave its patronage to the theatre in the form of royal patents. Many of the plays carry dedicatory prefaces or speeches addressed to a particular member of the royal family or aristocracy and many of the theatres established at the time still bear the name Theatre Royal.

Before extending our discussion into methods of deriving information about such important factors influencing initial conception as audiences and playhouses it will be useful to apply our method of enquiry to a play from a contrasting period. *A Doll's House* by the Norwegian playwright Ibsen was written in 1879 and once again contains a large number of statements concerning the nature of marriage. The play deals with the relationship between a husband, Torvald Helmer, and his wife Nora. Torvald has recently been promoted to the position of bank manager when his attractive wife is visited by an old friend, Mrs Christin Linde, who is now a widow. In studying the following short pieces of dialogue it should be possible to build up a picture of the underlying attitudes and assumptions. Consider each carefully:

(a) *Nora.* Oh yes Torvald, we can be a little extravagant now. Can't we? Just a tiny bit? You've got a big salary now and you're going to make lots and lots of money.
Helmer. Next year, yes. But my new salary doesn't start till April.

(b) *Nora.* ... Tell me, is it really true you didn't love your husband? Why did you marry him then?

(c) *Mrs Linde.* Well, a wife can't borrow money without her husband's consent.
Nora (tosses her head). Ah, but when a wife has a little business sense and knows how to be clever ...

(d) *Mrs Linde.* And you've never told your husband about this?
Nora. For heaven's sake, no! What an idea! He's frightfully strict about such matters. And besides he's so proud of being a man — it'd be so painful and humiliating for him to know that he owed anything to me. It'd completely wreck our relationship. This life we have built together would no longer exist.
(extracts (a)-(d) from Act 1)

(e) *Nora.* ... You see, Torvald's so hopelessly in love with me that he wants to have me all to himself — those were his very words. When we were first married he got quite jealous if I as much as mentioned any of my old friends back home.

(f) *Nora.* Don't look at me like that, Torvald!
Helmer. What, not look at my most treasured possession? At all this wonderful beauty that's mine, mine alone, all mine?

(g) *Nora.* It *is* true. I loved you more than anything else in the world.

(h) *Helmer.* You have loved me as a wife should love her husband. It was simply that in your inexperience you chose the wrong means. But do you think I love you any the less because you don't know how to act on your own initiative? No, no. Just lean on me. I shall counsel you. I shall guide you. I would not be a true man if your feminine helplessness did not make you doubly attractive in my eyes ... There is something indescribably wonderful for a husband in knowing he has forgiven his wife.

(i) *Nora.* We've been married for eight years. Does it occur to you that this is the first time we two, you and I, man and wife, have ever had a serious talk together? ... you're not the man to educate me into being the right wife for you.

(j) *Helmer.* But to leave your home, your husband, your children! Have you ever thought what people will say?

(k) *Nora.* What do you call my most sacred duties?
     Helmer. Do I have to tell you? Your duties towards your husband and your children.
     Nora. I have another duty which is equally sacred.
     Helmer. You have not. What on earth could that be?
     Nora. My duty towards myself.
     Helmer. First and foremost you are a wife and a mother.

(extracts (e) to (k) from Act III)

The whole tone of these fragments of dialogue suggests that we are on much more familiar territory than in *The Man of Mode*: this is the stuff of modern marriage guidance, of a great deal of our fiction and television drama. The questions raised here are within our experience although some of the opinions expressed are clearly quite unacceptable today. It is not necessary to be familiar with the whole play to detect that we are witnessing the breakdown of a marriage and that Nora makes the transition painfully from submission to a particular concept of a wife's role to independent self-assertion. Unlike the characters of the Restoration plays, these characters appear to have very *high* expectations of what marriage should be and achieve and consequently the failure of a marriage to attain such high ideals is a subject of tragedy rather than humour.

Each extract reveals something of the context of social attitudes and conditions in which Ibsen was writing. In (a), the husband and wife are discussing their changed financial circumstances in a way that suggests that they have both been aware of the need for economies and have, to that extent, shared a problem in a way that no characters from Restoration drama would have done. The wife, as in the Restoration plays, is shown as the more extravagant of the two and this traditional source of tension reveals not only a difference in temperament but a slightly uneven partnership. The view that women are really inferior managers and slightly irresponsible lies behind this exchange.

In (b), the incredulity of Nora that anyone should consider marriage for reasons other than love shows the basis on which she thought she was building her own relationship. Love as the only socially acceptable foundation for marriage is, in fact, the irony against which the action is played; but a major source of conflict is the social *ideal* of love, suggesting a sharing, *equal* partnership and the *reality* which assigns *unequal* roles to husband and wife. This reality is reinforced by the law, as shown in statement (c), and requires a rebellious and even devious woman if it is to be circumvented.

A very clear statement of the complex pressures and prejudices that lay behind the marriages of many nineteenth-century women is made in extract (d). Compare the almost sacred and reverential approach of Nora with the cavalier Mrs Sullen. Nora is reiterating the late nineteenth-century Protestant view of the sanctity of marriage: a relationship that had to be worked at, based on the father as head of the household and breadwinner, the wife as mother, homemaker and comforter and the home as the foundation of society. It is only against this background that we can understand the impact of the dialogue in (k), and appreciate why the audiences who first saw this play found it so indescribably shocking.

Both (g) and (h) show the sharing but male-dominated partnership; the husband's behaviour is governed by a common conception of how a husband *ought* to behave but to us he may have acquired a Jehovah-like self image. Infinitely more frightening is the extension of male dominance that sees the wife as the sexual possession of the husband, for it was by no means an uncommon nineteenth-century view that it was a wife's duty to provide sexual gratification regardless of her own feelings. That Helmer somehow manages to incorporate this belief into his supposedly caring concern for Nora is shown in his outburst in (f). In contrast with the possessiveness and concern for appearances, which appears to be the real root of Helmer's marriage, Nora has aimed at the ideal of love and is to pay a bitter penalty for it.

Other Plays from the Period as Sources

The need to cover up the cracks in marriages which failed to achieve the unity which society deemed desirable, the deeply painful experiences of the partners and the whole question of sexual taboo concerned a number of nineteenth-century dramatists. Ibsen's contemporary Strindberg showed in his play *The Father* (1886) how a marriage can become a living Hell, producing precisely the opposite effect to the desired state of bliss. Both Ibsen's and Strindberg's wife characters make a telling contrast to the self-effacing and eternally faithful wives we can find if we turn to Tom Taylor's *The Ticket of Leave Man* (1863) or T.W. Robertson's *Caste* (1867), although both these plays are credited with having contained elements of social comment, and we can build up a detailed picture of the problems of marriage in the second half of the nineteenth century if we compare all these plays with Sir Arthur Wing Pinero's *The Second Mrs. Tanqueray* (1893) which exposes many of the pressures and prejudices.

Observant students will also detect a growing debate in the wider issues of women in society; consider, for instance, the questions raised by such an apparently simple statement as the following from Strindberg's *The Father*:

> But I don't want to play the pimp and educate her just simply for marriage — if I do that and she stays single, she'll become one of these embittered spinsters. On the other hand, I don't want to train her for some masculine vocation that'll need years of study and be completely wasted if she does get married.

However unacceptable we find these views now, they form a vital part of the original context of the plays of the period. Dramatists were writing seriously about marriage for a very different kind of audience from the Restoration playwrights and again we can deduce something of the nature of that audience by an examination of the characters in plays by Ibsen, Chekhov, Strindberg or Wedekind.

In striking contrast to the leisured and titled characters of the seventeenth century the nineteenth-century plays are peopled by those who have worked to achieve their position, frequently in some profession such as banking, teaching, medicine, architecture or the armed forces. Many now enjoy comfortable middle-class affluence but because they may have climbed from humbler origins, their inferiors in the social scale will play an important role in the drama. A random selection of stage settings from the period reflects a deliberate lack of ostentation, emphasising the virtues of simplicity and sobriety: 'Dr. Stockmann's living room — humbly but neatly furnished', 'A large kitchen', 'Room in Grant's Cottage', 'The room occupied by Mary Edwards in Miss Willoughby's house — humbly but neatly furnished' and so on. When large houses are occupied, such as in Chekhov's *The Cherry Orchard*, they are shown as a financial burden to their owners or as the symbol of achievement through business acumen.

The inhabitants of such settings are often concerned by change: change of status, loyalty, belief or relationship; they are interested in the inner self, the effect of powerful personal drives and with the analysis of human conduct. At the same time, they are troubled by the need for outward respectability and for success as the middle-class world sees it. They seek happiness through the conscious working out of philosophical ideas and, above all, they subscribe to the Protestant work ethic: the view that unflagging self-help and industry bring their rewards in this life as well as in the life to come, and that a life of dissipation is rewarded by a Hell on earth.

Obviously such a range of topics would only interest a cross-section of the public who were familiar with the situations and problems under discussion. This was in fact the case, for the serious-minded audience for whom Ibsen and his contemporaries were writing consisted largely of those for whom the Industrial Revolution and the advance of science had brought increased affluence and education.

Interpretation and the Afterlife of Plays

So far we have been seeking to find out how much the playtext alone can tell us about social conditions and attitudes. We have seen that, in the characters of Etherege and Ibsen, behaviour is governed by a particular set of social assumptions. These are clearly embedded in the text of any given play and vary greatly from one period to another. Directors and performers will often use the production of a play from an earlier period to make statements about current issues. At times they delude themselves that the play was saying in *its* time what they want to say in *their* time but it is perhaps inevitable that a play will take on some quality of the age in which it is performed if it is to continue to

exist as a living work of art. Frequently the manipulation of a production to highlight a social or ideological point can be a fruitful and
stimulating exercise, as when Edward Bond translated Frank
Wedekind's play *Spring Awakening* (1891) for its first English
production at the National Theatre in 1974. Bond obviously felt a
considerable affinity with the play and in his lengthy introduction to
the published version wrote passionately of the failure of modern
industrial society; suggesting that *Spring Awakening*, though written
over ninety years ago, is almost *more* relevant now:

> The play isn't out of date. It becomes more relevant as our armies
> get stronger, our schools, prisons and bombs bigger, our means of
> imposing discipline more disciplined and veiled, and our self-
> knowledge not much greater.

This kind of attitude often gives rise to accusations of betrayal and
critics will argue that in a case like this Bond has used Wedekind's
play to serve his own purposes rather than respecting those of the
original work. Every new production involves a reordering of the
play's priorities and it is virtually impossible to draw a line between
the 'faithful' and the 'unfaithful' revival. Every performance is a
primary source for understanding aspects of the age in which it takes
place; we can, for example, learn a great deal about artistic trends in
the nineteenth century from records of Victorian productions of
Shakespeare, but we may learn very little about Shakespeare from the
same source. We shall need to examine carefully the question of
trying to reproduce the physical conditions of *original* performance
in order to achieve a true, authentic interpretation of a playwright's
intention. This must be considered alongside the broader problem of
theatre history, but for the moment we must deal with other means of
discovering factors which influenced the creation of a play.

Sources Outside the Play

Useful information for the student, director or actor in helping them
to establish the nature of the original play may be found by exploring:
(1) publications likely to have been influential and available to the
playwright and his potential audience; (2) private correspondence of
the playwright; (3) journals or newspapers of the time; (4) play
reviews; (5) programme notes or any introductory material that a

playwright might have written for his own work.

We can demonstrate the value of such sources if we continue, briefly, our consideration of Ibsen's *A Doll's House* and its effects on Strindberg. Ibsen returned to Norway in 1874, after an absence of ten years, to find the issue of women's rights a fierce debating point. John Stuart Mill's *On the Subjection of Women* had been translated into Norwegian in 1869 and provoked a mass of publications on the subject. Ibsen's play, therefore, gained enormous impact from its topicality and it is hardly surprising that, as Michael Meyer puts it, 'by the end of the century there was scarcely a civilized country in which it had not been performed' (Introduction to Ibsen, *Plays*, p. 11).

Ibsen's private correspondence reveals that the genesis of the play was, in part, dictated by the climate of opinion on women's rights and the inviolability of marriage and partially by his own personal experience. The critic Georg Brandes had suggested to Ibsen that a character from an earlier play, *The League of Youth*, who accuses her husband of having dressed her up like a doll and played with her, might form the basis of a future play. At a slightly later date Ibsen became involved with a woman whose predicament resembled that which the playwright created for Nora, and in 1878 we find him writing in some notes:

> There are two kinds of moral laws, two kinds of conscience, one for men and one, quite different, for women. They don't understand each other; but in practical life, woman is judged by masculine law, as though she weren't a woman but a man ...
> A woman cannot be herself in modern society. It is an exclusively male society with laws made by men and with prosecutors and judges who assess female conduct from such a standpoint.
>
> (*Plays 2*, p. 12)

We have now pieced together from some of the sources suggested a useful body of information which throws light on Ibsen's major concerns and by the use of further evidence from such sources many editors and historians have given a vivid picture of the reception accorded the play. This has been done most economically and stylishly by Michael Meyer (Ibsen, *Plays 1-4*).

What of the effect on Strindberg? The published version of *A Doll's House* together with the ferment it had created were both available to Strindberg when, in 1886, he read a magazine article by Paul Lafargue propounding a theory that the human family was originally a matriarchy. Strindberg's own deeply unhappy marriage, coupled with his contempt for Ibsen (the 'Norwegian Bluestocking' he called him), combined in a suspicion of women that was fuelled by the Lafargue article and he determined to write plays that would redress the injustice and damage which he felt had been done to men by *A Doll's House.* He accordingly wrote *The Father* in 1887 followed by *Miss Julie* in 1888, to which he provided a very revealing introduction. It is obvious that Strindberg was considerably affected by the intellectual climate of his times: his gloomy view of the relationship between the sexes as a struggle for dominance and survival clearly owed something to the ideas of Darwin and the emerging science of psychology with its concern for man's primitive, innate drives. By a careful check of dates we can see that Darwin's *Origin of Species* (1859), *The Descent of Man* (1871) and *The Expression of Emotion in Man and Animals* (1872) were all available in translation in Sweden by the time Strindberg was writing; furthermore only two years before he wrote *The Father* Freud arrived as a student at the Salpetrière clinic in Paris where he was to achieve a revolution in psychological investigation. In 1882, Tuke and Bucknill's textbook *Psychological Medicine* showed that even before Freud there was extensive interest and research into the workings of the subconscious mind.

Audiences

The intellectual climate that affects an author may also be expected to shape the opinions of his audience and the composition and assumptions of that audience form an essential element in the study of drama. The act of writing a play involves a commitment to communication with a public: every playwright desires a public hearing for his work. However much he may shun publicity, disregard reviews or hate watching his plays performed, his aim is to provoke a confrontation of his ideas with a live audience. He may despise his public, or wish to shock them; more commonly, he will aim to please them; but whatever his attitude, his awareness of them will shape the way in which he writes. Students of drama therefore need to be able to determine something of the playwright's attitude to his audience and of their ideological assumptions, as well as the social and economic conditions under which they live.

As an example, we can take some of Strindberg's remarks about his audience from a letter to Adolph Paul in 1907: '*Miss Julie* (without an intermission) has gone through its ordeal by fire and shown itself to be the kind of drama demanded by the impatient men of today: thorough but brief' (*Plays*, p. 3). Strindberg's sense of the 'impatient men' composing his audience was very different from George Etherege's idea of the people for whom he wrote *The Man of Mode*: members of fashionable society who brought a far more casual attitude towards sex to the theatre. Etherege's audience was in no hurry; they could afford to listen with mild amusement to a lengthy prologue written by Sir Car Scroope, Baronet!

The study of audiences, and of playwrights' attitudes towards them, is thus the first step in recreating any period play for a performance in the modern theatre. This emerges very clearly if we consider the problems of producing a play from the medieval period. In almost every important respect, the assumptions of the medieval audience were poles apart from those of contemporary theatre-goers. Let us imagine that we wish to stage *The Crucifixion* from the York cycle. We shall use a translation which makes the language intelligible to a modern audience, but even so much of the force that the play originally held is likely to be lost when we consider the broad differences in audience assumption set out in the columns below.

Huge discrepancies can be seen to exist between the attitudes and expectations of the two audiences. It follows that before a meaningful performance of the play can take place the audience must be transformed, made to shed some of its modern assumptions and 'play the part' of the medieval public. At a recent production of *The Passion*, a compilation by the National Theatre of medieval plays including the York *Crucifixion*, the director employed a variety of methods to induce something of this transformation in his audience. In the first place, he was clearly concerned by the discrepancy listed under (6) above. His solution was to use the Cottesloe auditorium, built as an open space resembling the court-yard of a late medieval inn. He cleared all the seats out and used every part of the space at some point in the action, thus ensuring that his audience moved around, sharing the space with the actors. Secondly, he drew the audience into the imaginative creation of the play's events at various points. For example, where the play dealt with the nativity of Christ, the cast distributed lighted candles to the audience, who then gathered round the scene of the birth at the centre of the floor space. By their action and positions, the audience found themselves contributing to the sacred significance of the scene. The lack of a common belief among

Original Audience	Modern Audience
(1) Familiar with Christian symbols and liturgy.	(1) Not generally aware of Christian symbols or imagery.
(2) Mainly illiterate.	(2) Entirely literate and mainly 'well educated'.
(3) Very familiar with the words of Bible story.	(3) Unlikely to be able to identify scriptural quotation or make cross-references.
(4) Assumes that the subject matter is the most important event in world history.	(4) Sceptical or doubting the truth of the historical event.
(5) Aware of theological and doctrinal points.	(5) Views the play as crudely realistic drama.
(6) Joins with the actors in celebrating redemption from sin.	(6) Watches the actors from a comfortable, expensive seat in the auditorium.
(7) Either a cleric, soldier, or manual worker on holiday.	(7) A middle-class, professional person who goes to theatres and buys drinks in the interval.
(8) Will be reminded of the need for regular church attendance.	(8) Regards church as irrelevant except at weddings and funerals.
(9) Familiar with story from visual representation in painting and sculpture — does not doubt Christ is God.	(9) Familiar with a rock-musical or a television play, both of which emphasise Christ's humanity.
(10) Used to acting which combines ritual qualities, verse-speaking and robust humour.	(10) Constantly exposed to 'realistic' acting on television.
(11) Regards life as part of a divine plan, largely inexplicable.	(11) Assumes rational, scientific explanations for everything.

members of twentieth-century British society was, for the space of the performance, overridden by the ceremonial force of the play's enactment of shared suffering and redemption.

The attempt to project oneself imaginatively into the situation of the original audience is part of the work of both student and director. Reviewers correctly identified this as one of the great achievements of the Royal Shakespeare Company's production *The Greeks*. Michael Coveny wrote:

> By telling a complete story, Mr. Barton has achieved the astonishing *coup* of suggesting what it must have been like to sit with an audience in Athens and relate the narrative to what the play-

wrights assumed their customers knew. (*Financial Times*, 10 July 1979)

It is the knowledge of this assumption that enables us to understand a playwright's purpose and achievement. We need also to establish what is *unfamiliar* to a modern audience and seek ways of presenting the plays in such a way that they become accessible and meaningful statements rather than interesting exercises in archaeology. Irving Wardle wrote of *The Greeks*: 'The story, addressed to a public coming fresh to the legends, is spell-binding' (*The Times*, 14 July 1979). What this production had successfully captured was the narrative dimension of Ancient Greek tragedy. It did this by refusing to allow its audience to treat the performance as after-dinner entertainment. Instead, it changed their expectations by performing three linked plays in the course of one day (as at the Ancient Greek drama festivals), beginning at 10.30 in the morning and continuing until 11 at night.

Much of the scholarship that is necessary to determine the conditions which prevailed when a play was first written depends on access to sources which may only be available to specialist researchers. Fortunately the trend in drama studies in recent years has resulted in scholarly editions of playtexts which bring together information from the various sources we have discussed to give a clear picture of the factors which need to be borne in mind when planning a modern production. Such texts too are usually accurate and show precisely the changes and accumulations of stage directions made by successive generations of performers, printers and editors. It is important, therefore, to check that the text you are using for any of the activities we have suggested represents the most recent scholarship available and the bibliography to Part III lists suitable editions.

Seminar Topics

(1) Printed below are extracts from Milton's tract on divorce entitled *Doctrine and Discipline of Divorce* and Farquhar's play *The Beaux Stratagem* which appear to be closely related. What investigations would be necessary before any informed speculation of one influencing the other?

Nay instead of being one flesh, they will be rather two carkasses

chain'd unnaturally together, or as it may happ'n, a living soule
bound to a dead corps.

(Milton)

Mrs. Sullen. I was ever so since I became one flesh with you.
Sullen. One flesh! Rather two carcasses joined unnaturally
together.
Mrs. Sullen. Or rather a living soul coupled to a dead body.

(Farquhar)

(2) All drama criticism is a product of its age and can tell us as much
about the ideas of the age in which it is written as it can about the plays
it discusses. What inaccuracies and prejudices can you detect in the
following extracts?

(a) The nineteenth century drama abandoned the Arthurian court
for the modern industrial slum, the shining pre-Raphaelite
romance for a passionate interest in the rights of women, public
hygiene and the disastrous results of failure to divorce.

(Audrey Williamson, *Theatre of Two Decades*)

(b) There is a piece being played at the Theater am Schiffbauer-
damm, in Berlin, called *Die Dreigroschenoper* (*The Threepenny
Opera*). An English visitor who omitted to buy the programme
would conclude that he had blundered into one of those combinations of drama, cinema, jazz and discord with which the name
of the Communistic Herr Piscator is associated. The production of
the piece is deliberately crude. Adopting the idea that it should be
a 'Threepenny Opera', the producers have provided a dirty cream-
coloured curtain about 10ft. high, worked by a primitive arrangement of strings, such as might be used in amateur theatricals.

(*The Times*, 25 September 1928)

Even the work of very good critics has to be read in the light of their
assumptions about the nature and function of theatre. What can you
deduce from the following extract about the writer's view of tragedy,
and which theory of tragic character underlies his judgement?

Lear's insanity is not the cause of a tragic conflict any more than
Ophelia's; it is, like Ophelia's, the result of a conflict; and in both
cases the effect is mainly pathetic. If Lear were really mad when

he divided his kingdom, if Hamlet were really mad at any time in the story, they would cease to be tragic characters.

(A.C. Bradley, *Shakespearean Tragedy*, 1904)

(3) Evaluate the success of a translation or adaptation of a play from a previous age which has recently been presented in the theatre; what were the problems involved in making the performance meaningful to a modern audience?

(4) In the light of your work on creating a character, what information concerning beliefs current at the time of writing would you need to prepare for a role in a given play by Shakespeare? How would you acquire such knowledge?

12 THEATRE HISTORY

Theatre history attempts to discover those factors of performance which have affected the interpretation of plays since their first showing. It is concerned with the design and function of playhouses and with the style and technique of the performers who worked in them. In order to obtain an understanding of these matters, theatre historians make painstaking searches through documents and archaeological evidence, drawing up records of statistics and dimensions. Their work is published in such journals as *Theatre Survey* and *Theatre Notebook* which contain articles giving precise measurements of stages and theatres, dates and venues of performances or careers of obscure actors in order that an accurate picture of some aspect of theatrical life may be obtained. The same experts meet at conferences to exchange their findings or disagree on the interpretation of some facts, while some enthusiasts go to the extent of building theatres in imitation of earlier playhouses: there is, for example, a reconstruction of 'The Globe' on the banks of the Mississippi and Nugent Monck's 'Maddermarket' theatre, which was built on the model of the Jacobean 'Blackfriars', is still in use in Norwich.

Piecing together an impression of past theatrical performances is a difficult task: archaeological evidence is scanty because many of the structures were made of wood or only intended to be temporary. Theatre buildings have always been the victims of the fluctuating fortunes of their owners and have often been torn down to make way for something larger and grander; altered to incorporate some new invention or sold off in an attempt to avoid bankruptcy. Others have been burned down or closed by government decree and most have been too concerned with the production of the moment to worry about preserving the past.

Actors and actresses too have left comparatively few records. For the most part they have lived wandering lives, enjoying, by most standards, little in social status or security, and the bills advertising their performances have been destroyed in favour of the latest sensation. If their *lives* are difficult to reconstruct, their *performances* are even more so: a few contemporary illustrations, a review, a prompt copy of a production or a faint wax cylinder recording may be all that remains of a performance which held an audience spellbound.

In spite of these difficulties, however, there has been a tendency in this century for scholars, directors and performers to want to learn more about the theatrical life of the past. Quite apart from the very considerable fascination this holds for any theatre enthusiast, this is justified by the growing realisation that there is a vital link between the playtext, type of theatre for which it was written and the style of acting prevalent at the time. We also now appreciate that acting styles are influenced both by the material being presented and by the theatre space in which the performance takes place.

During the present century there have been a number of notable attempts to present plays in conditions which, as far as possible, resemble those which existed in the theatre when the play was written. The intention has been to preserve the playwright's original vision but it has also been discovered that the juxtaposition of ancient practice with modern expectations has had a most powerful effect. Perhaps the best example of this may be found by looking at the work of William Poel (1852-1934), who had a considerable influence on subsequent production styles.

Poel made his first appearance as a rather indifferent actor in 1876, but it was as a scholar and director that he inspired a generation of producers and playwrights. His major concern was with authenticity in performance which naturally sprang from an insistence on using an accurate text. He was constantly seeking to rediscover original modes of staging, arguing that only by this means could an audience experience a play as the author intended. Many of Poel's ideas were seen as innovations in his day, though they may seem commonplace to us now. For example, writing of his 1901 production of *Everyman*, he claimed that is 'was the earliest instance in modern times of a return to the practice of characters approaching the stage through the auditorium', and idea that was taken up by Craig and Reinhardt. Since the turn of the century there have been so many changes in the theatre that few people would now think of this type of entrance as either remarkable or as a return to the past; in order, therefore, to understand the impact of Poel, we need to see his work in the context of the theatre of his day, against which he was in revolt.

In order to achieve his aim of giving authentic productions of plays, Poel had to form his own production company because no commercial management was sympathetic. He chose to concentrate on what he considered to be the greatest drama written in English,

Figure 1: William Poel's Production of *Hamlet* in the Carpenters' Hall, London, 1900

Poel himself played Hamlet. Photograph courtesy of the Victoria and Albert Museum.

that of the Tudor and Stuart period, and from 1894 to 1905 his 'Elizabethan Stage Society' mounted the first modern productions of Marlowe's *Dr. Faustus*, Milton's *Samson Agonistes* and the first production for four hundred years of *Everyman*. These, together with several Shakespearian plays, were performed in a variety of halls and courtyards and attracted considerable interest and critical acclaim.

We can see something of the nature of Poel's revolution by comparing an illustration of his staging of *Hamlet* in 1900 with a design for the same play by Hawes Craven used by the actor-manager Forbes-Robertson at the Lyceum theatre only three years earlier in 1897. The photograph on page 244 shows that Poel's production appears to be taking place on a reconstruction of an Elizabethan stage; by modern standards of research this is not a particularly accurate reconstruction but the intention is clear. There is no proscenium arch or row of footlights dividing the auditorium from the stage; the setting is non-representational and is obviously intended for use throughout the play. The characters, dressed in late Tudor or early Stuart costumes, dominate the picture. Poel's production looks small-scale, intimate and a little haphazard in grouping, but the interest is centred on the characters and what they are saying or doing. A row or two of uncomfortable-looking chairs suggest that this is not a modern commercial theatre but a hired hall and there seems to be little demand for sophisticated lighting effects. What Poel was trying to rediscover in such productions was the particular dynamic resulting from presenting a play in the type of theatre for which it was written. We can see that his *Hamlet* follows as many of the practices of the Elizabethan theatre as possible, including such features as the wearing of contemporary costume and the absence of scenery. We also know that he regarded preserving the integrity of the original text to be as important as its mode of staging.

By contrast, the illustration we have of Hawes Craven's design comes from a painting of the designer's intentions. However, this illustration was included in the published version of *Hamlet* compiled by the actor-manager Forbes-Robertson to coincide with his production and we know from prompt copies left by Irving when he used the same design, and from other illustrations made after the production, that this is how the stage would have appeared to members of the audience. The whole staging concept here is pictorial, designed to be seen through the frame of the proscenium arch. The sense of realism is achieved by minutely detailed architecture and

Figure 2: Hawes Craven's Design for *Hamlet* at the Lyceum Theatre, 1897

Gothic costumes; and the characters, almost dwarfed by the grandeur of the spectacle, employ gestures which seem to be part of the design. In order to achieve this picture, the actor-manager would have needed to employ elaborate late nineteenth-century theatre technology and the overall impression is of Shakespeare reinter-preted to suit the tastes and expectations of Victorian theatre-goers.

Perhaps the most significant difference between the two pro-ductions we are considering here is the relationship between the actors and the audience. Poel was able to direct the play knowing that it would appear perfectly natural for the cast to make direct address to the audience and he could argue that this is what Shakespeare intended; on the other hand for an actor to step from Hawes Craven's setting and speak directly to the audience would have seemed ridiculous and would have destroyed the illusion that the elaborate design was meant to create. Most nineteenth-century actor-managers were concerned with spectacle and to some extent concern for the text of the play itself was secondary; Shaw, one of the most trenchant critics of Lyceum productions, once lamented: 'How am I to praise this deed when my own art, the art of literature, is left shabby and ashamed amid the triumph of the arts of the painter and the actor?' (*Our Theatre of the Nineties*, vol. 1, p. 19). Poel felt convinced that Elizabethan drama could not be staged in the commercial theatre so dominated by the proscenium arch and 'realistic' scenery because he claimed that 'the atmosphere of Elizabethan drama is created through the voice, that of modern drama through the sight' (*Letters*, p. 95).

In his search to rediscover the 'authentic' Shakespeare Poel went to the earliest and most reliable sources for his information con-cerning the Elizabethan playhouse and the playtexts themselves. During the nineteenth century the plays had suffered a good deal of mutilation, partly on account of Victorian sensitivity to the more bawdy and explicit sexual aspects, and partly because actor-managers had attempted to reconcile the plays to the needs of the proscenium arch theatre: Poel therefore had no easy task. In order that famous actors could achieve startling scenic effects or dramatic entrances and exits for themselves it was found necessary to alter the sequence of scenes, transpose locations of events and cut or add speeches. Evidence for this is widespread: a recently discovered wax cylinder recording of Irving speaking a speech from *Henry VIII* reveals some extra lines inserted, and an examination of his prompt copy shows how these words were used to create a moving exit for the great actor as the curtain slowly fell. No wonder Shaw once remarked: 'Irving does not cut Shakespeare, he disembowels him!'

The acting edition of *Hamlet* from which our illustration is taken shows how Forbes-Robertson adapted the play for his own purposes, cutting out any lines with sexual undertones and locating the action of the scenes differently. The scenes from Act 2 onwards are described as follows:

Act II

Scene 1.   A Room of State in the Castle

Act III

Scene 1.   A Room of State in the Castle
Scene 2.   Another Room in the Same

Act IV

Scene 1.   The Orchard

Act V

Scene 1.   A Churchyard
Scene 2.   A Room in the Castle
Scene 3.   A Hall in the Castle

Justifying these changes and additions, Forbes-Robertson wrote in his Preface: 'I have ventured to transfer the scenes taking place in the house of Polonius to the Castle of Elsinore in order to avoid as much as possible a change of scene, and to allow more scope and freedom of movement to the characters.' We must remember that scene-changing in the Victorian theatre was indeed something to be avoided, for it involved large numbers of stage hands heaving on ropes and huge pulleys to send flats, wings and back-drops clanking noisily into position. But if Forbes-Robertson had taken Poel's solution and allowed a single open stage with a permanent setting to represent all the locations of the action and relied mainly on the text to set the scene, he would have avoided the problem altogether.

Scholarly research into playtexts and the acting conditions in past decades was very much in its infancy in the nineteenth century and actor-managers were faced with the problem of presenting to a public demanding spectacle, plays that were written for a type of theatre of which they were largely ignorant. The research in which Poel engaged enabled him to alert producers, directors and performers to the rich possibilities of ancient forms of staging. His work led to experiments with varying actor/audience relationships, ritual elements from Greek and medieval theatre and modern plays specifically created to exploit new theatre spaces based on early models. Producers such as Granville-Barker began to insist on a careful and intelligent analysis of the text, a trend reflected in his famous *Prefaces*, and bold experiments in scenic design followed; there was a new impetus to the study of theatre history.

A Student's Approach to Theatre History

From our brief consideration of the career of Poel in the context of late nineteenth- and early twentieth-century theatre we hope that a number of important factors have emerged. First we have seen the value of primary sources; most of the salient points concerning Poel's work emerged from a comparison of a photograph and a plate from 1900 and 1897 respectively. Obviously, experience in interpreting such evidence is desirable, together with some background knowledge to provide cross-references, but in any study of the theatre an ability to reconstruct from fragmentary sources is essential.

Secondly, we must be aware that theatre history is being made with every peformance, and the ephemera: programmes, producers' notes, playbills, lighting or prompt copies, costume designs and so on need to be preserved and catalogued for research purposes. Poel's own work has passed into theatre history and his productions are now studied as assiduously as he studied the performances of the past; we can only obtain an accurate view of his work by a careful consideration of all the surviving evidence and although much of the material has been conveniently gathered in books, there are still unexpected lines of development to be traced.

Thirdly, we have seen how theatre history must establish connections between the playtext, the performance space, the style of design and the manner of acting. By changing the performance space, and its relationship to the audience, Poel was able to develop a new manner of acting which revealed Shakespeare's plays in a new light. In the place of rather statuesque, self-consciously beautiful images, audiences discovered the full-blooded, rapid narrative rhythms of Elizabethan and Jacobean drama.

Stage Directions

The first published texts of Shakespeare's plays contain almost no explicit stage directions. Any indications about methods of staging therefore have to be gleaned from the kind of research into theatre history that we have been discussing. In addition, certain inferences can be made from the statements of some of Shakespeare's characters about actors, clowns or theatre performance. Hamlet's advice to the players to 'suit the action to the word, the word to the action' and not to 'o'erstep the modesty of nature' has frequently been cited as evidence that actors of the time were fond of unnaturally large gesture and melodramatic delivery. But without being certain what standards these things are to be measured against, it is difficult to arrive at more than the most impressionistic conclusions. Later playtexts usually include stage directions which, in the case of nineteenth-century writers, may be very long indeed. But even when the author has taken care to set down exactly how he wishes his play to be staged, there may be very considerable problems of interpretation in matching his directions with current theatre practice. Below are printed six sets of playwright's directions concerning the settings for certain scenes in their plays. Let us consider what valid deductions may be made from each of these, taken from a number of contrasting periods of theatre history.

(1) The set should be constructed realistically with no attempt to distort its dimensions, shapes, objects or colors. No objects should be introduced which might draw special attention to themselves other than the props demanded by the script. If a stylistic 'concept' is grafted onto the set design it will only serve to confuse the evolution of the characters' situation, which is the most important focus of the play.

(True West, Sam Shepard, 1981)

(2) Scene IV. A View of the Country, 1st grooves.
Act II Scene I. A View of the Downs, The Fleet at Anchor, 6th grooves.

(Black-Ey'd Susan, Douglas Jerrold, 1829)

(3) Here entreth Nichole Newfangle and bringeth in with him a bagge, a staffe, a bottle, and two halters, going about the place shewing it to the audience singing thus ...

Here entreth Rafe Roister and Tom Tospot in their doublet and
their hose, and no cap nor hat on their head, saving a night-cap
because the strings of the beards may not be seene.

(*Like Will To Like*, Ulpian Fulwell, *circa* 1568)

(4) *Act One*

A spacious garden in Karsten Bernick's house. Downstage left, a
door leading to Bernick's room: upstage in the same wall is a
similar door. In the centre of the opposite wall is a large entrance
door. The rear wall is composed almost entirely of fine clear
glass, with an open door giving on to a broad verandah over
which an awning is stretched. Steps lead down from the verandah
into the garden, part of which can be seen enclosed by a fence and
a small gate. Beyond the fence is a street, the far side of which is
lined with small wooden houses painted in bright colours. It is
summer and the sun is shining warmly ...

Act Four

The same ... it is a stormy afternoon, already twilight; during the
scene it grows gradually darker.

(*The Pillars of Society*, Henrik Ibsen, 1877)

(5) *Act I. Sc. I.*
Enter D'Amville, Borachio, attended.
Act I. Sc. II.
Enter Old Montferrers and Charlemont.
Act I. Sc. III.
Enter Castabella, avoiding the importunity of Ronsard.
Act II. Sc. I.
Music, a banquet. In the night. Enter D'Amville, Belforest,
Levidulcia, Ronsard, Castabella, Languebeau Snuffe at one
door; at the other door Cataplasma and Soquette, ushered by
Fresco.
Act II. Sc. V.
Enter Levidulcia into her chamber.
Act III. Sc. III.
Enter Charlemont in prison.

The Atheist's Tragedy, Cyril Tourneur, 1611)

(6) *Act I. Sc. I.*
A room in Boniface's Inn. Enter Boniface, running.

Act II. Sc. I.
A gallery in Lady Bountiful's House. Enter Mrs. Sullen and
Dorinda, meeting.
Act II, Sc. II.
A room in Boniface's Inn. Enter Aimwell, dressed and Archer.
Enter Boniface, Hounslow and Bagshot at one door, Gibbet at
the opposite.

(*The Beaux Stratagem*, George Farquhar, 1707)

Discussion

Using various stage directions and instructions as sources of theatre
history has its dangers. We may well be obliged initially to indulge in a
good deal of conjecture in the interpretation of certain statements in
the texts before having the opportunity of checking our findings and
testing our theories by reference to other sources. Furthermore, it
must be appreciated that stage directions are sometimes the work of
later editors; this is particularly the case with 'acting editions' which
contain directions added by London producers. We can see therefore
that it is essential to use a scholarly edition of the playtext where there
are clear indications of the authenticity of the original stage
directions. Later additions to these directions do, of course, tell us
something about the stage conventions of the period in which they
were added but they are notoriously difficult to date accurately.

Statement (1) belongs to an age in which stage technology is so
advanced that it is quite reasonable for the playwright to demand that
his setting exactly resembles the real world. Unlike (4), which makes
similar demands however, this writer is concerned that his intentions
should not be distorted by 'stylistic' design. This gives us an interesting insight into how at least one contemporary writer responds to the
trend in modern theatre design. Is it the case, we should now ask, that
recent designers have tended to distort the shapes and dimensions of
objects to give a different view of reality? And in so doing have they
taken the focus away from the action of the play to the set design
itself? Photographic evidence of scenic design in the modern theatre
is plentiful and we can check to see if Sam Shepard's barely concealed
anxiety is justified.

One of the most lavishly illustrated journals of contemporary
theatre is the Soviet publication *Teatr* which each month contains a
section of recent set designs. Issues for the past five years show quite
clearly a trend of 'distorted reality' in the work of theatre designers

and the general impression is that the set should make its own powerful visual statement contiguous with the statements of the text and action of the play.

We cannot pursue this line of enquiry now without superficiality and those who wish to study this aspect of modern theatre must make their own investigations into the work of influential designers and playwrights. An interesting starting point, however, is the question of visual symbolism in modern drama which may be considered in relation to playwrights from Ibsen to Beckett.

Extract (2) may well send us in bewilderment to a reference book such as *The Oxford Companion to the Theatre* and in this case we shall not be disappointed as that volume contains a very full article under the entry 'Groove'. A key word here, perhaps, is 'view', which suggests that a picture painted on the shutter which ran in the groove simply provided a background against which the scene was played. The inclusion of so specific a reference to 'grooves' in the playtext makes it clear that, at least at the time of writing, they were a permanent feature in playhouses. We need to determine the period during which this was the case. There is no mention of grooves in our extracts (4) or (5), for example, but we must notice that (5) demands no scenic devices whereas (4) obviously requires something three-dimensional. It might, however, be reasonable to conjecture that the scene changes demanded in (6) could and would have been achieved by sliding painted shutters in grooves even though the text, which is not so obviously based on a prompt copy as (2), makes no mention of this fact. At this point we must resort to theatre archaeology. An examination of plans and theatre buildings which have survived from the eighteenth and nineteenth centuries sometimes reveals the existence of grooves on the floor and above the stage and by this means it is possible to date their use with some accuracy.

Extract (3) gives us information of a quite different sort, but equally valuable in piecing together a picture of past performances. The characters who enters bringing his props with him has no scenic background to establish the context of the action. This and the much extended example under (5) are excellent illustrations of what Poel meant when he observed that early drama created its 'atmosphere' through the voice. The instruction 'going about the place' must lead us to speculate that some form of open staging was envisaged, possibly including direct access to the audience. From this tudor 'Interlude', like another of its kind, *Thomas More*, we also learn something of the type of false beard worn by actors, a type which was obviously still in use when Bottom came to select his beard for his performance as Pyramus in *A Midsummer Night's Dream*. Information from extract (3) also suggests that Elizabethan plays were staged in contemporary costume.

Extract (4) is a remarkable contrast, for here the setting is given with as much detail and precision as if it were a novel. The use of the terms 'upstage' and 'downstage left' identifies the theatre of the proscenium arch and the entire concept demands a high level of sophistication in scenic construction. In such a setting it would be inconceivable for the actor to behave as he is asked to do in extract (3), for this is a realistic play in which the audience looks through the 'fourth wall' into the private world of the characters. Most striking of all are the demands for lighting effects which presuppose a high level of control over the lighting apparatus and it is necessary to go to other sources for information concerning the nature of such equipment available in 1877. Reference to *The Oxford Companion to the Theatre* (under 'stage lighting') or *The Revels History of Drama in English*, vols. 6 and 7, shows that this was the era of gas lighting, the use and control of which had been brought to a high level by Irving at the Lyceum. Two notable studies, Terence Rees's *Theatre Lighting in the Age of Gas* and Richard Southern's *Victorian Theatre*, will now provide us with almost all we could wish to know about this aspect of theatre history; it only remains actually to see the gas taps and jets that are still visible in some theatres and to make that essential imaginative reconstruction of how a performance by gaslight would have looked with the help of contemporary accounts.

No such visual subtlety was possible in the theatre for which Tourneur was writing in 1611. Extract (5) gives so little indication of setting that we are forced to conclude that the stage is bare. In his famous dialogues entitled *On the Art of the Theatre*, to which we have referred in our section on staging, Edward Gordon Craig discusses the issue of the sparsity of stage setting directions in old plays, and concludes that playwrights of the last one hundred and fifty years, who have indulged in much greater specificity, have intruded into the territory of the stage director (designer or director). In our example, there are so many short scenes that realistic scenery would have proved almost impossible in any case, but the constant suggestions of movement, particularly of entrances and exits, do impose certain physical features on the setting. We are provided with a clue to the most important of these features in Act 2 Scene 1, where it is clearly stated that there are two doors and they are mentioned in such a way

Figure 3: The Swan Theatre Stage, *c.* 1596

Johanne de Witt's sketch copied by Arend van Buchell. The only contemporary pictorial evidence of the interior of an Elizabethan playhouse.

as to suggest that they were permanent architectural features of the playhouse. The precise positioning of the doors in the rear stage area of Elizabethan and Jacobean playhouses has been hotly disputed by scholars, largely because there is so little pictorial evidence of the appearance of these early stages. However, the famous drawing by de Witt (1596) of the interior of the Swan Theatre (from which all subsequent illustrations and reconstructions have taken their inspiration) shows the two doors. Most reconstructions also include a gallery above the stage to house the musicians mentioned in our extract.

The banquet 'in the night' poses a problem because we know from other sources that performances took place in an open-air theatre, in the afternoon. Judging by the frequency with which theatres were burned down, flaming torches may well have been used but the playwright may simply have relied on the 'atmosphere' created by the voice: the mention of the owl and the scene ending with bedtime.

The permanent doors anticipated by the 1611 playwright were also presupposed by the writer of *The Beaux Stratagem*, though extract (6) contains several pointers to the effect that these doors were no longer in the *rear* of the stage. The alternation of the location of the scene between 'a room in Boniface's Inn' and 'a Gallery' suggests that a fairly substantial change of scenery is envisaged; incorporating the fixed door in the rear wall would have been difficult and if a solid backdrop were used they would have been hidden altogether. Furthermore, the suggestion of 'meeting' hints at the doors having been on opposite sides of the stage. Conjecture needs the reinforcement of pictorial evidence and fortunately the theatre of the eighteenth century is better documented than that of earlier periods. Illustrations of plays in performance between 1733 and 1825 (often taken from printed editions of the plays themselves) show a pair of doors, one on either side of the stage, in *front* of the proscenium arch. In perhaps the most famous of these contemporary prints, the 'screen scene' from Sheridan's *The School for Scandal* in 1777, the 'proscenium doors' as they have come to be known are particularly evident.

It is an item of considerable interest to theatre historians to determine for how long the proscenium doors persisted as a permanent feature of play houses, what their effect was on the performance and production style and how performances were also affected by having members of the audience seated in boxes at the side of the stage, as we can clearly discern from the *School for Scandal*

Figure 4: The Famous Screen Scene from Sheridan's *School for Scandal*

An engraving showing Drury Lane Theatre in 1777 from Wilkinson's *Theatrum Illustrata*. The shaft of light falling across the stage has been interpreted by many scholars as evidence for side lighting.

illustration. A model piece of research on aspects of this topic appeared in Robert Hume's 1979 article on the Dorset Garden Theatre in *Theatre Notebook*, showing the care and detail which is necessary to present a full picture of the theatre in other periods. At the conclusion of this section you will find suggestions for embarking on an original piece of theatre research and it must be emphasised that exploring the history of one particular building or the career of a specific actor or actress will provide far more valuable insights than over-generalised histories of the stage.

Performance and Style

Theatrical performances are governed by conventions, traditions, physical conditions, audiences and a whole range of personal factors including the physique and voice of the actor or his response to the material of the play. Sometimes we identify one particular performer with a role: we speak of 'Gielgud's Hamlet', 'Sybil Thorndike's St Joan' or 'Olivier's Richard III'; at other times we credit a performer with having 'created' a part and all subsequent attempts at that role operate in that shadow. As we have seen, however, the art of the theatre is essentially ephemeral and the problems involved in imaginative reconstruction of past performances are enormous. If we are forced to rely on eye-witness accounts we find them coloured by the theatrical traditions of the day and the personal prejudice of the author. For example, many devotees of Irving, including Craig and Bram Stoker, attempted in their reminiscences to give an impression of the great actor's unusual diction, which included rendering the long sound 'my' as 'mi'. It was only with the recent discovery of a wax cylinder recording of Irving's voice that it was realised that reports of the strangeness of his pronunciation had produced a wildly exaggerated impression and that, by modern standards, his style was remarkably natural. Further research has established that all mid-nineteenth-century actors contracted 'y' into 'i', and so Irving was only following tradition.

Among the most serious of early attempts to preserve elements of great acting for posterity was that of Joshua Steele in his *Prosodia Rationalis* (1779). Steele invented a system of notation to show all the subtle changes of voice: inflections, pace, pause and volume used by the famous actor David Garrick. He applied his system to Garrick's speaking of the soliloquy 'To be or not to be' from *Hamlet* and he notated a version of the speech as performed by an old style 'ranting' actor. Steele claimed that by reading the speech back from his notated version it was possible for a student to come very near to Garrick's or a ranter's performance. Interesting as the experience of reconstructing the vocal rendering of a speech may be, it does, of course, only provide a fragment of the complex nature of live performance and there is, as yet, no entirely satisfactory way of recapturing a moment of theatre.

Almost every 'new' approach to acting, whether it be pioneered by Garrick, Irving or Shakespeare in Hamlet's advice to the players, is greeted as more *natural* than the style it aims to replace. Strindberg longed for actors and actresses who would turn their backs on the audience, Stanislavsky aimed for naturalistic behaviour from his performers, yet in our section on acting we have seen how elusive the ultimate natural style has always been. It is as if the theatre is constantly struggling to find a natural style but the very fact that it is concerned with *performance* renders it unattainable. The possibility of a more natural style has undoubtedly increased when playwrights have produced dialogue which sounded like real human beings using everyday language, but changes in styles of writing, from verse to prose, verse 'rediscovered', the pause-packed prose of Pinter, ritualistic language and so on, have both affected and been affected by styles of acting. At the same time, the performances we see in the theatre are based on the way people behave outside the theatre; the way people talk, move, dress, sing or eat provides the basis for ideas we may have on what constitutes acceptable acting; as we have noted in our section on social conditions, however, these factors are all subject to changing fashion. Furthermore, the theatre lags behind the outside world and it is still possible to see acting performances in the theatre today which preserve modes of speech and social conduct that were common twenty years ago. Thus any attempt to state categorically that acting at a certain period was always like this or that is quite impossible and the best we can do is to acquaint ourselves with details available about particular performers and set this against what we can discover of social and acting conventions and theatre conditions of the time.

Actors are constantly struggling with the problem of *appearing* to speak or move naturally at the same time as being seen and heard by hundreds of people: the larger the playhouse, the greater the problem. It is only in comparatively recent years that any systematic scheme for training actors in the necessary skills has become available in Europe or the USA; prior to that actors simply learned their craft by a kind of apprenticeship in a 'Stock Company'. Acting traditions were certainly preserved more easily under this system than they are today, when subsidy and stage schools offer both the opportunity and the incentive for experiment.

Evaluating Sources

The difficulties of reconstructing past performances have been shown to be considerable. Illustrations can show us actors or actresses in various poses and using various gestures but these are always static, whereas the frozen image relates to past or future movement which we cannot see the picture. There are some remarkable early films of such actors as Forbes-Robertson but the jumpy movements and two-dimensional view give a distorted impression of live performance. With the increased status of actors during the last century and the popular demand for literature, many performers wrote their 'memoirs' and these, together with surviving prompt copies, can give striking pictures of theatrical life and the way in which certain parts were acted. Such information is far less readily available for earlier centuries and the evidence must be pieced together much more laboriously.

Study the following passages concerning some aspect of live performance and discuss the nature of the information that can be gleaned from each.

(1) Whenever there is Danger of a Riot, always act an Opera; for Musick drowns the Noise of Opposition.

(J.P. Kemble's journal, 1791-2)

(2) It seemed almost as if a being of a superior order had dropped from a higher sphere to awe the world with the majesty of her appearance. Power was seated on her brow, passion emanated from her breast as from a shrine; she was tragedy personified. In coming on in the sleepwalking scene, her eyes were open, but their sense was shut. She was like a person bewildered, and unconscious of what she did. Her lips moved involuntarily — all her gestures were involuntary and mechanical. She glided on and off the stage like an apparition. To have seen her in

that character was an event in everyone's life, not to be forgotten.

(Hazlitt on Mrs Siddons as Lady Macbeth)

(3) Behold her now with wasted form, with wan and haggard
countenance, her starry eyes glazed with the ever-burning
fever of remorse ... whether walking or asleep the smell of the
innocent blood incessantly haunts her imagination. 'Here's
the smell of the blood still: all the perfumes of Arabia will not
sweeten this little hand.'

(Mrs Siddons's notes on Lady Macbeth)

(4) ... a convulsive shudder — very horrible. A tone of imbecility
audible in the sigh.

(A spectator describing Mrs Siddons's performance of
the same scene in 1784)

(5) In the fifth [act] when the news was brought, 'The queen, my
Lord, is dead.' he seemed struck to the heart. Gradually
collecting himself he sighed out 'She should have died here-
after!' then, as if with the inspiration of despair, he hurried out,
distinctly and pathetically, the lines '... Tomorrow and
tomorrow, and tomorrow ...' rising to a climax of desperation
that brought the enthusiastic cheers of the close-packed
theatre. All at once he seemed carried away by the genius of
the scene. At the tidings of 'the wood of Birnam moving' he
staggered, as if the shock had struck at the very seat of life, and
in the bewilderment of fear and rage he could just ejaculate the
words 'Liar and slave,' then lashing himself into a state of
frantic rage ended the scene in perfect triumph.

(Macready describing Kemble's final performance as
Macbeth in 1817)

(6) Helene Weigel spoke the sentences as if they were in the third
person, and so she not only refrained from pretending in fact
to be or claim to be Vlassova, and in fact to be speaking those
sentences, but actually prevented the spectator from transfer-
ring himself to a particular room, as habit and indifference
might demand, and imagining himself to be the invisible eye-
witness and evesdropper of a unique intimate conversation.

(Brecht discussing his wife's performance in notes on
The Mother, 1933)

(7) In the central part [of *Mother Courage*] Helene Weigel is
never allowed to become a bawdy and flamboyant old darling;
her performance is casual and ascetic; we are to observe but
not to embrace her. Twice, and agonisingly, she moves us: once
by the soundless cry which doubles her up when she hears her
son being executed: and again when, to avoid incriminating
herself, she must pretend not to recognise his body. She walks
towards it, wearing a feigned, frozen smile that does not budge
from her lips until she has stared at the body, shaken her head
and returned to her seat. Then her head slumps and we see,
collapsed and petrified, the sad stone face of grief. Elsewhere,
even in Paul Dessau's magnificent songs, we must never
sympathise with Mother Courage; she has battened on the
Thirty Years War, and must suffer for her complicity by losing
her daughter and both her sons.

(Kenneth Tynan on the Berliner Ensemble's production
of *Mother Courage* in London, 1956)

(8) I have few illusions of being able to persuade the actor to play
to the audience and not with them, though this would be
desirable. I do not dream that I shall ever see the full back of an
actor throughout the whole of an important scene, but I do
fervently wish that vital scenes should not be played opposite
the prompter's box as though they were duets milking
applause. I would have them played at whatever spot the
situation might demand. So no revolutions, but simply
modifications ... A word about make-up, which I dare not
hope will be listened to by the ladies, who prefer beauty to
truth. But the actor might well ponder whether it is to his
advantage to paint an abstract character upon his face which
will remain sitting there like a mask.

(Strindberg, Preface to *Miss Julie*, 1888)

Performance Theory and Practice

It will be obvious from our discussions in this section that we are
neither providing nor advocating a conventional 'history of drama'.
There clearly are some benefits in studying key texts from selected
periods and traditions in order to acquire an over-view of the
development of drama and such an approach will rely on the great

plays which have survived in performance or simply in print. But this creates a number of problems. So-called 'great plays' may have been deemed worthy of study because of their literary rather than their theatrical merit, for we must remember that prejudice against the study of drama as a performing art as opposed to a branch of literature has been, and to some extent remains, strong. Plays selected and considered in the quiet of the study provide, at best, an incomplete picture and by looking at other sources we can see that some of the most interesting and creative periods in the history of drama were those from which few plays have survived. The fact that a play has not survived is not necessarily a guide to its merits either. The whole business of staging a play is so complex and costly that thousands of good plays, and perhaps some great ones, have simply been lost or remained on the page. A musician wishing to revive some music from a past age gathers together a group of instrumentalists or singers, provides them with copies, has a couple of rehearsals, gives one performance, and the public is satisfied; but the revival of a play will involve the learning of many lines, the blocking of moves and enough performances to repay the time and effort (or the management) involved.

In recent years there has been a growing appreciation of the fact that playwrights have gained much of their impetus from the advances in performance style, technology and public taste which took place in what have frequently been considered 'bleak periods' in drama and that many of the playwrights working in these periods (such as the early to mid-nineteenth century in Britain) were craftsmen of considerable skill. One of the most striking facts to emerge from studies in the careers of performers and the history of playhouses is the vast repetoire of once popular and now forgotten plays which engaged the energies of actors and actresses and the interest of audiences. If we add to this the fact of the rapidly changing tastes of the public we can see how unreliable a guide to quality is survival. Some kinds of play are more durable than others; in situation comedy and melodrama, the essence of the drama lies in the action and not in the words, so such plays appear to have little merit on paper. Moreover, even enthusiastic critical acclaim cannot guarantee the continued, long-term success of a playwright. Consider, for example, some of the comments written about the plays of Stephen Phillips, who had a number of very successful productions in the early years of this century:

a thing of exquisite poetic form

necklets of perfectly matched pearls

so fiery coloured; so intense, the character so largely projected, the action so relentlessly progresses till the final drops of awe are wrung from us.

Any young playwright reading such criticism of his work might be forgiven for assuming that he had achieved lasting recognition as one of the world's great dramatists, yet who knows or cares about Stephen Phillips today? In fact, Phillips died, dispirited and forgotten, within a few years of those words have been written and, in the event, far more lasting success was achieved by his publisher's office boy, Ben Travers. No doubt, the critics who so lavishly praised Phillips considered themselves as discerning, cultured and sophisticated as do their present-day counterparts, but as a guide to whether Phillips's plays are worth our consideration (or if not, why not) they tell us nothing. It is doubtful if modern theatre criticism is likely to be any more helpful to future students except that the critics always reveal something of the context of the writing and original production of the plays. Such contextual issues, with which this section has been concerned, can help to explain why certain plays are popular at certain times, and what world events (the First World War in Phillips's case) bring about changes in taste.

Projects

The various topics we have discussed may now be conveniently brought together in two projects:

(a) Performance Project

We shall centre this work around the play *The Country Wife* by William Wycherley, which was first acted in 1675. The extract to which our suggestions relate is Act 2 Scene 1, A Room in Pinchwife's House, but a knowledge of the entire play is necessary and an initial reading of the complete text should precede the activity.

Using the approaches outlined in this chapter you might prepare to perform the scene in the following way.

(1) Research into seventeenth-century acting styles by looking at as

many contemporary illustrations as possible and reading a specialised study on the subject: *The Ornament of Action* by Peter Hollands. Lyn Oxenford's *Playing Period Plays* and Clive Barker's *Theatre Games* will provide some useful acting exercises and it will be helpful to listen to, and if possible learn the steps of, a seventeenth-century dance such as the Sarabande.

(2) As with our previous consideration of Restoration plays, look particularly at the view of marriage presented in this scene and have this in mind as you begin work on characterisation.

(3) This scene is particularly rich in allusions to the historical conditions of the day; note especially the information concerning the status of actors, the behaviour of audiences and Pinchwife's attitude to the theatre. How might all this affect your playing of the scene and how might you attempt to recreate some of the original conditions?

(4) After careful research into the staging techniques of the period, construct a small stage in your studio with proscenium doors, a forestage and audience seating at the side. Now play the scene using an imaginative reconstruction of the original staging and employing the doors as entrances and exits. Note, for example, how the opening moments of the scene with 'Pinchwife peeping behind at the door' works in this setting and how his later entrance becomes effective. Decide also into which door Pinchwife eventually bundles his wife on the lines 'In baggage, in'.

(5) Using your stage with some live audience in position give careful attention to the many 'Asides', 'Whispers' and 'Aparts' in the scene. N.B. Use a scholarly edition of the play. We suggest either the version in the Regents Restoration Drama Series (Edward Arnold) edited by Thomas Fujimura or that in the New Mermaid Series (Benn) edited by John Dixon Hunt.

(6) Devise a series of improvised scenes based on the themes of this scene.

(7) Much of the scene is taken up with witty discourse: try playing the scene very rapidly with each remark 'thrown out' to the audience. What is the effect on the style of performance?

(8) Research and design costumes for the scene and discuss how these might affect performance, or preferably discover this by making and wearing such costume.

(9) Research the careers of any actors and actresses who have played in *The Country Wife* at any time and attempt to establish their views on the roles and their critics' reactions to their performances.

(b) Theatre History Research Project

We have already suggested that investigation into the history of particular theatres is a far more useful and interesting activity than relying on general surveys. Discovering the past of lost or surviving theatres is not so daunting a task as it may seem and you are encouraged to delve into the theatre history of your own town or village. As a guide use the following article by the theatre historian Paul Ranger which originally appeared in the journal *Speech and Drama* but has been modified by its author for inclusion in this book. Paul Ranger, who made a most successful research project into the old theatres of Winchester, concentrates here on the eighteenth and nineteenth centuries which are the most promising for most beginners, but if your location holds other possibilities the *methods* suggested here are equally valid.

A Ground Plan for Research: Eighteenth- and Nineteenth-Century Provincial Theatre

Paul Ranger

The hundred years from 1750 to 1850 were the heyday of the provincial theatre. Nearly every country town and, indeed, many a village boasted of its own theatre. It is surprising that the history of so few of these enterprises has been written up. At first sight the task may appear daunting to an inexperienced researcher but I hope that this ground plan will encourage readers to start looking for material and subsequently to become the author of a particular theatre's story.

A distinct pattern of development can be observed repeatedly. Until about 1750 groups of players arrived in towns to give dramatic performances that were in reality illegal. These would normally be held in barns, warehouses or wooden sheds situated in the courtyards of inns; the improvised theatre was rough and ready, consisting of little more than an unsteady platform, a green curtain and a few bits of scenery. After 1750 the more stable of companies tended to make a long-term conversion of a permanent building such as a malt house or silk mill within which they gave regular seasons. In such set-ups Sarah Siddons and John Philip Kemble began their acting careers before they graduated to the two London patent theatres of Drury Lane and Covent Garden. After 1788, when an Act of Parliament was passed allowing companies licitly to give performances of plays in one place for up to sixty days at a stretch, managers sank some of their capital into purpose-built theatres and the next ten years saw a great mush-rooming of these, many of which, in some shape or form, are still standing. It is these that are waiting to be discovered.

As a starting point in one's research it is a good plan to consult in your local reference library volumes of the *Victoria County History of England* that refer to your home area. Details of the locations of theatres are often stated in this work — although if no mention is made of one, that does not necessarily preclude further investiga-tions!

Descriptions of the Provincial Theatres

Several writers have prepared sets of notes on provincial theatres. With the exception of the first of these listed below the notes are still in manuscript form. It is necessary therefore to write to the relevant depository and ask for photocopies of the pages referring to the theatre in which you have an interest. It is worth pointing out that the space in the Theatre Collection of the Victoria and Albert Museum in which the Peter Davey Notebooks are kept is limited and that an appointment has to be made to see them.

(1) *The Theatric Tourist.* James Winston (London, 1805) (Birmingham Reference Library, Language and Literature Section)

James Winston was himself an actor and theatre manager. For the benefit of London Actors proceeding to the provinces in the summer months he wrote this directory of out-of-town theatres. A proof copy is in Birmingham together with many of the letters that Winston received at his address in the Tottenham Court Road from provincial actors of whom he had sought information. In conjunction with the book a series of plates showing external views of some of the theatres was issued.

(2) *The Theatric Tourist Notebooks.* James Winston (TS1335.211, Harvard Theatre Collection, Harvard College Library, Cambridge, Mass., USA)

Winston planned to present his *Theatric Tourist* in a number of issues, but after the first eight his project failed. The notebooks therefore cover many more theatres than the printed work does. The fourth notebook contains a number of sketches by the author that were later used in the production of the plates. Some measured drawings are of particular interest. An index to the theatres described is given in an article by C. Beecher Hogan in *Theatre Notebook*, vol. 1, no. 7 (1946), p. 87, published by the Society for Theatre Research.

(3) *The Douglas Notebook.* William Douglas (Johannesburg Public Library, Market Square, Johannesburg, South Africa)

William Douglas continued the work of James Winston approximately fifty years later. Two notebooks are extant, this one, the less informative of the pair, in Johannesburg, and a second in New York. The Johannesburg notebook relies heavily on quotations from a topographical work entitled *The Beauties of England and Wales.*

(4) *The Douglas Notebook.* William Douglas (New York Public Library, Fifth Avenue and 42nd Street, New York, NY 10018, USA)

A wide range of theatres is dealt with here. Some early matter is culled from Winston but the date summaries take us to the mid-nineteenth century. Douglas makes mention of many of the later managers of theatres which is helpful in compiling a history.

(5) *The Peter Davey Notebooks* (Theatre Collection, Victoria and Albert Museum, South Kensington, London SW7)

When Davey retired from the managership of Portsmouth Theatres Ltd, he set himself the task of writing an epic history of the south of England theatres in the eighteenth and nineteenth centuries. Unfortunately he died whilst still at the collecting stage and his notes are in fifty bound exercise books at Kensington. Provincial newspapers and actors' memories supply many of the dates and whilst the former are accurate Davey rarely checked the latter. However the notebooks are still a valuable source of information.

Newspapers and Periodicals

(1) Provided that a local newspaper is published early enough it can give a week by week impression of the fortunes of the theatre.

Advertisements appear regularly and there are comments on the plays in the news columns. Sometimes the criticism is written by the manager himself with the result that the 'puffs' are over plauditory. Public libraries usually have a run of originals or microfilms. In areas where local newspapers were late in starting one may need to look further afield for a journal which gives a general coverage and this may be housed in a library some distance away. A useful book for tracking down such locations is the *British Union Catalogue of Periodicals*, J.D. Stewart, M.E. Hammond and E. Saenger (London, 1955). The eighteenth-century stocks of the British Library Newspaper Library, Colindale Avenue, London, NW9 (01-205-6039) are depleted by war damage, but the nineteenth-century collection is extensive.

Points to notice in the advertisements are:

(a) the name of the manager of the theatre;
(b) date and time of performance;
(c) titles of plays;
(d) members of the company where given;
(e) under whose patronage the performance took place;
(f) prices and disposition of the seating;
(g) addresses from which tickets may be obtained — this is sometimes an indication of where the actors lodged.

At this point your researches will indicate that each manager owned a number of theatres and that his company travelled around the circuit from one town to another giving a series of performances at each for a season. The seasons would often coincide with important social events such as race meetings and fairs. A glance at the advertisements will reveal, too, that a different play was given each night with a number of repetitions throughout the season. An evening at the theatre consisted of a main piece, an interlude of songs, tricks, dances and recitations, and an after piece which often took the form of a farce.

Interesting details about the construction of the theatre and alterations to it should also be noted. The installation of gas lighting, for example, brought with it all sorts of problems and at some theatres this forms a saga in itself. Unexpected happenings to the stage hands and to the actors were usually newsworthy — counterweights fell on carpenters, often seriously injuring them; actresses sometimes gave birth in the wings in the course of a performance; and the firing of muskets on the stage as part of the show set the scenes on fire more than once.

(2) *The Monthly Mirror* (in 30 vols., London, from 1795)

This is a general literary magazine which gives biographies of actors, notes on London productions and also, rare tit-bits, news of what is happening in the provinces. It is bound in half-years with an index to each volume.

Playbill Collections

Often newspapers only give the performances for the first few days of the week and playbills augment this information. They also give complete cast lists and it is one of the joys of research to trace what becomes of a member of 'our' company. It is possible to discover the type of role (the stock type) that an actor played by comparing the characters noted on a number of the bills. Usually the bills were posted up outside the theatre and at inns and coffee houses. Within the theatres they served as programmes. When George III visited the Theatre Royal at Windsor the bills were printed on silk and were eagerly collected as souvenirs once the royal family had left. Silk posters and programmes were similarly used for some Victorian municipal entertainments.

(1) Playbills (The Reading Room, The British Library, Great Russell Street, London, WC1)

This is the largest collection of playbills in England. Manchester, Newcastle and Chester are fully represented and numbers of small towns such as Bungay, Huntingdon, St Neots and Thetford are also well documented. It must be noted that a reader's ticket is to be applied for in advance of visiting the British Library. This is usually only given to post graduate readers — but a special case may be made if the material is unobtainable elsewhere.

(2) The provincial files (The Theatre Collection, Victoria and Albert Museum)

The files contain not only playbills but also newspaper cuttings, prints, photographs and the odd unexpected item. Under 'Chelmsford' I recently discovered a prompt book belonging to Richard Barnett who was manager there during part of the nineteenth century.

(3) Playbills (The John Johnson Room, Bodleian New Library, Broad Street, Oxford)

A small but representative collection is housed in the ephemera room keeping company with menus and sauce bottle labels.

(4) Birmingham Central Library

A large collection of playbills is kept in the reference library that relates especially to the Midlands and to performances of Shakespeare's plays.

(5) Folger Shakespeare Library, Washington, DC, USA

An amazing number of bills have found their way here. The librarians are most helpful and will send lists of bills if you advise them of the towns in which you are interested. It is possible to get photocopies and microfilms made.

(6) Playbills are also to be found in the local history collections of the larger public libraries; in the county record offices; in local museums and archive collections; and in the offices of old-established newspaper printers.

Dr Frederick Wood compiled a handlist of collections of playbills in England and America which was printed in *Notes and Queries,* 1 June 1946 (pp. 222ff). However it must be remembered that some collections were partly destroyed by bombing in the Second World War.

Biography

Newspapers and bills will supply the researcher with lists of actors. It is then worth amassing information about such actors' lives and the theatres in which they played. A short list of recommended contemporary books offering potted biographies is given below:

The Thespian Dictionary (London, 1805)
Biographia Dramatica. D.E. Baker, I. Reed and S. Jones (London, 1812)
Dramatic Biography and Histrionic Anecdotes. William Oxberry (London, 1825)
The Georgian Era (London, 1834), vol. 4

Many eighteenth-century actors, whether or not they were endowed with literary ability, either wrote their own memoirs or caused others to do so on their behalf. Once the above dictionaries have been consulted it is well worth checking the catalogue of the British Library for the title of a particular actor's biography. Such people had the happy knack of working in a variety of companies and so tended to comment on many different theatres, their managers and audiences as well as their fellow actors. As an indicatory guide a few names and the areas in which the actors worked are given:

> *Memoirs of His Own Life.* Tate Wilkinson (London, 1790)
>   Hampshire and Yorkshire
> *Memoirs and Adventures of Mark Moore.* Mark Moore
>   (London, 1795) Midlands and the south coast
> *Memoirs of an Unfortunate Son of Thespis.* Edward Cape
>   Everard (London, 1818) Hampshire, Gloucestershire and
>   Berkshire
> *Retrospections of the Stage.* John Bernard (London, 1830)
>   Somerset
> *Memoirs of a Manager.* Henry Lee (Taunton, 1830)
>   Manchester, Oxfordshire, Berkshire, Somerset

Books published at the beginning of the nineteenth century are now rare and one may have to enlist, through a local public library, the help of the Central Lending Library in finding copies.

Local Collections and Topographical Works

(1) The local history collection is usually housed in the public library and quite often may only be used for reference. Town and country directories give details of the theatres together with the shops and other premises that surround them. One may also look up the builder of the theatre and the names of the people from whom tickets may be bought. Several valuable directories are:

> *The Universal British Directory* (1793)
> *The Beauties of England and Wales.* E. Wedlake and J. Britton
>   (London, 1801)
> *The London and Provincial Directory* (1823)

Local histories and guide books of the period must not be neglected. Memoirs of residents can also contain useful information. Charles Knight, editor of a local paper in the first half of the nineteenth century, gives an excellent description of the Windsor Theatre in his biography *Passages of a Working Life*.

It was not an exclusive theatre. Three shillings gave the entrance to the boxes, two shillings to the pit and one shilling to the gallery. One side of the lower tier of boxes was occupied by the court. The King and Queen sat in capacious armchairs with satin playbills spread before them. The orchestra, which would hold half a dozen fiddlers, and the pit, where some dozen persons might be closely packed on each bench, separated the royal circle from the genteel parties in the opposite tier of boxes.

Sometimes local history scrapbooks are available. At Chertsey, for example, I consulted the Wetton Scrapbook. Wetton was a printer and not only playbills, but also tickets, local views, letters and so on were mounted in this compendious volume.

(2) The county record office can also be a haven. Such material as the licence to perform for sixty days, leases showing plans of the theatre, sale notices giving not only a map but also listing the effects, may all be found here.

Correspondence

Correspondence relating to a small theatre is very difficult to discover, and yet, either published or in manuscript, it can be worthwhile. It was at Winchester College that I came across the letters of Mrs Sarah Williams to her husband who was chaplain to the Speaker of the House of Commons in which she described the hullabaloo surrounding the building of Winchester's New Theatre in 1785 and the attempts of a solicitor to prevent it opening until an effigy of him was publicly burned. Again, local circumstances differ so greatly that it is only possible to advise the reader to enquire of local historians about the possibility of such letters.

You might well discover that a person of some consequence visited your local theatre and that his, or her, letters (or diaries) have been published. When I was working on Lord Barrymore's theatre in Wargrave in Berkshire I found, for example, the published letters of Mrs Lybbe Powys most useful. Another instance: the Margravine of Anspach often visited the Newbury Theatre and there are oblique references to this in the comedies that she herself wrote and performed in at her private theatre just outside the town. This obviously is a variant on casual comments in correspondence.

General Reference Works

So far we have been dealing with material 'of the period', but now we must break away from that convention and mention a number of more recent general works.

(1) *The Dictionary of National Biography*

This has entries for a number of the better known eighteenth-century players. To each article is appended a list of source material.

(2) *English Theatrical Literature.* J.F. Arnott and J.W. Robinson (London, 1970)

This labour of love, many years in the making, lists writings, including a full section on biographical material, about the theatre in the seventeenth and eighteenth centuries. A handy cross reference system has enabled the work to be bound in a single volume. It is based on an earlier work by Robert Lowe published in 1888.

(3) *The Theatre of the British Isles.* A. Lowenberg (London, n.d.)

Entries are arranged principally under towns. Within these references are made to poems, theses, magazine and newspaper articles dealing with the theatre in that locality. A most useful pamphlet, published by the society for Theatre Research.

(4) *Discovering Lost Theatres.* John Kennedy Melling (Tring, 1969)

A slight and by no means scholarly work, but one full of infectious enthusiasm. Melling deals with 'lost' theatres, playhouses that are now cinemas, and former theatres that became offices or warehouses.

(5) *A History of English Drama.* Allardyce Nicoll (Cambridge, 1962), vols. 3 and 4

No doubt the reader will wish to know more about the plays performed in his own particular theatre and this standard work of reference will supply the need. Early chapters admirably sketch in the developmental background.

(6) *The Benefit System in the British Theatre.* St V. Troubridge (London, 1967)

Only a brief acquaintance with actors' memoirs will make the reader realise that the benefit system was complicated and full of pitfalls.

The late Sir St Vincent in his book explains how this system, together with the implied patronage, worked.

(7) *All Right on the Night.* V.C. Clinton Baddeley (London, 1954)

A popularly written book full of direct explanation. Clinton Baddeley takes a number of theatrical terms ('clap-trap'; 'giving out the play'; 'half price'; 'keeping places'; 'length', and so on) and by relating these to context entertainingly makes their meaning clear.

(8) *The English Theatre in Wales in the Eighteenth Century.* Cecil Price (Cardiff, 1948)

If you are working in Wales then this invaluable book helps to place your research in a context.

(9) Two other area studies are not only informative, but provide a clear model of presentation.

The Georgian Theatre in Wessex. Arnold Hare (London, 1958)

Rogues and Vagabonds. Elizabeth Grice (Lavenham, 1977)

The latter is a study of the circuits in East Anglia.

(10) The study of a single theatre is often presented in the form of a pamphlet. Two meticulously researched and attractively presented examples which may well serve as models are:

The Theatre Royal Bristol. Kathleen Barker (Bristol, 1969)

The Georgian Theatre, Richmond, Yorkshire. Richard Southern and Ivor Brown (Richmond, 1962)

(11) It may well be that you wish to know more of the plays presented in the theatres of the late-eighteenth and early-nineteenth centuries. To obtain those of Sheridan presents no problems but useful anthologies of lesser known works are:

Eighteenth Century Tragedy. Michael Booth (ed.) (London, 1965)

Eighteenth Century Comedy. W.D. Taylor (ed.) (London, 1965)

(12) The most comprehensive recent survey of old theatre buildings is:

Curtains! Or a New Life for Old Theatres. Curtains Committee (Eastbourne, 1982)

(13) Periodicals are also a useful source of reference. Three that I have found especially fascinating to dip into are:

All the Year Round. This magazine was edited for a while by Charles Dickens and contains many articles on various aspects of the theatre, especially on the technical side.

Theatre Notebook. This is the journal of the Society for Theatre Research. Back numbers give detailed notes on some of the works I have mentioned — there are, for example, several articles on Winston's *The Theatric Tourist.* The occasional index volume makes cross-referencing easier.

Notes and Queries. An indexed magazine of literature and the arts to which reference has already been made. Contributors receive a feedback to their articles through the correspondence columns. A patient use of the index will lead to further avenues of exploration.

Visits to Theatres and Sites

Armed with an array of facts one is then ready to have a look at the sites of the buildings on which one's work is based. Sometimes, of course, the edifice is still in use as a theatre. Recently I went to Henley on Thames to see the Kenton Theatre built in 1805 under the direction of Penley and Jonas and still going strong. In such instances there is a strong hope that bills, admission tokens and other examples of ephemera remain. Some buildings are in use as shops (the theatres at Banbury, Gosport and Chichester, for example) and one will need to hunt around, with permission, to find objects such as a disused pay box. Domestic buildings sometimes cover the site. In Arundel the garden of a house in Maltravers Street was once the floor of the pit and a small section of the gallery has been turned into a rockery. But in so many instances, as in Wells next the Sea, there may only be a memory in the name of a road — Theatre Lane.

Approaches and Methods

Research implies an orderliness in keeping one's materials. Although the following points seem pedantic, experience has shown me the need to be systematic in collecting materials. Each theatre that I work on has its own loose leaf binder. I can then enter into that file information relating to the building and to the companies that performed in it. With each book that I consult it has become habitual to record: the full name of the author, the full title of the book, the place of publication and the date of publication. I also keep a marginal note of the page numbering alongside the information. It is necessary to be able to distinguish one's own summary of the information from direct quotation and here an indentation for all quotations is a useful ploy. A sturdy pocket inside the cover of each file is useful for keeping photographs in. In addition to the theatre files I have found a series of biography files and files relating to plays useful in my research. These are arranged in alphabetical order. As the material grows a simple cross-referencing system is necessary: an index built up on small record cards is one answer.

When I began my forays into theatre history I concentrated on one theatre in Winchester, the Market House Theatre of 1620, and eventually wrote up my researches in the *Hampshire County Magazine* (February 1974). This then expanded into a study of later Winchester theatres until the last of the managers, ruined by debts, packed the show in. An edition of the *Proceedings of the Hampshire Field Club* (1976) has been devoted to this further development. Readers may care to consider the possibility of having off-prints made, as I have done, from a limited edition to be sold commercially in bookshops and museums. An exhibition of playbills in the City Museum and an accompanying slide lecture helped to announce the publication. Modest trumpeting is no bad thing. Additionally I wrote, in a more popular style, articles for the local newspapers.

Expanding to work on other theatres, I discovered that occasionally a modern theatre manager would welcome a brief article for one of his programmes: the Theatre Royal at Windsor, for example has an attractive magazine programme, *Curtain Up,* which formed a suitable outlet for a description of Henry Thornton's management of the Windsor Theatre in the eighteenth century. similarly the pamphlets issued by local history associations are a further means of promulgating one's researches: the work by Kathleen Barker mentioned in the section on general reference works was issued by the Bristol branch of the Historical Association. *Theatre Notebook* and *Nineteenth Century Theatre Research* are both journals which publish articles on original aspects of investigations.

An alternative method of approach is to take the life of a theatre manager and to concentrate on that. This usually means that, in order to cover his early days, several circuits have to be studied. Names of managers abound — there was Thomas Trotter working in Sussex based at Worthing for much of his life; or the redoubtable Mrs Baker, unable to read or write, but with a formidable array of actors in Kent. Needless to say this approach requires more time and travel than the straightforward history of a single building. Difficulties arise in the publication of such a work, for its purely local quality has gone — an obstacle I ran up against when I presented for publication a study of Henry Thornton's highly elaborate circuit in the Home and southern counties of England. An expedient I employed was to offer, at cost price, a typescript of my research to the librarian of each of the counties in which Thornton had managed a theatre. In all cases the offer was accepted and this means that each county has a record of the manager's work in at least one of its local history collections.

A third and yet more complicated approach is to take the circuits of a region and compare their working. The general reference section mentions two such area studies.

Writing up the research material offers its own challenges and is outside the scope of an article merely intended to set people on a quest of discovery. It is to be hoped, however, that these few pointers will lead a number of enthusiasts to present their work in either article or book form. May it go well with you!

REFERENCES

A. Playtexts and Scholarly Editions

Calderon (1976) *The Great Stage of the World*, trans. George
  Brandt, University of Manchester Press, Manchester
Centlevre, Susannah (1968) *A Bold Stroke for a Wife*, ed. Thalia
  Stathas, Edward Arnold, London
Chekhov, Anton (1980) *The Cherry Orchard*, trans. Michael
  Frayn, Methuen, London
_____ (1980) *The Cherry Orchard*, trans. Trevor Griffiths,
  Pluto, London
_____ (1980) *The Cherry Orchard*, trans. Ronald Hingley,
  Oxford University Press, Oxford
Cibber, Colly (1967) *The Careless Husband*, ed. W.W. Appleton,
  Edward Arnold, London
Cibber, Colly and Vanbrugh, Sir John (1969) *The Provoked
  Husband*, ed. Peter Dixon, Edward Arnold, London
Dryden, John (1981) *Marriage a la Mode*, ed. Mark Auburn,
  Edward Arnold, London
Etherege, Sir George (1966) *The Man of Mode*, ed. W.B.
  Carnochan, Edward Arnold, London
Farquhar, George (1978) *The Beaux Stratagem*, ed. Michael
  Cordner, Benn London
_____ (1978) *The Beaux Stratagem*, ed. Charles Fifer, Arnold,
  London
Fulwell, Ulpian (1972) *Like Will to Like* in *Tudor Interludes*, ed.
  P. Happé, Penguin, Harmondsworth
Ibsen, Henrik (1980) *Plays 1-4*, trans. Michael Meyer, Methuen,
  London
Jerrold, Douglas (1972) *Black Ey'd Susan* in *Nineteenth Century
  Plays*, ed. George Rowell, Oxford University Press, London
Molnar, Ferenc (1979) *The Guardsman*, trans. Frank Marcus,
  Methuen, London
National Theatre (1980) *The Passion,* Rex Collings, London
Phillips, Stephen (1921) *Collected Plays,* Macmillan, New York
Pinero, Arthur Wing (1936) *The Second Mrs. Tanqueray*, French,
  London

_____ (1936) *Trelawney of the Wells*, French, London

Robertson, Tom (1982) *Plays*, ed. William Tydeman, Cambridge University Press, Cambridge

Shakespeare, William (1897) *Hamlet* (acting edition), as arranged for the stage by Forbes-Robertson, The Nassau Press, London

Shepard, Sam (1981) *True West*, Faber, London

Steele, Richard (1967) *The Tender Husband*, ed. Calhoun Winton, Arnold, London

Strindberg, August (1964) *Plays*, trans. Michael Meyer, Methuen, London

Taylor, Tom (1972) *The Ticket of Leave Man* in *Nineteenth Century Plays*, ed. George Rowell, Oxford University Press, London

Tourneur, Cyril (1976) *The Atheist's Tragedie*, ed. Brian Morris and Roma Gill, Benn, London

Vanbrugh, Sir John (1977) *The Provoked Wife*, ed. James Smith, Benn, London

Wedekind, Frank (1981) *Spring Awakening*, trans. Edward Bond, Methuen, London

Wycherley, William (1977) *The Country Wife*, ed. J. Dixon Hunt, Benn, London

B. Memoirs and Journals

Allen, Percy (1922) *The Stage Life of Mrs. Sterling*, Fisher Unwin, London

Bassham, Ben L. (1978) *The Theatrical Photographs of Napoleon Sarony*, Kent State University Press, Kent, Ohio

Benson, Sir Frank (1930) *My Memoirs*, Benn, London

Boaden, James (1896) *Memoirs of Mrs. Siddons*, Gibbins, London

Courtenedge, Robert (n.d. [c. 1920]) *I Was an Actor Once*, Hutchinson, London

Craig, Edward Gordon (1957) *Index to the Story of My Days*, Hulton, London

Graham, Joe (1930) *An Old Stock Actor's Memories*, Murray, London

Harvey, Sir John Martin (1930) *Autobiography*, Sampson Low, London

Maude, Cyril (1927) *Behind the Scenes with Cyril Maude by*

Himself, Murray, London

Poel, William (1929) *Monthly Letters*, Werner Laurie, London

Saintsbury, H.A. (ed.) (1939) *We Saw Him Act: A symposium on the Art of Sir Henry Irving*, Hurst and Blackett, London

Shaw, George Bernard (1932) *Our Theatre of the Nineties*, Constable, London, vol. 1

Toynbee, William (ed.) (1912) *Diaries of William Charles Macready*, Chapman and Hall, London

C. Histories of Individual Theatres

Handley, Ellenor and Martin Knina (1978) *The Royal Opera House Covent Garden* (a history from 1732), Fourlance Books, London

Hume, Robert (1979) 'The Dorset Garden Theatre: A Review of Facts and Problems', *Theatre Notebook, 33* (1)

MacCarthy, Desmond (1966) *The Court Theatre, 1904-1907*, University of Miami Press, Florida

MacDermott, Norman (1975) *Everymania, a History of the Everyman Theatre, Hampstead* 1920-1926. Society for Theatre Research, London

Morley, Malcolm (1966) *Margate and its Theatres*, Museum Press, London

Pope, W. Macqueen (1945) *The Theatre Royal, Drury Lane*, W.H. Allen, London

Ranger, Paul (1978) *The Lost Theatres of Winchester, 1620-1861*, City Museum, Winchester

D. Secondary Works on Theatre History

Bentley, G.E. (1968) *The Seventeenth Century English Stage*, University of Chicago Press, Chicago and London

Brockett, Oscar G. (1977) *History of the Theatre*, Allyn and Bacon, London and Boston

Craik, T.W. (ed.) (1976-82) *The Revels History of Drama in English*, Methuen, London

Gielgud, Kate Terry (1980) *A Victorian Playgoer*, Heinemann, London. Contains a review of Forbes-Robertson's *Hamlet*.

Hartnoll, Phyllis (1968) *A Concise History of the Theatre*, Thames and Hudson, London

_____ (ed.) (1967) *The Oxford Companion to the Theatre,* Oxford University Press, London

Holland, Peter (1977) *The Ornament of Action: Text and Performance in Restoration Comedy,* Cambridge University Press, Cambridge

Hughes, Allan (1980) *Henry Irving Shakespearean,* Cambridge University Press, Cambridge

King, T.J. (1971) *Shakespearean Staging, 1599-1642,* Harvard and Oxford University Presses, Cambridge, Massachusetts, and Oxford. .For a full discussion of doors, hangings, etc.

Nagler, A.M. (1959) *A Sourcebook in Theatre History,* Dover, London and New York

Oxenford, Lyn (1974) *Playing Period Plays,* J. Garnet Miller, London and Chicago

Price, Cecil (1973) *Theatre in the Age of Garrick,* Blackwell, Oxford

Rees, Terrence (1978) *Theatre Lighting in the Age of Gas,* Society for Theatre Research, London

Richards, Kenneth and Thomson, Peter (eds.) (1972) *The Eighteenth Century English Stage,* Methuen, London

Rowell, George (1973) *Theatre in the Age of Irving,* Blackwell, Oxford

Russell, Douglas (1980) *Period Style for the Theatre,* Allyn and Bacon, London and Boston

Southern, Richard (1971) *Victorian Theatre,* David and Charles, Newton Abbot

Speaight, Robert (1954) *William Poel and the Elizabethan Revival,* Harvard University Press, Cambridge, Massachusetts

E. Other References

Barker, Clive (1977) *Theatre Games,* Methuen, London

Barker, Harley Granville (1963) *Prefaces to Shakespeare,* Batsford, London

Bradley, A.C. (1904) *Shakespearean Tragedy,* Macmillan, London

The Curtains Committee (1982) *Curtains! Or a New Life for Old Theatres,* John Offord, Eastbourne

Darwin, Charles (1962) *Origin of Species,* new edn. Macmillan, London

Steele, Joshua (1779) *Prosodia Rationalis,* printed privately,
    London
Williamson, Audrey (1951) *Theatre of Two Decades,* Rockliff,
    London

F. Journals

Speech and Drama: the Journal of the Society of Teachers of
    Speech and Drama
Teatr: the Soviet Journal of Theatre
Theatre Notebook: the Journal of the Society for Theatre
    Research
Theatre Quarterly: now ceased publication
Theatre Survey: the Journal of the American Society for Theatre
    Research.

INDEX OF ACTING TERMS

INDEX OF NAMES AND TITLES

285